Family Man, Family Leader

Family Man, Family Leader

Biblical Fatherhood as the Key to a Thriving Family

Philip Lancaster

THE VISION FORUM, INC.
San Antonio, Texas

"Where there is no vision, the people perish."

The Vision Forum, Inc.
4719 Blanco Rd., San Antonio, Texas 78212
1-800-440-0022
www.visionforum.com

ISBN-10 1-929241-83-6
ISBN-13 978-1-929241-83-5

Cover Design by Shannon G. Moeller
Typesetting by Jeremy M. Fisher

"Where Next?", circa nineteenth century, by Edward Frederick Brewtnall (1846-1902).
Watercolor on canvas, 18½ x 28¾ in., Private Collection / Christopher Wood Gallery,
London, UK / Bridgeman Art Library.

PRINTED IN THE UNITED STATES OF AMERICA

To my father,
Truman O. Lancaster,
with deep thankfulness
for providing me with a living example
of Christian manhood

Contents

CHAPTER 1

Is Revival On the Way?

Behold, I will send you Elijah the prophet before the coming of the great and dreadful day of the LORD. And he will turn the hearts of the fathers to the children, and the hearts of the children to their fathers, lest I come and strike the earth with a curse.

Malachi 4:5,6

I must be one of the few Christian men who lived through the 1990s and never went to a Promise Keepers rally. That's right, I never spent a weekend with fifty thousand pumped-up men in a stadium singing, praying, and listening to inspiring speakers talk about what it means to be a man. While I did watch the news reports about the climactic PK gathering in Washington, D.C. toward the end of the decade, that's about as close as I came.

So how can I presume to write about Christian manhood if I haven't been part of the biggest men's movement of our times, of history, for that matter? Well, I have been somewhat preoccupied with another Christian movement, one that, I must admit, hasn't been exactly a men's movement. In fact, to be quite honest, it is still more of a women's movement—but I have been busy trying to change that.

My wife, Pamela, and I started home schooling our children in 1984 and began attending support groups and conferences for home schoolers. One of the things we noticed in those early years was that the women were doing nearly all of the teaching in most home schools. They were also providing most of the leadership and labor connected with the support groups, publications, and state organizations for home educators. Besides feeling socially out of place among all those ladies, I had to wonder if something was askew on a more fundamental level. After all, I thought, didn't God call men to be the leaders in their families—and everywhere else, for that matter?

Over the years we began to see a small but significant countertrend: more and more men were taking an active role in their family education program, and men were, in increasing numbers, assuming the roles of leadership in the auxiliary organizations. We have done what we can to encourage this development. Since the early 1990s we have been publishing a magazine, *Patriarch*, which has this subtitle: "Equipping men to be godly leaders in family, church, and society." It has been satisfying to see many previously passive and uninvolved men begin to discover what it means to be the leaders of their homes.

Both the Christian men's movement and the home education movement have captured my attention for one very good reason: they just might be the heralds of a great work of

God in our generation. Yet, while I'm hopeful, I'm not confident as to how things will go.

To understand both my fascination and my ambivalence, take a look at two portions of Scripture. The first is the very last three verses of the Old Testament. The second is the record of the very first words of revelation spoken in the New Testament era (by the angel Gabriel).

> Remember the Law of Moses, My servant, which I commanded him in Horeb for all Israel, with the statutes and judgments. Behold, I will send you Elijah the prophet before the coming of the great and dreadful day of the LORD. And he will turn the hearts of the fathers to the children, and the hearts of the children to their fathers, lest I come and strike the earth with a curse. (Malachi 4:4–6)

> He will also go before Him in the spirit and power of Elijah, "to turn the hearts of the fathers to the children," and the disobedient to the wisdom of the just, to make ready a people prepared for the Lord. (Luke 1:17)

Isn't that amazing? According to the infallible Word of God, there is something vitally important about fathers. Fathers are the subject of the last breath of Old Testament revelation, and they are once again in the angel's announcement proclaiming the coming of the Messiah.

Both references describe the work of God through His prophet John. John's ministry was to prepare the people of Israel to receive God's Son, Jesus Christ, and thus to inherit the kingdom of grace and salvation that Jesus would establish. This was nothing less than the turning point of all history.

Pay close attention to what we have here. This is God's own definition of true revival. The turning point of all history is characterized by a double "turning" in the lives of individual men: they turn to their families and they turn to the wisdom of the just, which means that they return to the only source of wisdom for righteous living, God's revealed will in His Word. God says that John (who was the "Elijah" of the prophecy) would "turn the hearts of the fathers to the children and the hearts of the children to their fathers." In Luke the angel repeats this idea and speaks of a second "turning," that of "the disobedient to the wisdom of the just," which parallels the call of Malachi to "remember the Law of Moses." The optimum spiritual condition of people is when the fathers turn their hearts toward their families and when the people return to God's Word as their standard for how to live.

Notice how critically important these matters are. Taking the two passages together, this twofold spiritual condition is necessary, negatively, to avoid God's curse on the land and, positively, to make ready a people who are prepared to receive Jesus and be part of His work in the world.

True revival is not about getting charged with emotion at a church meeting. It is about submitting to God by being family men and by obeying His Word.

FAMILY MEN

How exciting! By God's grace we may be living at another turning point in history. Both the Christian men's movement and the home education movement have called men to reconsider what it means to be a man and a father. They have challenged fathers to commit themselves to the calling of family leadership. In response, men by the millions have turned their hearts toward home.

These two movements represent the greatest hope for revival that this nation has seen in recent history because, through them, men are being reminded of one of God's highest priorities. And fathers returning to the calling of shepherding their families is evidence that God is, once again, preparing a people through whom he can spread His kingdom with power, just as in Jesus' day.

Most home schoolers began to teach their children at home simply because they believed it was the best option for their children. Few began with any grandiose visions of restoring families or catching a wave of spiritual renewal. Yet in the process of bringing education back to the home, many have come to find that their choice has opened their eyes to a new vision of family life—how to raise children, the roles of husbands and wives, and the relationship of the family and the church. They have begun to see possibilities for a deep reformation in their lives that they never dreamed of when they first kept Johnny and Susie home from school.

In a similar manner, many of those who have been moved by the call to be a "promise keeper," a committed family man, have seen their lives changed, along with those of their wives and children. They have dedicated themselves to reordering their priorities, leading their homes, and becoming men of integrity and sacrificial love.

What is so earth-shaking about a man turning his heart to his family? It is the movement of a father's heart out of the sphere of immediate, temporal, and self-centered concerns toward the sphere of long-range, even eternal, concerns. A man who shares God's priorities sees in his children his (and his wife's) most important mission in life. He sees in them the foundation of many generations, generations which he can shape for God, and which God can use to shape history, through the power of Christ and His gospel.

A godly man should embrace the role of husband and father because he embraces God's grand plan for history. The Lord's goal is, in Christ, "to reconcile all things to himself" (Col. 1:20). Christians are God's agents of reconciliation in this age (2 Cor. 5:18), through which Christ spreads His gospel and kingdom. The godly man wants to prepare a quiver-full of well made children-arrows (Ps. 127:4,5) with which he can participate in the defeat of God's enemies. Turning his heart to his family is the best way a father can turn his heart to his Lord.

When a father makes his family his priority, it is inevitable that the hearts of his children will be turned to him. There is no generation gap when fathers do their job. Quite the contrary: there is a solid generational bond. How can a child turn against his father when their hearts are bound together? For that child to rebel would destroy his own heart as well as his father's. With the heart of the children won to their father and their father's God, the cause of Christ in the world can go forward through the generations. There is no speedier path to fulfilling the Great Commission of Jesus to his followers: to make disciples of the nations.

BACK TO THE BIBLE

I am truly encouraged by the evidence that God is working as millions of fathers want to be family-centered. However, I am looking for indications of the other "turning" that marks a time of true revival: returning to God's Word, the Bible, as the source of wisdom for how to live in a way that is pleasing to God.

Now millions profess belief in the inerrancy of God's inspired Word and intend to live by its teachings. But the fact is that, despite such professions of high regard for the Bible, few demonstrate this by practicing what the Bible says in day-to-day life. There are not even many evangelical Christians who read Scripture with regularity, much less spend time in serious study of the Book and how to apply it to daily life.

Not surprisingly, then, there is a lack of knowledge about what the Bible actually teaches. When it is read, it is too often regarded as a source of mere spiritual and emotional lift, a tranquilizer to help a man cope with the stress in his life. How many men today open the Word daily to understand the truth God has revealed and how it applies to their everyday responsibilities?

This ignorance of God's Word is evident specifically when it comes to understanding what it means to be a man and how exactly a father should turn his heart toward his family. The jargon of psychology and the assumptions of feminism too often lurk in the sermons, books, and articles that shape a man's view of his masculine callings. So while many Christian fathers want to become family men, they do not have a clear roadmap, derived from the Bible, to get them there.

With this in mind, here is a sober warning from Hosea 4:6:

My people are destroyed for lack of knowledge. Because you have rejected knowledge, I also will reject you from being priest for Me; because you have forgotten the law of your God, I also will forget your children.

Today, God's people are being destroyed due to their lack of knowledge of God's Word. Sheer ignorance is epidemic. But worse is the rejection of the Bible's clear teachings when those doctrines run counter to the current wisdom of our culture. The Lord says He will reject those who so disregard His wisdom and no longer allow them to be His priests who represent Him and carry out His work in the world. Further, he warns of a generational curse: "I also will forget your children." Failing to turn our hearts to the "wisdom of the just" (Luke 1:17) by learning the Bible and doing what it says will undermine our efforts to turn our children's hearts to ourselves and to the Lord.

You see, both "turnings" must come together. You cannot be the family man God wants you to be unless you also turn to His Word as the source of wisdom for how to do that and everything else in life. And this means doing what God says when the world, or even the church, says you are foolish for doing it. A longing to discover the will of God, repentance for failures to conform to His will, and a determination to put His will into practice at all costs—these attitudes have marked any God-sent revival from the time that John prepared a people to follow the Messiah. When the Holy Spirit works renewal in the hearts of people, He leads them to embrace the Bible as the sole standard for what to believe and how to live.

The secret of genuine success in life is found in the Lord's command to Joshua when he called him to lead the armies of Israel to conquer enemy territory:

> This Book of the Law shall not depart from your mouth, but you shall meditate in it day and night, that you may observe to do according to all that is written in it. For then you will make your way prosperous, and then you will have good success. (Joshua 1:8)

God says that success comes to those who know His Word and put it into practice. The Bible isn't just a feel-good book. Yes, it enables a man to know God in a personal and satisfying way. But it is much more. The Bible contains God's marching orders for Christian men, telling them how to take back territory from the enemy and advance the cause of Christ and truth. Without a disciplined study of the Word with faithful adherence to its commands and living out its patterns of wisdom, we will not succeed in being family men, nor will we understand the meaning of true manhood.

The jury is still out on the Christian men's movement and the home education movement. Will they produce men who are truly men by God's standard? Will they succeed in raising up a generation that God can use to spread the kingdom of Jesus, "a people prepared for the Lord"? Or will these efforts prove to be a flash in the pan, fads that got men excited for awhile but bore no long-term fruit? Lasting fruit only comes from abiding in

Christ (Jn. 15:5), and abiding in Christ means doing what God says. "If you love Me, keep my commandments" (14:15). Will the new generation of family men be those who are also radically committed to being men of the Book?

I pray it may be so. I desperately want to see both elements of genuine revival because the need in our day is so desperate.

THE WORST OF TIMES

"It was the best of times; it was the worst of times." The opening words of Charles Dickens' *A Tale of Two Cities* would seem to apply to our own times as well.

You and I live at a moment of history that is simultaneously terrible and wonderful. Terrible because of the condition of the society in which we are destined to live out our lives. Wonderful because of the unprecedented opportunities to make a difference in the destiny of a nation and the world.

We must maintain this perspective and fasten our eyes in two directions at once. On the one hand, we must be soberly realistic about the dreadful condition of our beloved country; and on the other hand, we must be joyfully realistic about the power of God to change the course of history through us.

This two-pronged realism—about the reality of sin's effects and the reality of Christ's victory over the effects of sin—is our best preparation for being men who make a difference in the twenty-first century and beyond.

Take a realistic look at the worst of times. What do we see as we look out across this great land today? We see the tragedy of a nation squandering its inheritance. We see a land that once was characterized by virtue, liberty, wealth, and power now fallen to a state of corruption, bondage, poverty, and impotence.

In a land that once blushed at the mention of fornication, we now have public officials promoting sodomy as a normal lifestyle. Where gambling once was reserved for the secretive back rooms of shady establishments, our elected leaders now prey on the covetousness of the populace to satisfy their insatiable lust for more of somebody else's money to spend. In a land that consciously crafted a republic out of principles found in the Bible, we now find a student suspended for saying grace quietly over his lunch at a public school. A once-virtuous nation has corrupted itself. If the pinstriped barbarians stalk the corridors of power today (and they surely do), they are only a reflection of the barbaric hearts of the citizens who gave them power.

In a land where once the patriot's cry, "Give me liberty, or give me death" was met with heartfelt consent, we now find a people who prefer living in slavery. Like children, citizens cry out to the government to take care of them, to guarantee them a job, an income when they don't have a job, security in old age, care for their children, and health care. And with each empty guarantee the paternalistic guardians gain more power as the citizens give up their wealth and relinquish the freedom that can only remain with those who take responsibility for themselves.

At one time the United States of America was the world's largest creditor, the engine of production that lifted the whole world up the ladder of prosperity. Today our nation has the notorious distinction of being the world's largest debtor. The reckless and immoral spending addiction of both major parties has brought our economy to the very edge of bankruptcy. Sometime in the not-too-distant future it is entirely possible that the United States of America will have to either default on its mountain of debt or inflate the economy into economic ruin. One way or the other we could enter a period of our national history that will make the Depression of the 1930s look like a picnic.

In my lifetime I have witnessed the rapid acceleration of this decline of virtue, this abandonment of liberty, and this squandering of wealth. It is painful to see our beloved nation in decline.

The problem does not rest solely with out-of-touch politicians and overzealous bureaucrats. Consider also the state of our churches and families. These institutions provided the fertile soil out of which our great republic grew, and it is the decline of the family and the church that has preceded and contributed directly to the decline of our nation as a whole.

The church is in a sad state today. Never mind the mainline denominations that have long-since abandoned biblical faith; we're talking about the Bible-believing church. Here, too often, we see *much ado about nothing*. There is talk of revival without the reality. The church today measures its success by the numbers on its rolls, the size of its offerings, or the volume of its worship bands—rather than by the holiness of its members.

When was the last time you heard of a church rebuking members for gossip, admonishing men for the immodest dress of their wives and daughters, or excommunicating a member for adultery? Today's evangelical church may take a strong stand on fundamental doctrines like the divine nature of Christ and the inspiration of Scripture, but it too often denies this Christ and this inspired Word by not practicing a true Christian lifestyle. The pattern of life of most Christians is so much like the world around them that they blend right in and cannot serve as salt and light.

The family, too, is in decline among Christians. Believing fathers generally fail to play their God-given role as the spiritual leader of their families. Christian fathers in times past led their families in twice-daily family worship. Today most Christian fathers reinforce the pervasive humanism of our culture, denying the practical relevance of God to the lives of their children by failing to worship Him together with their families in the home.

Christian mothers too often neglect their home-centered role for the empty promise of fulfillment in the workplace, while they warehouse their children in daycare centers. Parents send their children to secular schools where God is outlawed, and they allow them to watch trashy movies and listen to vile music—and hang out with those who do the same. After years of training in the ways of rebellion through godless schooling, debauched entertainment, and peer association, Christian parents are somehow surprised when their teenagers rebel, forsaking the God of their fathers.

Christian homes look too much like the world around: the same roles for parents, the same schools, the same entertainment, the same divorce statistics—is it any wonder that our nation is in decline?

It is painful to consider the factors that make these the worst of times, but it is vital for us to be realistic about the problems so that we can also be realistic about the solutions.

THE BEST OF TIMES

The very things that make these such terrible times in which to live are what also make them such exciting times. Never before has there been a greater need for men who will commit themselves to live for Jesus Christ, not just in words, but in the whole fabric of their lives.

One of the basic human longings, placed in a man's heart by God Himself, is the desire to make a difference. My Christian brothers, you have such an opportunity, you have such a mission.

We must be realistic about the terrible condition of our families, churches, and nation. But we must also be utterly realistic about the power of God that is at work in those who walk in obedience to His revealed will in the Bible. God can change the world through you and me. Look at what He accomplished through that motley collection of twelve fishermen.

The course of history has literally been shaped by the quiet choice of men and women to obey God and walk in His way no matter what the cost. I truly believe that history in the twenty-first century will be shaped by the choices that you and I make in the next few years.

God doesn't need a majority. The Bible tells us that He is looking over the earth, scanning it for those whose hearts are fully committed to Him in order that He might strengthen them (2 Chron. 16:9). He just needs a few good men to turn our nation around.

These are the worst of times. Let's be realistic. But these are also the best of times. Let's also be realistic about the victory of

Jesus Christ and the power of God to renew our land. What a great moment to live as a Christian man! What an opportunity to make a difference!

Here is a prediction from the book of Isaiah:

> Those from among you shall build the old waste places; you shall raise up the foundation of many generations; and you shall be called the Repairer of the Breach, the Restorer of Streets to Dwell In. (Isaiah 58:12)

Whether we are the ones who fulfill that prediction depends on how we respond to the challenges we face. There are many "waste places" around us that require repair and restoration, as we have already seen. But how do we make those repairs? How do we become those who lay the foundations of many generations?

THE HOME RULES THE NATION

It is the home that determines the rise and fall of churches, nations, and civilizations. It is the decline of the family, and specifically the Christian family, that underlies the general decline we witness about us today. And it is only the restoration of the Christian home that holds any hope for the larger restoration of church and society. In this connection, hear the insight of Theodore Cuyler:

> For one, I care little for the government which presides at Washington, in comparison with the government which rules the millions of American homes. No administration can seriously harm us if our home life is pure, frugal, and

godly. No statesmanship or legislation can save us, if once our homes become the abode of profligacy.

The home rules the nation. If the home is demoralized, it will ruin it. The real seed corn whence our Republic sprang was the Christian households represented in the *Mayflower*, or the family altar of the Hollander and the Huguenot.

All the best characters, best legislation, best institutions, and best church life were cradled in those early homes. They were the taproot of the Republic, and of the American churches.[1]

"The home rules the nation." Our national crisis is a consequence of the crisis of the home, and the crisis of the home is a crisis of male leadership. Men have abandoned their calling to be the spiritual leaders of their families, to be the builders of Christian character, the teachers of Christian doctrine, and the models of Christ-like faith and virtue. They have abdicated their responsibility to be the guardians of that wellspring of Christian civilization: the Christian family. Because men have forsaken their families, we are losing a civilization.

"The home rules the nation." Therefore the most important work in America today is the restoration of the Christian family. Now listen closely and consider. I truly believe that those reading this book embody more potential to renew our nation than is represented in all the executives, legislators, judges, and generals who inhabit the marbled halls of Washington. If it is true that the home rules the nation—that the welfare of church, state, and larger society are determined by the welfare of the family—then national renewal can only begin with family renewal. And family renewal must begin with a restoration of family government, the recovery of the role of spiritual leadership by men in their homes.

The future of America lies squarely on the shoulders of men like you all around this land. What higher calling, what nobler mission than this? Our task is nothing less than the restoration of our civilization, our nation, our churches—and it all rests on our actions in restoring our own homes.

Does the task seem too great? Think how Zerubbabel must have felt. A remnant of the people of God had returned to their land after seventy years of exile. They were trying to rebuild the temple that had been destroyed by the Babylonians. The work was hard, the hands few, the opposition great. What was the Lord's message to the man in charge? "'Not by might, nor by power, but by my Spirit,' says the Lord Almighty" (Zech. 4:6). God's work never depends on mere human power, fortitude, or numbers. It depends on the presence and power of His own Spirit. His Spirit working through a few obedient men will accomplish more than all the lofty expressions of merely human power.

It may be that the decline of America has gone too far, that God will not now allow a restoration to our former greatness. That is up to Him. Our mission is the same in any case: to restore our homes so that they become Bethels, houses of God. However depraved and mournful and anxious the people around us may yet become, our homes can be sanctuaries of righteousness and joy and peace. But we have hope that the Lord has preserved a remnant who want to reclaim spiritual leadership. It may not be too late for America.

Returning to Biblical Patriarchy

We must return to the *biblical patriarchy* that characterized this nation at its beginnings. Weldon Hardenbrook in *Missing from Action: Vanishing Manhood in America* explains the root meaning of the word:

> The biblical term *patriarchy* is derived from two words in the Greek language—*patria* (taken from the word *pater,* "father"), which means "family;" and *arche,* which means "beginning," "first in origin," and "to rule." A patriarch is a family ruler. He is the man in charge.

Recent generations of men have retreated from their calling to be patriarchs, to provide the spiritual direction for home and society. The male leadership role has been relegated merely to the spheres of politics and business. Men have abandoned the truly formative institutions of civilization. They have left the home, the education of children, and most of the work of the church to women, and they have also failed to give any effective moral direction to the political and commercial spheres which they continue to lead.

Reinforcing the effects of their own abdication of responsibility, men have also had to contend with emasculation at the hands of destructive cultural forces. Feminism hates men, and it especially hates men who act like men, men who take charge. Civil government undermines the male role of provider by taking on the care of children, the elderly, and the needy. Boys are feminized as they are shaped mostly by females in the home, the schools, and the churches. The masculine inclination to lead and protect is thwarted by efforts to create the new "sensitive" (and sad to say, "feminized") man.

It is time for men to look back to the past so that they can look to the future with hope. They need to repent for generations of failed leadership and reject the feminizing pressures of today. They need to again accept the burden of godly leadership.

Patriarchs are men who walk with God and fear Him only, who accept responsibility for leadership, and who follow the example of Jesus who led through service. God's chosen nation Israel was founded by the patriarchs. America was set on its blessed course by Christian patriarchs. By God's grace we, too, can become godly patriarchs so that succeeding generations may live under a blessing instead of a curse.

If we are to return to the blessedness of biblical patriarchy, how do we go about it? Where do we begin? We must not create some man-made system that exalts men over women, as if men are inherently superior. We certainly must not mimic such silly antics as those recommended by Robert Bly in his book *Iron John*. He calls for men to rediscover the "mythopoetic" roots of masculinity through reenacting primitive male group rituals as they gather around campfires, beat drums, wear animal skins, and carry spears. We must also go beyond the Christian men's movement which has men promise to stay married and stay home at night—good beginnings, but hardly a sufficient definition of manly responsibility.

To be truly Christian men we must get back to the Bible and to the God of the Bible. The goal of this book is to present the foundations of biblical patriarchy as revealed in God's Word. After a brief look back in history to discover how men and their families have fallen so far since colonial times, we will look at what the Bible teaches about manhood and fatherhood, with particular emphasis on how God the Father and Jesus Christ are models for the Christian man.

The goal of this study is to restore what has fallen and "raise up the foundation of many generations." It is to rediscover the long-lost knowledge of the Bible as it relates to men and their primary calling in the home. It is to equip men with food for study and meditation so that they "will have good success" as they work to turn their hearts toward their families.

My immediate hope is to build on the promise of the Christian men's movement and of home schooling and help them both to carry through to long-term fruitfulness. That will only happen as we get back to the Bible and back to biblical patriarchy.

This may indeed be another turning point in history in terms of the progress of the gospel and the kingdom of Christ. Time will tell whether we follow through on our good beginnings. May God make it so!

CHAPTER 2

Whatever Happened to Families?

Brethren, do not be children in understanding; however,
in malice be babes, but in understanding be mature.
1 Corinthians 14:20

One of the first rules of land navigation is that you have to know where you are before you can figure out how to get where you are going. If I hand you a road atlas of the United States and ask you to plot a course to Tishomingo, Mississippi, you won't be able to do that if you don't know on what piece of ground you are standing at the moment. The directions you take will be quite different starting from Atlanta, Georgia, than they will be if you begin in Spokane, Washington. (Even this former Army Reserve chaplain learned that much about map reading when he was in the service!)

Do you know where you are standing, or sitting, at this moment? If you are bright enough to be reading this page, I'm quite confident the answer is, yes. Locating ourselves physically is not a great challenge, after all. As I write this I'm in a trailer in the woods on a hillside off Firehouse Road in the Blue Ridge mountains, Floyd County, Virginia, USA. Sorry, I can't give you the exact latitude and longitude, not having any GPS equipment handy.

Let me ask you another question. Do you know where you are standing historically and culturally at the moment? I'm not just talking about things like your nationality, your language, and the century in which you live. Do you realize where you stand in the flow of events and ideas that have shaped our whole society, its ways of thinking and its manners of living?

Do you know what factors have influenced your educational choices; your choice of vocation; your music preferences; your ways of relating to elderly relatives; your family's dress and appearance; your view of children, of money, of marriage and divorce; your views of welfare, of global warming, of the military, etc.?

The answer is that history and culture have shaped you, as they have me. We are all the products of the modern world, and we are all influenced by its ideas and by the social and economic structures that make it up. It is true that we are also shaped by subcultures within this larger culture: for example, the South or the North, the city or the country, the university or the trade school. But these subcultures contain very little variation within the main themes of the dominant culture of Western society.

In order to carefully plan our route toward the destination that God sets before us as Christian fathers, we must understand the culture that has molded us. We need to be like "the sons of Issachar who had understanding of the times, to know what Israel ought to do" (1 Chron. 12:32). For us to know what to do at the present time we need not only to know the Bible, we also need to have an "understanding of the times" in which we live so that we know how to *apply* the Bible in a way that will make a difference to our families and, by God's grace, to the whole culture.

This chapter is designed to help us figure out where in the world we are. We will look briefly at the historical trends and ideas that have formed the world around us and that have affected our views of manhood, the family, and the roles of fathers. With this accomplished, we can then take up the Bible as our map and compass and begin to plot out the course toward the God-ordained goal of biblical patriarchy.

THE GOOD OLD DAYS

Now don't get me wrong, I don't have any desire to go back to the 1600s. I'm quite happy to have running water, sewage systems, electricity, telephones, cars, and the computer on which I am typing this book. Not to mention, with my wife in mind, vacuum cleaners, automatic washers and dryers, electric grain grinders, and bubble-gum-flavored antibiotics for the little ones' earaches.

I'm not talking about technology when I refer to times past as "the good old days." I'm talking about family life. And there is no question whatsoever in my mind that the seventeenth and eighteenth centuries in America were much better in that regard than today.

For folks back then, as for most people through most of world history, life was centered in the home and the surrounding community. Here is Brian Abshire's description of that period:

> Before the Industrial Revolution, most people lived in small communities. The same families lived in the same locales for generations, since the family was tied to the land. Mom and Dad usually came from the same community and therefore shared a common cultural background, values and sense of identity. Children were an asset; every extra pair of hands meant the farm could produce more food (or the craftsman more products). Mom's domestic skills, baking, cooking, sewing, etc., were desperately needed in the home. Children worked closely with their parents from a young age. Dad worked with the sons in the fields (or at his craft), Mom with the daughters in the house. Children learned not only skills, but character and values at the same time.[2]

As late as the early nineteenth century over ninety percent of American families lived either on farms or in small villages. This rural way of life centered on the homes of the communities, each having its own vibrant economy, with each member of the family contributing something to the provision of the home. Since children were an obvious economic asset, there were lots of them, with the average mother bearing seven children in her lifetime.

Although fathers were no more perfect in the old days than today, the social organization back then made it much less of a challenge for a man to turn his heart toward home. Here is how the Hories state it in *Whatever Became of Fathering?*

> Up until the Industrial Revolution, life in Europe—and,
> for the most part, in America—was centered within
> the framework of the home. The father worked in the
> immediate vicinity of the home. Not only was he available
> to his children, but the children were also included in his
> work. The sons were his apprentices; he was the one who
> taught them how to farm or to work with the tools of
> the trade. It was taken for granted that the sons would
> pursue his vocation as adults. They worked with the
> father in order to perpetuate his enterprise. Since each was
> dependent upon the other, their closeness engendered a
> mutual trust.[3]

The role of fathers in these homes was clearly defined: the
father was the leader; and it did not occur to anyone to challenge
this biblical notion. In *Missing from Action: Vanishing Manhood
in America*, Weldon Hardenbrook confirms this.

> … [C]olonial families were also unquestionably overseen
> by men. It was a paternal society. Like Abraham, Isaac, and
> Jacob of old, colonial men held to the patriarchal model
> of family structure. "Both society and household were
> frankly patriarchal in the seventeenth century based on the
> supreme authority of men as fathers," writes professor of
> history Mary Ryan. "Women were subject to fathers and
> husbands within the household, and barred from positions
> of independence and authority outside it."[4]

Fathers ruled their homes, with their wives by their sides as their vital domestic partners, and with both being an integral part of their children's daily lives. A mutual love and confidence was the bond that held the family together under the father's oversight and direction.

The extent of respect for a father's authority can be witnessed in this example taken from *Virginians at Home*, by Edmund S. Morgan, shared in Mr. Hardenbrook's book:

> In 1708 Ann Walker, an Anglican married to a Quaker, objected in court to having her children educated as Quakers, but the Court, while acknowledging her own freedom to worship as she chose, instructed her not to interfere in any way with the instruction of her children, even forbidding her to expound any part of the Scriptures to the children without her husband's consent. Such complete support for the husband's authority is all the more remarkable in view of the fact that the Anglican Church was the established church of Virginia, to which all the members of the court doubtless belonged.[5]

This total oversight of the home by men led to a very natural and consistent result: men were also the leaders in the churches and the communities, as well as in business and civil institutions. As Mary Ryan writes in *Womanhood in America*, "Only the patriarch of the family… could rise to leadership in political, cultural, and religious affairs."[6]

This patriarchal way of life was a wholesome balance of order and freedom, authority and relationship, which is what

God designed the family to be. Rev. Abshire again:

> Work, recreation, religion, and welfare were all family oriented and contributed to a sense of identity and belonging. Children had both economic as well as social incentive to maintain close family ties. They inherited the land, expanding the family's economic basis. The extended family assisted during emergencies. The sociological background therefore reinforced biblical family values.[7]

The "frankly patriarchal" society of early America was the ideal environment for a man to live out his biblical duties to lead and love his family and to train up his children in the Lord.

However, things were soon to change, and on a scale unprecedented in history.

The Exodus of Fathers

Historical trends do not begin on a particular date on the calendar, but there is general agreement that the Industrial Age was ushered in by the invention of the steam engine by James Watt in 1764. It took some decades for this new source of mechanical power to be perfected and used on a wide scale, but once it did, it changed the shape of society. Following the steam engine came the development of many other machines that harnessed this great power, applying it to the accomplishment of tasks and to the production of goods which before had required the labor of man or animals. This led to the creation of factories and systems of mass production.

Industrialism made an impact on the home in several negative ways. First, and most significantly, *industrialism took fathers away from their wives and children.* The factories needed the laborers and paid cash wages. So men left their farm or trade and went to work for other men in the task of mass production. Thus began what we now take for granted: the father who is away from his family for most of the day, earning his wages so that he can buy the goods manufactured in the factories. The shift of the focus of production from the home to the factory led to fathers shifting their attention from their families to their jobs. As Alan Carlson stated it, "In this new order, the home became separated from the factory and the office, a revolutionary shift in human living patterns."[8]

Second, *the need for home production and the small trades gradually diminished.* If a factory can make candles by the millions and sell them cheap, why should a mother and her girls labor to make candles themselves? The same question could be asked in regard to fabric, clothing, baskets, soap, butter, and so many other products formerly manufactured by the cooperative efforts of the family members in the home. Thus industrialism left women to run the homes while having less meaningful work to do there.

As to the trades, how can a cobbler stay in business when shoes made in factories are available for a fraction of the cost? Think also of the blacksmith, the wheelwright, the tinsmith, and the tailor, not to mention, in time, the butcher, the baker, and the candlestick maker. If these tradesmen had not already closed shop to go work in the factory themselves, they soon went out of business simply because of a lack of demand for their goods. And what would they then do but go work in the factories themselves? Home- and community-based manufacturing thus became obsolete.

Third, *children lost their significant place in the family and in the hearts of their fathers.* With the loss of home production, children became, over time, economic liabilities instead of assets, consumers instead of producers. The quite natural result was that families had fewer and fewer children. For Christian families this meant that there were fewer "arrows" produced to carry on the task of spreading the kingdom of Christ.

Fathers no longer directed the day-to-day affairs of their homes; nor could they now train their sons to follow them on the farm or in the family trade since there was no more farm or trade. But the economic shift was not the most significant effect of this new cultural trend. The truly tragic effect was the loss of relationship between a father and his children. With the father gone so much of the time, the development of mutual trust and love, previously taken for granted, was now greatly hindered.

Yet More Challenges

Aside from its direct affects on family structure and relationships, industrialism created a new type of society that put further strains upon the home. *Urbanization,* a natural result of the need to bring together large business enterprises and the workers they need to function, overwhelmed the family unit. Instead of relating to a few other families of similar values in small communities, families now were lost in a sea of anonymous faces, with fewer significant relationships. Cities also tended to become concentration points for the baser of human tendencies and the temptations of evil became more readily accessible to family members. The effects of urbanization at its extremes can now be found, on the one hand, in the anonymity of the modern suburbs where people often don't know their next-door neighbors, and, on the other hand, the inner-city "neighborhoods" where derelict buildings hold derelict children and "father" is strictly a biological term.

Modern *transportation*, another direct result of industrialism, has created unprecedented mobility. First the train, then the automobile, and finally the airplane have made it easy for families to move in pursuit of better jobs and more income. Gradually the ties of location were severed and families moved about at will with little or no regard for what used to be known as the "home place," the community of extended family and friends that made up the world of families in "the good old days." Transportation also has made it easier for children to leave the home, whether on Friday night for a date or to set up their own apartment in a city far away.

Yet another product of industrialism, *consumerism* has eaten away at the heart and soul of the family. Those who mass produce goods naturally find it necessary to create a mass market for their products. So they use mass media to quite literally brainwash the population into buying their products. Family members, who used to be producers, are now consumers. The consumer mentality amounts to a materialistic focus in the heart of a person, and at its worst, it becomes a continual, insatiable lust for more and more manufactured things that, he thinks, will make him feel good or boost his self-esteem. Such a movement of the soul is contrary to the spiritual, God-centered preoccupation to which Christian parents and children are called.

A final perverse effect of industrialism is its intrinsic tendency toward the progressive *acceleration* of its other effects. All of the family-damaging trends increased their pace throughout the twentieth century. One noteworthy example: the two world wars drew women into the workforce in great numbers in order to support the war effort because the men were away fighting and dying. It has since become the norm for women to work out of the home—and who can blame them when there is no one at home and no work to do there?

At the beginning of the twenty-first century the family is a mere shell of its former self. At its best it is the mere nuclear family, cut off from kin, living in anonymous cities, without productive work in the home, and with both parents working and the children away at school. With each family member feeling the centrifugal pull of out-of-home commitments, they hardly have any time together. The father's heart is at his job, the children's hearts with their classmates and friends. Add to this the mind-numbing and soul-destroying distractions of contemporary music, television, and movies—the latest "blessings" of our industrial-technological society—and you round out the picture of the challenges Christian fathers face in attempting to become true family men once again.

Is Wealth Worth the Price?

I said before that I am not willing to turn the clock back and return to pre-industrial times, but I have to ask: Is it worth it? Has the fruit of the Industrial Age been worth the price? Of course I realize that what's done is done, and so it may appear pointless to even raise the question. But my concern in asking it is not so much to evaluate an historical trend, as it is to try to sharpen in us the trait of discernment. Remember what set apart the sons of Issachar: they had "understanding of the times" and so knew what to do next.

There is no debating the marvelous blessings that have come with the giant strides technology has taken in the last two hundred years. I could not produce *Patriarch* magazine as I do, virtually by myself, if it weren't for computers and laser printers and scanners. And don't even get me started on the value of the Bible program I have on both my desktop and laptop computers which includes scores of commentaries and study books, multiple versions of the Bible, including Greek, Hebrew, and Latin, and advanced search capabilities that work with lightning speed. Such a tool greatly enhances the potential productivity of Bible study time.

The cumulative effect of families having a myriad of such tools at their disposal is that we are truly the wealthiest generation to have inhabited the earth. Each of our domestic servants—be it the computer, the dishwasher, or the car—enhances our material quality of life the same or even more than if we had a cadre of human servants. Freeing us from the demands of drudgery, we have more time available for nobler pursuits. This is beyond doubt a great blessing.

My question, though, is whether these blessings are worth the price we have paid for them as a society and as families. Reflecting on the changes industrialism brought, Rev. Abshire comments, "These changes in culture undermined and destroyed the sociological foundations that had held the family together from antiquity."[9] Addressing the same subject, the Hories conclude, "The material rewards were often great, but the price was high: the loss of family ties."[10] Are the material blessings worth the social and spiritual costs?

My answer is an unequivocal, "No!" If I had to choose, I would rather be in a materially poor society where families were intact and fathers were bound to their children than to be in a rich society with families fragmented to the point of practical dissolution. Material prosperity is not worth the price of family destruction.

The next question is this: Is family disintegration a necessary effect of material improvement? In other words, do we have to choose either material prosperity or family health? And a related question: Am I suggesting that we need to all become farmers or tradesmen and return to the agrarian patterns of the past in order for families to survive?

There are some profound and complex issues inherent in these questions that, frankly, I don't know that I am capable of addressing. Suffice it to say that there is no inherent contradiction between technology and wealth on the one hand, and family health and solidarity on the other. And no, I don't believe the only solution is a return to an agrarian way of life, though that would be an excellent choice for some families and communities.

I believe the real problem is rather that *Christians have failed to be discerning in their response to developing technology and the social changes it has brought*. This is the real issue, not technology itself. Christian men too often went off to work at the factories without a thought for how this would alter home life. Many fathers have moved every few years to pursue a higher income without considering the toll this takes on family members and their connections to other significant people. Men have been caught up in the flow of social change without any serious reflection or discussion about how these changes affected their fundamental duties.

Given how far we have come through the industrial/technical social transformation, I believe the only thing we fathers can do now is to become self-conscious about every choice we make from this point forward. Fathers need to ask, "Will this choice enhance the spiritual and relational dimensions of my family's life? Will it turn my heart to my children and theirs to me? Is this choice compatible with the principles and commands of Scripture?" If the answers are yes, we can proceed. If no, then we had better stop and think about other options.

Technology and the wealth it brings can be a blessing or a curse. We have allowed them to be a curse because we have indiscriminately followed wherever technology and money have led, justifying the spiritual costs by the material gains. It's time for men to stand up in the face of technological progress and increasing wealth and say, not "Stop," but "Wait." Wait until we can evaluate the total effects of this change before we embrace it. Is the technically more advanced white bread really what we want to eat, in light of the nutritional needs of the body? Is that promotion and raise really worth uprooting my family once again?

Let me repeat again for emphasis: men need to *understand the times* so that they know what they ought to do.

Significant as it is, industrialism is not the only trend that has affected modern views of manhood, the family, and the roles of fathers. We will look, more briefly, at three other significant developments before we close this chapter.

The Government as Father

Paralleling the rapid progress of industry and technology has been the growth of the paternalistic state. Today the civil government ("the state") has taken over most of the functions that used to be overseen by fathers in their homes.

Since the dawn of time families have provided the lion's share of the care and nurture needed by human beings from cradle to grave—that is, until modern times. In the past families brought children into the world and cared for the young. Parents taught their children to read and gave them the essential knowledge they needed to take their place as adults in society. Father and mother were adept at the healing arts and ministered health care to the sick among their family. Aged family members were cared for in the homes of their children or other relatives. Extended family members would take in widowed and orphaned relatives or see that their needs were met. The home was a child-care center, a school, a health provider, an old folks home, an orphanage—whatever it needed to be to care for its own.

The state has taken over more and more of these responsibilities. It began around 1840 when the states began to create the public schools and mandated the attendance of children through compulsory attendance statutes. This was a remarkable and profound cultural change. Whereas the father and mother had been the ones to indoctrinate their children, shape their character, and oversee their socialization, this task was now transferred to the state schools that proved to have a much different aim than what Christian parents had. The schools sought, and still do, to create the model citizen, one who can find his place in the modern economy, one who will be loyal to the values of socialism and tolerance or whatever the current doctrines of political correctness may be.

Since the Great Depression of the 1930s the taxpayer-financed welfare apparatus has grown enormously. All in the name of benevolence, several family functions have been usurped by the state. Most notable among these, and the most expensive, is the Social Security system, which promises financial and medical care for the aged. What families used to do out of a sense of loving obligation, the state now does, poorly, through a program of coerced income transfer. It is similar with the programs that feed the poor and provide support for single mothers with children. These "welfare" programs are a direct attack on fatherhood, not only since the state provides what a father ought, but because the father must be out of the home for the woman to qualify for support.

We could go on about government medical programs which are not only very costly to taxpayers but which also increasingly erode the liberty of families to make medical decisions. Or we could address how financing the welfare state has placed a huge economic burden on families, making it very difficult to get by on the father's income alone, and forcing women into the workplace. But we would quickly get beyond the scope of our present concern.

One final example of the state's usurpation of family duties deserves mention, however, since it is such a direct attack on parental sovereignty over children. Alan Carlson, of the pro-family Howard Center for Family, Religion, and Society, in a speech some years ago, addressed the doctrine of *parens patriae*, or "the parenthood of the state," which first made its appearance around 1840. He said:

> Twisting ancient English chancery law to a new purpose, a Pennsylvania court used the term to justify the seizure and incarceration of children, over the protests of families, when the natural parents were deemed "unequal to the task of education or unworthy of it." Reform schools, the "child saving" movement, the juvenile justice system, and the vast child abuse and neglect apparatus, all built on the *parens patriae*, representing as it did the family's surrender of its protective function to the state.

This legal perversion has been developed to the point where today an anonymous call to a "child-abuse hotline" can result in parents losing custody of their children without any legal process whatsoever.

So the state has become the father to the nation, and men have allowed it. We can't simply blame the politicians and judges, though they deserve blame. Fathers by the millions have been passive in the face of the ongoing assault against their families. Someone has called it "responsibility drift." Men have been glad to relieve themselves of some of the burdens of fatherhood, and the state has been only too happy to take them over.

IDEOLOGIES VS. MANHOOD

So far we have been addressing social and political factors that have restructured our society in ways detrimental to fathers and families. We should also take note of the influence of ideas: the philosophical attack on the family.

Christian thought dominated the West from the time of the Roman Empire to the Renaissance of the fifteenth and sixteenth centuries. At that time a revival of interest in the ancient wisdom of the pagan Greeks began to lay the groundwork for what in time came to be called "humanism." By the late eighteenth century philosophers were boldly denouncing the Christian concept of God, and the "Age of Enlightenment" enshrined the notion that man is the measure of all things. Despite the powerful and lingering influences of the Reformation, the God of the Bible came to be regarded, among the intelligentsia, as an embarrassing relic to be discarded. God as the Father who personally cares for his creatures and personally punishes sin was set aside in favor of an impersonal god who made no ethical demands. Eventually even this idol was abandoned in favor of a materialistic and evolutionary interpretation of reality.

With the loss of both God the Father and of His authoritative Word as the standard by which to order all of life, Western society lost the foundation that had underlain the patriarchal social system, which thus no longer had a theoretical basis for its existence. Without the solid ground of revealed truth as a foundation for belief and for social organization, Western culture began to substitute what have come to be called ideologies.

My dictionary defines "ideology" as "visionary theorizing." These theories generally have to do with the vision of remaking human life and culture according to whatever pattern the theory espouses. Western civilization has been driven by anti-Christian visionary theories that are antithetical to Scripture and which, in particular, are very unfriendly to the God of the Bible and to biblical manhood. Yet one common characteristic of ideologies is that they are notoriously pushy. They do not tolerate opposition in their drive to remake society in their image.

One humanist ideology that has grown dominant in the last century or so is that of egalitarianism, known more commonly by its most visible and vocal manifestation, feminism. Egalitarianism is a perversion of the sound idea that "all men are created equal"—sound, that is, as long as you understand this to mean that everyone has equal dignity before God and thus should be treated equally before the law. In other words, no favoritism. However, this notion has been twisted to mean that all people should be regarded as equal in every way, and differences should be eliminated, as far as possible.

Feminism says that women are equal to men. That, of course, is true in regard to the inherent worth and dignity of the person and the equally important roles both play in society. That is a biblical idea. However, feminism teaches something very different. It denies the propriety of role differences between the genders and the order of authority that God has established for home and society, and at this point it is in radical rebellion against God, His creation, and His revealed will in the Bible.

Many of the political battles of the last century have involved applications of this ideology, including the unsuccessful drive to pass the Equal Rights Amendment (ERA) and the more recent successful effort to force women into the previously all-male Virginia Military Institute. This philosophy has been a huge blow to biblical manhood and the family. It provides a theoretical basis for denying the man's leadership role in home and society, and it encourages women to abandon their God-given, home-centered calling. The effects have been devastating to family life in the societies where this anti-Christian message prevails. Feminism is a direct assault on the Bible and the God of the Bible, and it has been relentlessly molding this society toward its utopian vision.

Some of you may wonder if I'm not still fighting old battles as I address the dangers of feminism. After all, the heyday of feminism seems to have passed with the failure of the states to ratify the ERA. But what you need to see is that, while the political agitation in its favor may have subsided, the philosophy of feminism has won the battle for our culture. With or without the ERA, feminism has triumphed. Its assumptions have become the assumptions of our whole society, including Christians, who have been passive before its advances, if not downright accommodating.

I was cast into a major depression the day I saw an article in a leading Christian men's magazine with the title, "Why We Need Feminism." How did the author speak about this anti-Christian, man-hating movement?

> Christians need feminism… I want to argue that feminism
> is more right than wrong. In fact, I think feminism is

fundamentally a Christian idea....

[The author's future wife] didn't call herself a feminist, and we rarely discussed the topic. But what seemed so obvious—so logical—to us was that God had given us each a vocation. That we would be equal partners in sustaining a household....

Modern feminism has Christian roots. Begun in the mid-nineteenth century in America by seminary-trained Elizabeth Cady Stanton and Quaker Susan B. Anthony...

I think Jesus was a feminist... And so modern feminism can be seen as a work of restoration, continuing the revolution started by Jesus... In many ways, feminism is simply Christian common sense.[11]

What hope is there for the Christian men's movement when feminist propaganda passes editorial muster at one of its principal publications? A couple of verses come to mind: "This I say, therefore, and testify in the Lord, that you should no longer walk as the rest of the Gentiles walk, in the futility of their mind" (Eph. 4:17). "And do not be conformed to this world, but be transformed by the renewing of your mind, that you may prove what is that good and acceptable and perfect will of God" (Rom. 12:2). If there is to be any hope of lasting fruit from the men's movement, Christian men need to purge their minds of the futility of the feminist lie, and they need to renew their minds by grounding their view of the world in the Bible alone.

This problem of accommodation and compromise in the face of evil brings me to a final factor that has influenced the modern notions of family, manhood, and fatherhood.

Feminized Churches and Doctrines

The churches should have been a refuge for Christian fathers seeking guidance and solace in the face of all the challenges to biblical manhood and the family that we have addressed thus far. I am sad to say, they have failed in that task. Actually, if we are to be honest, they are a large part of the problem.

First, instead of standing up and challenging the direction modern society has taken, *the church has acquiesced to the culture at every turn.* In the liberal denominations this has taken the form of accommodating feminism and embracing whatever new idea the God-haters have come up with, to the point where they are now in the process of embracing practicing sodomites and considering them for the ministry instead of calling them to repentance and offering them the forgiveness of God and His grace to live a new life. The mainline churches have simply followed the cultural drift, accepting the ideology *du jour* with fawning gusto.

Sadly, the evangelical churches have also largely failed to recognize and address the destructive trends of Western culture. In their case it is mostly the result of a faulty theology that teaches that Christians should not bother engaging the culture. This attitude has been rooted in an understanding of Scripture that truncates the application of the gospel: the gospel is about "spiritual" things, not earthly matters like schooling, politics, and business. This has then been reinforced by a pervasive tendency to think that it's no use getting exercised about such things since Jesus could come back at any time.

Most churches have allowed themselves to be transformed by the influence of the industrial/business model for organizations, with efficiency and bureaucracy as their hallmarks. Activities, organizations, and committees are multiplied while vital relationships are too often lost in the process and families are fragmented into age-segregated and functional subgroups as soon as they walk in the church door. True body life is too often lost as churches pursue the mega-church model, however small they might actually be.

Ironically, both liberal and evangelical churches have taken a passive, we might even say feminine, posture toward the culture: allowing the culture to act upon the church rather than the church acting upon the culture. The church is supposed to be feminine in relationship to God, but masculine with reference to the world. Christians should take a more aggressive posture toward culture, the kind suggested by the words of the apostle Paul: "For though we walk in the flesh, we do not war according to the flesh. For the weapons of our warfare are not carnal but mighty in God for pulling down strongholds, casting down arguments and every high thing that exalts itself against the knowledge of God, bringing every thought into captivity to the obedience of Christ" (1 Cor. 10:3-5). Rather than taking thoughts captive for Christ, Christians have allowed their own thoughts to be taken captive by the humanistic philosophies and ideologies of the modern world.

The second way the church has been part of the problem instead of the solution in the cultural drift is that *it has largely abandoned the virile doctrines of the early church and the Reformation.* Instead of the Bible's masculine *doctrine of salvation* in which an initiating God acts with efficacious love to subdue His chosen people to Himself, much of the church now proclaims a passive God who offers His love but would not think of imposing His love on His bride. The pallid Jesus stands at the door and knocks, hoping we'll let Him in. God is no longer presented as the very archetype of masculine power and love. This kind of feminized doctrine has contributed to the proliferation of feminized men who stand fearful even before their wives. If God is feminized, what chance do Christian men have?

The church has also become largely *antinomian* (a word which means "against law"), and this has contributed to its ineffectiveness in addressing issues of morality and social order. Christians today are scared to death of the law of God. After all, didn't Jesus set us free from the law? Of course he did: we are no longer condemned by the law. Praise God! But the moral law of God is binding on all men at all times, and the Christian rejoices in the law of liberty (Jas. 1:25) which shows him how to please God. He understands that "all Scripture is given by inspiration of God, and is profitable for doctrine, for reproof, for correction, for instruction in righteousness, that the man of God may be complete, thoroughly equipped for every good work" (2 Tim. 3: 16,17). In short, the Christian man loves the law (the Word) of God, meditating on it day and night (Ps. 1:2). Those who don't think God's revealed will (his Word, his law) applies to them are not inclined to conform their lives to the patterns of this law, and they are likely to accommodate themselves to the winds of cultural change, however lawless.

A final destructive doctrine of the modern church, which has especially hindered its ability to respond to the dissolution of the family, is its *individualism*. The Bible teaches the solidarity of the human race in Adam and of the elect in Christ. It teaches a solidarity of family in which fathers are tied to their children and their children's children. The Bible's view of life is covenantal: God works with groups of people, not just with individuals, as he accomplishes His purposes in history. He deals with families, with churches, and with nations. God saves individually, but not apart from a consideration of the family of which the person is a part. "But the mercy of the LORD is from everlasting to everlasting on those who fear Him, and His righteousness to children's children, to such as keep His covenant, and to those who remember His commandments to do them" (Ps. 103: 17,18). God works through families as families, not just through individuals. The loss of this vision of life has diminished the significance of the family in the minds of Christian men and made it more difficult for them to stand against the modern assaults on the family.

Taking 'Old Paths' Into the Future

Thus says the LORD: "Stand in the ways and see, and ask for the old paths, where the good way is, and walk in it; then you will find rest for your souls. But they said, 'We will not walk in it.'" (Jer. 6:16)

When a people who used to walk in wisdom go astray to their hurt, the smart thing for them to do is to return to the old paths so that they can find rest once again. As a culture we used to do the family thing right, but over the last few generations we have lost our way to the point that we won't even survive as a culture given our current course. It makes sense to get back to the ways that worked. It makes sense to get back to biblical patriarchy.

Unfortunately it is likely that most men will reject this call, even among Christians. There is a strong inertia that will hold men back, and that force is another ideology of the modern world. It is the absolute conviction that new is better than old. This is a logical corollary to the doctrine of evolution: everything is improving over time. So what could the past possibly have to teach us?

Add to that the visceral reaction against the word "patriarchy" among those indoctrinated by feminism, and the crowd thins even more. But we use this term for several very sound reasons (cf. Appendix A), one of which is that it identifies the ideological battle of our day and forces a choice upon the person who hears the term: feminism or patriarchy? You can't live in both worlds.

Many men will say of the old path, "We will not walk in it." But that needn't stop you and me. Let's adopt the attitude expressed by Job:

> For inquire, please, of the former age, and consider the things discovered by their fathers; for we were born yesterday, and know nothing, because our days on earth are a shadow. Will they not teach you and tell you, and utter words from their heart? (Job 8:8-10)

We need the humility to realize that we don't know very much at all. We need to learn from the past, from our forefathers, who will still speak to us from their hearts if we will just listen.

Even if the crowd doesn't follow, even if the larger culture continues its path toward destruction, you can do it right in your home. You don't control the world, but by God's design, you do control your own choices and your own household.

Doing it right starts with understanding what you have done wrong, and a large part of that is simply a matter of understanding the times in which you live. We've all been led astray, but we can get back on course.

Let's set our eyes on the future because that is where we and our children are going to live. But as we do, let's learn the lessons of the past so that we understand the times in which we live today.

Let's take the "old paths" into the future.

Now that we have figured out where we are, we can take the Bible in hand as our map and compass and figure out where the Lord wants us to go.

CHAPTER 3

The Man is Responsible

But I want you to know that the head of every man is Christ, the head of woman is man, and the head of Christ is God.

1 Corinthians 11:3

We've all heard of a spineless man. He's the one without courage. But why "spineless"? An analogy is designed to help us understand something by picturing it for us. So picture this: a man who literally has no backbone. What would he look like?

He couldn't stand up. He would fall in a heap. Just like the timid man can't stand up to his boss, or his wife, or even his children. He collapses in a pile when faced with opposition. It's easier to let the other person have their way. So spinelessness is a pretty good image of a man who lacks the courage to stand up for himself and for what is right.

Leaders need backbones. They need to be able to stand up straight, make decisions, and get others to follow them. A weak man in authority won't be effective and won't last long, at least if he himself has a man with a backbone as his boss.

Ideological feminists hate men with backbones. Men who have the courage to exercise authority are at the top of their enemies list. That's why the only men who can get along with them are, well, spineless men who are willing to bow to their egalitarian theories.

But it's worse than this. The feminists don't just want spineless, feminized men—they want a spineless world. They want to do away with all traditional (read "biblical") authority structures, which are invariably described as "oppressive" and (gasp) "patriarchal."

Although it was more popular back in the '70s, surely you have seen the bumper sticker, usually found on a car with a woman driver, that states simply, "Question Authority." That is a fitting motto for our modern age. And I don't think the message is suggesting that we ask polite, respectful questions of those in authority over us. It is a call to question the very existence and legitimacy of authority. Ours is a radically anti-authority age.

Authority, however, is inevitable. It is inescapable because the ultimate authority, God, is inescapable, and because He has established authority structures as the very framework of existence.

Authority establishes order, and this order is like the skeleton in a body. It is the strong principle that holds everything together and enables each part to function. Imagine a man's body with the bones removed. What would he look like? No skull, no jaw, no arm and hand bones, no ribs, no thigh bone connected to the knee bone. He would look more like a puddle than a person. Bones are essential to life. They provide the hidden strength and structure that allows the organism to thrive.

The order established through God's authority is to the universe as a skeleton is to a body. It provides the structure and strength that allows the creation to function, both physically and spiritually.

What are called "the laws of nature," such as gravity and inertia, is the order by which the universe operates and without which its very existence would be impossible. The laws themselves, of course, are simply an expression of God's authority and power. The force that holds the physical universe together is the personal God. The eternal Son, who was at His Father's side during the process of creation as a "master craftsman" (Prov. 8:30) is also the one in whom "all things consist" (Col. 1:17). God creates and preserves His physical creation through the structures we recognize as the laws of physics.

Although modern ideologues deny it, the universe is not only material. It has a spiritual/personal dimension, and this spiritual element also operates by laws that God has established as part of the very fabric of creation. One of these laws is the principle of headship or authority, and it is this law which provides the necessary order in which persons, angelic and human, can interact and carry out their God-given purposes in harmony. We have hints of authority structures beyond this world in the Bible's references to "principalities and powers in the heavenly places" (Eph. 3:10; cf. Col. 1:16; 2:15). We will be looking at the evidence that God has also established such structures for mankind in this world.

Authority is not everything. It is simply the framework in which relationships can thrive, love can blossom, and everyone can work together with one mind to the glory of God. Jesus said, "If you love Me, keep My commandments" (Jn. 14:15). True love cannot exist outside of submission to God's authority.

The modern world is seeking love, success, and fulfillment apart from the authority structures that God has ordained. This quest must always end in futility. Without submitting to the laws by which God has ordered life, there can be no love, no success, and no personal fulfillment.

Recently I have heard news reports of two fatal train wrecks. In both, as in all such disasters, the train cars were strewn about the crash site in a spectacle of chaos and destruction. As long as the engine stays on those two parallel rails, the train is fine; but once it gets de-railed, calamity is inevitable. The tracks are not the most important thing about that mode of transportation; the goods that are shipped or the people that are transported are the purpose of the system. But if the tracks are ignored, the whole system will become unworkable and downright dangerous.

It is similar with our families in God's world. As long as our family train stays on the tracks of God's Word and His revealed patterns for life, we can live in peace and blessing. When we jump the rails and try to plot our own course—well, "train wreck" is a pretty good description of what we get in our homes and in the nation. God's order of authority is what keeps us on track.

EVEN GOD OBEYS THIS LAW

At the opening of this chapter we placed the key text for understanding all of this authority business, 1 Corinthians 11:3. It reads: "But I want you to know that the head of every man is Christ, the head of woman is man, and the head of Christ is God."

Although it is not stated in this order, here is the picture that we get from the verse:

GOD THE FATHER
⇩
CHRIST
⇩
MAN
⇩
WOMAN

In context this picture is used by the apostle Paul in support of his admonition to the Corinthian saints to exhibit proper role relationships between men and women while praying or prophesying.

As to the word "head," its use elsewhere in Scripture shows that it refers to one who holds a superior position in reference to another. "And He put all things under His feet, and gave Him to be head over all things to the church" (Eph. 1:22). As head over all things, Christ had all things under His feet, which is to say in an inferior position. "And He is the head of the body, the church, who is the beginning, the firstborn from the dead, that in all things He may have the preeminence" (Col. 1:18).

As the Messianic king, Christ has the preeminence, the place of supreme prominence and superiority. A person who is head of someone holds a position of authority over that person. Speaking only in terms of *position* and not worth, the head is the superior and the one under the head is the inferior within the order of authority.

We tend to focus immediately on the fact that man is the head of woman, and that is, after all, the reason Paul wrote the sentence. But there are two very striking truths revealed in this verse that go beyond mere human relationships.

First, *there is a structure of authority within the Godhead.* "The head of Christ is God." "God" here obviously refers to God the Father to whom Christ constantly alluded with deference and submission during His earthly ministry (e.g., Luke 22: 42; John 17:4). The Son submits to the Father, and the Holy Spirit submits to the Father and the Son (Jn. 14:26; 15:26). Before there was a creation, authority existed for all eternity among the divine persons. Authority is eternal. Given this truth, it is apparent that authority is not just a temporary and unhappy expedient imposed upon mankind because of sin. It is a fundamental principle of reality, a law that even applies to God (which is to say, it is a part of His own nature).

Second, *a structure of authority ties God and mankind together.* Those who believe the Bible reject the "chain of being" myth that teaches that God and man are simply on different rungs of the ladder of being, and thus man can, in principle, become God. Rather we believe in the radical transcendence of God: He is totally separate from His creation and He has an entirely different quality of being. However, there is a connection between God and man. Our verse teaches that God and His creation are joined by ties of authority (as other passages teach they are joined by ties of love). As God is the head of Christ, so Christ is the head of man. So while there is no chain of being, there is a chain of authority that joins heaven and earth.

Both of these truths demonstrate the absolutely fundamental nature of authority structures. Authority and order exist in the Godhead, and authority and order tie the creatures to their Creator. So the feminists can "question authority" all they want, but that won't change a thing. They still exist in the world as it is, not as their fantasies would have it, and it is an orderly world, structured by authority. The choice for any man or woman is to get in line with God's order or suffer the train wreck that results from rebelling against His plan.

Authority structures are God's very creative solution to the problem of how to mesh multiple wills in a common purpose, so that the human race can live in peace and take dominion over the earth. If every person does what is right in his own eyes, there is chaos. When many wills are brought together under the harmony and order created by authority structures, each person's energies are freed to work to the fullest advantage and directed to the highest good of all and to the glory of God. Order does not stifle—it liberates.

Before we leave 1 Corinthians 11:3, let's just note one other thing: *both the man and the woman are under authority, and each must practice submission.* The verse begins by saying that the man is under the authority of Christ. The man is not a god who may do as he wishes. Nor, then, is the woman alone in having to submit to authority; the man has to do that, too. Even Christ himself, the second person of the Trinity, must practice submission to his Father. *Everyone*, including God, is in this chain of authority. Each person has a different role to play depending upon where he or she is in God's order.

The importance of recognizing and bowing to God's authority structure is evident in the Gospel account of Jesus' healing of the centurion's servant:

> Now when Jesus had entered Capernaum, a centurion came to Him, pleading with Him, saying, "Lord, my servant is lying at home paralyzed, dreadfully tormented."
>
> And Jesus said to him, "I will come and heal him."
>
> The centurion answered and said, "Lord, I am not worthy that You should come under my roof. But only speak a word, and my servant will be healed. For I also am a man under authority, having soldiers under me. And I say to this one, 'Go,' and he goes; and to another, 'Come,' and he comes; and to my servant, 'Do this,' and he does it."
>
> When Jesus heard it, He marveled, and said to those who followed, "Assuredly, I say to you, I have not found such great faith, not even in Israel!" (Matt. 8:5-10)

Why did Jesus describe the centurion's faith as so great? He recognized the ability of Jesus to heal his servant, but others also trusted Jesus in this way. What made his such a "great faith" seems to have been the centurion's recognition of how Jesus' authority related to his power. This soldier recognized that authority works through a chain of command, that the one in charge does not need to carry out the work directly but can delegate authority and project his power without being present at the point where his will is executed. The centurion thus showed exceptional insight into how the kingdom of God works.

An essential ingredient of true faith in God is an understanding of how He works His will in this world. Faith does not just grasp the reality of God and His power, it also recognizes the means by which God executes his power. In other words, faith perceives and submits to God's authority structures.

In the Beginning

To get the full picture of God's plan for the human race, including the authority structure He has ordained for mankind, we need to consult the first three chapters of Genesis. We find the creation of mankind first mentioned in chapter one:

> 26 Then God said, "Let Us make man in Our image, according to Our likeness; let them have dominion over the fish of the sea, over the birds of the air, and over the cattle, over all the earth and over every creeping thing that creeps on the earth."
> 27 So God created man in His own image; in the image of God He created him; male and female He created them.
> 28 Then God blessed them, and God said to them, "Be fruitful and multiply; fill the earth and subdue it; have dominion over the fish of the sea, over the birds of the air, and over every living thing that moves on the earth."

From this passage we learn that mankind, both male and female, are made in the image of God to have dominion over the whole earth. For this task they need to multiply and fill the earth, so God blessed them to that end. Just as God rules the whole universe, so He has made mankind to rule this planet. It is primarily in his having this delegated power to rule that man images God. Man is king of the earth, but he is a steward answerable to God. To use a theological term, man is God's vice-regent upon the earth.

Genesis 2 gives a fuller description of what happened when God made mankind. Let's look at the key portions of the chapter.

> 7 And the LORD God formed man of the dust of the ground, and breathed into his nostrils the breath of life; and man became a living being.
> 8 The LORD God planted a garden eastward in Eden, and there He put the man whom He had formed....
> 15 Then the LORD God took the man and put him in the garden of Eden to tend and keep it.
> 16 And the LORD God commanded the man, saying, "Of every tree of the garden you may freely eat;
> 17 "but of the tree of the knowledge of good and evil you shall not eat, for in the day that you eat of it you shall surely die."
> 18 And the LORD God said, "It is not good that man should be alone; I will make him a helper comparable to him."
> 19 Out of the ground the LORD God formed every beast of the field and every bird of the air, and brought them

to Adam to see what he would call them. And whatever Adam called each living creature, that was its name.

20 So Adam gave names to all cattle, to the birds of the air, and to every beast of the field. But for Adam there was not found a helper comparable to him.

21 And the LORD God caused a deep sleep to fall on Adam, and he slept; and He took one of his ribs, and closed up the flesh in its place.

22 Then the rib which the LORD God had taken from man He made into a woman, and He brought her to the man.

23 And Adam said: "This is now bone of my bones And flesh of my flesh; She shall be called Woman, Because she was taken out of Man."

24 Therefore a man shall leave his father and mother and be joined to his wife, and they shall become one flesh.

In this passage we see that God did not create the man and the woman simultaneously. He created the man out of the dust, placed him in the garden, gave him his dominion task of caring for the garden, warned him not to eat from one of the special trees in the garden, brought the animals to the man so that he could name them and discover his need for a more suitable helper, and finally created the woman out of the man and brought her to him.

THE MAN IS THE LEADER

Let's now look more closely at Genesis 2 in an effort to discern God's authority structure for mankind. In several ways within this chapter it is abundantly evident that God created the man to be the leader and the woman to be his subordinate (as a companion and helper). This picture of the human race is consistent with the principle declared in 1 Corinthians 11:3: man is the head of woman.

First, *the man was created first.* God the Creator fashioned the man out of the dust of the ground, breathed into his nostrils the breath of life, and man thus became a living being (v. 7). The woman was not formed until sometime later (v. 22). The man's prior creation suggests his superior status, in terms of authority.

Our conclusion is confirmed by an explicit statement in the New Testament. In 1 Timothy Paul is giving instructions for Christian worship. He writes, "Let a woman learn in silence with all submission. And I do not permit a woman to teach or to have authority over a man, but to be in silence. For Adam was formed first, then Eve" (vv. 11-13). The reason Paul gives, by inspiration of the Holy Spirit, for his prohibition against women teaching men or exercising authority over them is simply that Adam was created first. The clear implication is this: the fact that God formed the man first is proof of his position of headship.

Second, *God dealt directly with the man.* Before the woman was even created, God gave Adam his dominion assignment (v. 15), laid down the moral law to him (vv. 16,17), and assigned him the task of naming the animals (vv. 19,20), which was also part of his job as ruler of the earth. God's first interactions with mankind—very significant interactions—were with the man alone. Nor, after He created Eve, did the Creator repeat to her the things He had said and done with Adam. This suggests the priority of Adam's status before the Creator. God spoke to the head and laid out the groundwork for life before anyone else was there. That was sufficient to get the job done because Adam was then responsible to teach his wife what God had said, and apparently he did this since Eve was aware, for example, of God's commandment (3:3).

Third, *the woman was created from the man.* While Adam was made from the ground, Eve was fashioned from a rib (or the side) of Adam (v. 22). By God's miracle of creation, Eve derives her very being from Adam. Her existence is dependent upon him. She is, in fact, a completion of the man. When she was presented to Adam he declared, "This is now bone of my bones and flesh of my flesh" (v. 23). Then God pronounced his blessing upon marriage in verse 24, ending with "and they shall become one flesh." The woman came from the man and is returned to him in marriage. That is why the key marriage passage in Ephesians 5 uses this kind of language: "So husbands ought to love their own wives as their own bodies; he who loves his wife loves himself. For no one ever hated his own flesh, but nourishes and cherishes it, just as the Lord does the church" (vv. 28,29). A man should regard his wife as a part of himself because, in terms of her origins, this is exactly who she is.

If there were any doubt about this reason for viewing the man as the leader, it is removed by 1 Corinthians 11:7,8:

> For a man indeed ought not to cover his head, since he is the image and glory of God; but woman is the glory of man. For man is not from woman, but woman from man.

The fact that the woman came from the man establishes his position of superiority over her as her head.

Notice, too, that verse 7 describes the man as the image and glory of God, while the woman is the glory of the man. While both the man and the woman were made in God's image (Gen. 1: 27), he reflects that image directly and she reflects it derivatively by reflecting the glory of the man from whom she was made. The constituent parts of their humanity are the same for man and woman (mind, will, emotions), and they both reflect God in their knowledge, love, holiness, etc. However, since the man has the position of headship, he reflects God in this additional way, while the woman does not. Her glory is in relating to her head and reflecting him. Both man and woman are the image of God constitutionally and ethically; the man is also the image of God in terms of his position.

The language of this verse can leave no doubt that the man is the superior in the relationship. And please remember: Scripture here is addressing authority structure, not inherent worth and dignity. To say that the man is the woman's superior is a statement about their place in God's order of authority, not about the value of either.

Fourth, *the woman was created for the man*. The Lord seems to have gone to some lengths to be sure Adam understood this. Only after parading the animals before him (v. 19), and thus showing him how alone he was, did God create Eve (vv. 19,20). She was created to meet Adam's need for companionship and for help in his dominion task. She was a "helper comparable" to him (v. 20). He couldn't do the job alone. He certainly couldn't be fruitful and multiply by himself (1:28)! She was the perfect provision for his need since she could comfort him with her presence as his companion, assist him in his work as his helper, and bear his children so that there would be more dominion workers.

In 1 Corinthians 11 Paul uses yet another argument to bolster his case for exhibiting proper role relationships. In verse 9 we read: "Nor was man created for the woman, but woman for the man." This corroborates the conclusion we drew while looking at Genesis 2. The headship of the man is displayed by the fact that the woman was created to be his helper.

Fifth, *the man named the woman*. In the Bible, having the prerogative of naming someone always indicates a position of authority over the one named. Think of parents naming their children, or of Jesus giving new names to some of His disciples (e.g., Simon to Peter). Adam exercised his authority over the animal kingdom by naming the animals (v. 19). Then after the woman was created Adam called her "Woman" (v. 23), and he later named her "Eve" (3:20).

Sixth, *the man and the woman together are called "man."* In Genesis 1 we read: "So God created man in His own image; in the image of God He created him; male and female He created them" (v. 27). Both "male and female" at the end of the sentence are encompassed by the designation "man" at the beginning. We find a similar statement in chapter 5, verse 2: "He created them male and female, and blessed them and called them Mankind in the day they were created." The word translated "mankind" is the Hebrew word *adam*, which means man and is also the name of the first man.

The reason the generic word for humankind is the male term is because the male is the head of the human family and of his wife in particular. In calling Eve by her husband's name in Genesis 5:2, God has given us, in effect, the first instance of the introduction we always hear at weddings: "Ladies and gentlemen, it is my privilege to introduce to you Mr. and Mrs. Adam!" It is proper for a woman to take her husband's name when she becomes his wife because he is now her head, and this headship is expressed in their common name. When a married woman maintains her maiden name and refuses to take her husband's surname, she is signaling a rejection of his headship over her.

THE LEADER IS ACCOUNTABLE

A seventh and final evidence from Genesis that God created the man to be the leader is seen in the fact that *the man was held responsible for the fall into sin, even though the woman sinned first.*

Let's first take a look at the passage that records that fall and its aftermath. This is from Genesis 3:

> 1 Now the serpent was more cunning than any beast of the field which the LORD God had made. And he said to the woman, "Has God indeed said, 'You shall not eat of every tree of the garden' ?"
> 2 And the woman said to the serpent, "We may eat the fruit of the trees of the garden;
> 3 "but of the fruit of the tree which is in the midst of the garden, God has said, 'You shall not eat it, nor shall you

touch it, lest you die.'"

4 Then the serpent said to the woman, "You will not surely die.

5 "For God knows that in the day you eat of it your eyes will be opened, and you will be like God, knowing good and evil."

6 So when the woman saw that the tree was good for food, that it was pleasant to the eyes, and a tree desirable to make one wise, she took of its fruit and ate. She also gave to her husband with her, and he ate.

7 Then the eyes of both of them were opened, and they knew that they were naked; and they sewed fig leaves together and made themselves coverings.

8 And they heard the sound of the LORD God walking in the garden in the cool of the day, and Adam and his wife hid themselves from the presence of the LORD God among the trees of the garden.

9 Then the LORD God called to Adam and said to him, "Where are you?"

10 So he said, "I heard Your voice in the garden, and I was afraid because I was naked; and I hid myself."

11 And He said, "Who told you that you were naked? Have you eaten from the tree of which I commanded you that you should not eat?"

12 Then the man said, "The woman whom You gave to be with me, she gave me of the tree, and I ate."

13 And the LORD God said to the woman, "What is this you have done?" The woman said, "The serpent deceived me, and I ate."

14 So the LORD God said to the serpent: "Because you have done this, You are cursed more than all cattle, And more than every beast of the field; On your belly you shall go, And you shall eat dust all the days of your life.

15 And I will put enmity between you and the woman, And between your seed and her Seed; He shall bruise your head, And you shall bruise His heel."

16 To the woman He said: "I will greatly multiply your sorrow and your conception; In pain you shall bring forth children; Your desire shall be for your husband, And he shall rule over you."

17 Then to Adam He said, "Because you have heeded the voice of your wife, and have eaten from the tree of which I commanded you, saying, 'You shall not eat of it': "Cursed is the ground for your sake; In toil you shall eat of it all the days of your life.

18 Both thorns and thistles it shall bring forth for you, And you shall eat the herb of the field.

19 In the sweat of your face you shall eat bread till you return to the ground, for out of it you were taken; for dust you are, and to dust you shall return."

Satan comes in the form of a cunning serpent and begins his temptation of the human race with the question he has been using ever since (after all, it worked well then!): "Has God indeed said…?" The human family has always been susceptible to this subtle attack on God's authority. God speaks clearly in His word, yet someone will ask, "Did God really mean that? Is that really what the Bible means?" How else can we account for the accommodation of Christians to the lies of feminism and evolution, for example? Satan opens the door to our minds and hearts with a subtle invitation for us to become the judges of God's Word. "Why don't you just think about what God says. Is that right?" Before long, the attack becomes less subtle: "You will not surely die." Having allowed ourselves to sidestep God's authority slightly, we end up swallowing the whole lie.

The long and short of the story is this: Eve fell for the lie; checked out the fruit, making herself the judge of whether it was good to eat or not; ate the fruit; gave it to her husband who obligingly ate it, too; and their consciences bothered them so they hid from God behind leaf-clothes and bushes.

What happens next is what is interesting for the purposes of our current topic. "Then the LORD God called to Adam and said to him, 'Where are you?'" Remember, Eve sinned first. Adam just went along. But God comes to him and points his finger in his face, as it were, and demands an accounting from him. After Adam mumbles some excuses, God presses his questions on him, "Who told you that you were naked? Have you eaten from the tree of which I commanded you that you should not eat?"

The point is that Adam is responsible, even though it was Eve who sinned first. *He* was in charge. God gave *him* the commandment. God was holding *him* accountable. This is the way it works with leadership. The head answers for all those under his authority.

Adam was not only acting for himself. He was the head of the whole human race, not just Eve, and when he sinned the whole race fell into sin. "Therefore, just as through one man sin entered the world, and death through sin, and thus death spread to all men..." (Rom. 5:12). This is how seriously God takes headship!

After God's relentless confrontation, Adam played the coward and tried to pin the fault on Eve. "The woman whom You gave to be with me, she gave me of the tree, and I ate." We can even hear a subtle attempt to blame God: It's the woman *you* gave me who led me into sin. So our first father failed to take responsibility. (Now you know where we got it!)

One final evidence of Adam's unique accountability is found in the words the Lord used as He began to pronounce the curse upon him: "Because you have heeded the voice of your wife..." (v.17). To Eve, God simply pronounced her punishment (v. 16), but to Adam he began by identifying the first form of his transgression. The real sin of Adam lay in listening to his wife's invitation to sin and then following her rather than being the leader he was created to be. The head failed to lead and allowed the tail to wag the dog.

So God's holding Adam accountable is the seventh and final evidence in these passages that God designed the man to be the head of the human authority structure—from the beginning. Before leaving the scene in the garden, however, let's consider more carefully what went wrong there and what we can learn from it.

MALE PASSIVITY: THE ROOT OF ALL EVIL

Since Adam was the head of the human race, we might have expected that he would be the one to take the lead and drag his wife and all the rest of us into sin. But what we see actually unfold in the garden is that, while he retains his formal authority as representative head of the race (and it is indeed his act that doomed us all), Eve becomes the *de facto* leader and Adam the follower as they rebel against God. In the midst of the formal acts of disobedience (eating the fruit) we find another perversity at work: the breakdown of the proper relationship between the man and the woman.

If indeed there was a breakdown of that relationship, what was the nature of the failure? Clearly Adam was supposed to lead in the relationship, not Eve. Yet she took the lead into sin. While she is guilty for her part in getting out from under her husband's authority, the leader is always the one who bears responsibility for the relationship. When she attempted to take the lead, he should have resisted, asserted his authority, and refused to go along with her. Instead, he followed her. So they both erred in a kind of reversal of roles.

More specifically, Adam failed in his leadership by not protecting his wife. The serpent sought out the more vulnerable of the two to work his wiles (Gen. 3:1; cf. 1 Tim. 2:14). Where was Adam? Why did he not step in and shout the serpent down when he questioned the Word of God? It appears from the language of Genesis 3:6 (he was "with her") that Adam was present but simply passive and ineffective in his role of leader-protector. Though the text is not explicit, it seems as if Adam simply watched his wife be beguiled into sin and then went with the flow and sinned with her. It is explicitly clear that he followed her into sin. It is implicitly clear that he was passive even before that and failed to lead his wife by providing protection against their spiritual enemy.

So it would seem that the context of the specific acts of disobedience (eating of the tree) was a general failure of obedience to God's created order for the marriage relationship. It would not then be too much of a stretch to say that the first sin was Adam's passivity and his failure to lead and protect his wife. It was this failure that led to her being tempted and succumbing to sin. Even if some may doubt that inference from the passage, it is certainly clear that it was Adam's passivity that led to his sharing the fruit that his wife offered him. Any way you slice it, the passive male appears to be a major factor in the entrance of sin into the world. We might even put it this way (to borrow a phrase from our Lord): the passive male is the root of all evil. If Adam had been an active leader-protector instead of a passive follower, the curse would not have been pronounced on the world.

Sin did not just sneak up on the first couple and tackle them. They fell because of their own passivity in the face of temptation. In their hearts they did not resist the evil suggestions of the serpent that contradicted God's words. They yielded, they took the easy path of acquiescence rather than saying "No" to the tempter. Likewise, the passivity of Adam in relationship to the tempter and to Eve led directly to the Fall. He failed to guard her and to lead her. Instead he yielded to her leadership and ultimately to that of Satan. Thus began the sordid saga of human history.

The well-being of the whole creation rests on the proper functioning of the various authority arrangements that God has established. Satan was a high angel who stepped out of his role and rebelled against God's order. He came to earth to wreak havoc with the perfection God had created here. Eve got out from under her human authority, Adam, and instead of seeking his leadership took the initiative in rebellion and led her husband into sin. Adam failed to take the lead in the temptation episode and chose instead to accept the leadership of Satan and of his wife. *The story of the entry of sin and misery into the world is the sad tale of a series of failures to submit to God-given authority and to exercise God-given leadership.*

Our focus is on the man because, again, he is the one God put in charge and the one He holds accountable. Unfortunately men from Adam onward have inherited his penchant for avoiding the demands of their leadership calling, especially in relationship to their wives and family. Men today have almost totally abdicated their calling as family leaders. Whatever remnant of leadership energy they have tends to be directed to interests outside the home—business and recreation, in particular. But it was a *failure of home leadership* that thrust the world into darkness, and this is still the most costly form of leadership failure.

Before we leave Adam, let's take a little break from the heavy (but essential) ideas we've been considering and see what we can learn from the account of Adam and his failure. What were the qualities that Adam failed to display in the face of Satan's attack on his family that would have enabled him to be the spiritual leader God created him to be? As we answer that question we can discover ways to help improve our own performance as leaders as well.

ALERTNESS

The first quality Adam lacked was *alertness*. We can perhaps understand that he had never faced a threat before. Living in a perfect environment did not prepare him to expect an attack, especially the subtle, crafty attack that the serpent waged. Adam's devotion to his Creator, however, and God's clear commandment with its equally clear warning should have caused Adam to be vigilant. He should have been alert to any attack on God's veracity or any suggestion of rebellion against His authority. The very warning *not* to eat of the tree should have made him super-alert to any suggestion to the contrary.

However, it appears as if Adam was asleep at the wheel. Satan was allowed unimpeded access to Eve and was offered no resistance by Adam. Even if one gives Adam the benefit of the doubt and assumes he was unaware of the Eve-serpent dialogue, he definitely failed the alertness test when Eve made her proposition to him. There is no sense of vigilance at all: "She also gave to her husband with her, and he ate" (Gen. 3:6). And he ate. Period. No protest. No resistance. No alertness to the danger the act represented. "And he ate."

We, too, often fail in our leadership at home through a lack of watchfulness to danger, or through a general lack of alertness to other opportunities to show leadership. We, too, are often asleep at the wheel, just letting things happen and hoping for the best.

Are you aware of the temptations your wife and children are facing this week? Or are you just waiting for the results of their yielding to temptation to blow up in your face? Talk to them. Find out what is in their minds and their hearts. Keep track of who they spend time with, what they read, what they view on the screen, and the music they hear. Is the serpent working his wiles on your little flock? Are you alert to the dangers faced by those under your command?

INITIATIVE

The second quality needed by both Adam and his heirs is *initiative*. A man with initiative makes things happen. A man without initiative waits for things to happen to him and to his family. Adam waited to see what would happen when the serpent confronted Eve. He waited to see what she would say when she approached him after eating the forbidden fruit. He didn't initiate action, he reacted—and reacted poorly.

Our first father should have stepped up to the plate when the serpent threw his pitch toward Eve. He should have intervened in the dialogue. And if he didn't know about that conversation, why not? Was it not his responsibility to keep the commandment of God and assure it was kept by Eve who was under his authority? Further, when offered the fruit by his wife, why did he not at least at that point seize the initiative, rebuke her error, and confront the serpent? But no, Mr. Adam was what we now know only too well: your basic passive male. Avoiding action. Reacting to problems in a way that causes the least flack in the short term. "Yes, dear. I'm sure it's a very good piece of fruit. Whatever you say, dear."

So how are you at showing initiative? Is your leadership style at home characterized by your setting the agenda, asking the questions, requiring accountability? Or do you just go with the flow, hoping for the best? Do you make things happen in your family life, or are you just a passive passenger in the family vessel, letting others steer the ship or letting it drift wherever it will? You are the leader, the protector, and the teacher of your family. Each of these roles implies the need for you to be proactive. Remember, one day the Lord will seek you out as he did Adam in the Garden and ask an accounting for your leadership in the home.

COURAGE

The third quality lacking in Adam but needed by us all is *courage*. This is closely related to the last. Men seem congenitally fearful of exerting authority in the home and taking the initiative required to be effective. They are afraid they might be wrong in the choices they make. They are afraid of what their wives and children will think, or whether the family will even follow their leadership.

We don't know what Adam was feeling, but why didn't he stand up to his wife? It would have taken courage to contradict her, to correct her. He may have risked her displeasure. There seems to be nothing worse for the average man than to have his wife unhappy with him. The easy thing for Adam was to go along. It was also easier than confronting that wily serpent.

The alluring thing about cowardice is that it seems to make everybody happy. Failing to stand for principle or to correct those who are in the wrong keeps things peaceful. Of course, it may lead the whole human race into millennia of sin and misery, but hey, it keeps the wife happy today! The failure of manly courage has cost the world dearly.

Our nation is cursed today with men who are afraid to be leaders at home. For so many men their greatest desire is simply to keep peace within the family—no matter what the price. What the wife wants she gets, what the children want they get, unless the demand is so outrageous that Dad has to get angry and then sulk about their forcing him to take a stand.

Do you take your stand to lead your family according to principle even when they disagree, or when others outside the family don't understand? Are you willing to risk being unpopular for a time with your wife and children because you take a stand to protect them from evil companions and environments? Is pleasing God more important to you than pleasing men (or women, or children)? One sure mark of a leader is his willingness to take actions that bring him under attack from those who don't share his understanding of what it means to please God. The family leader is a man of courage because he fears God.

VISION

A fourth quality lacking in Adam and in too many of his heirs is that of *vision*. We're talking about long-term vision, the ability to look beyond immediate concerns to the future implications of today's decisions. Surely Adam was not thinking about the future at all when he took the fruit from Eve. He must not have reflected too much on what the Lord meant when he threatened

FAMILY MAN, FAMILY LEADER

him with death. He certainly must not have thought about what harm would result for his wife and children. Would he have taken the fruit if he had paused to reflect on the millennia of pain and suffering that would be caused by this one bad choice?

Our Lord was an example of a man with vision. Hebrews tells us of, "Jesus, the author and finisher of our faith, who for the joy that was set before Him endured the cross, despising the shame..." (12:2). The immediate prospect of the cross was enough to cause our Lord grim agony as he prayed in another garden, Gethsemane. Yet he was able to press on through what became the most horrendous personal nightmare of human history because he could foresee the future blessing His choice would bring to the human race. Adam's lack of vision damned mankind. Jesus' clarity of vision led him to become the world's Savior.

Men today lack vision. Their time horizons are very short, extending only to the next paycheck, the next vacation, or the next promotion. But godly men must be able to gauge the effects of their present choices on their children and their children's children. They must picture the future. They must see it and allow it to motivate their present actions. Their time horizons must extend even past their grandchildren and into eternity as they learn to weigh every action in light of its eternal implications.

What are the long-term implications of the choices you make today? What difference will it make that you have (or neglect) family worship and Bible instruction? How will your grandchildren be affected by your prayer life today? How will your children be shaped by your choice of vocation? By where you choose to live? By the church to which you belong? By how you choose to educate them? By your policies concerning peer-grouping or entertainment or driving privileges? The choices you make today, even many that may seem insignificant, will shape the lives of your descendants and reverberate through eternity. Adam didn't think ahead. Jesus did. You and I must.

A Sense of Responsibility

The final quality absent in Adam but needed by all men is a *sense of responsibility*. This is that quality which is well expressed in the proverbial expression, "The buck stops here." We have already seen that Adam not only failed to exercise his duty, he also failed to take responsibility for his failure, preferring instead to blame his wife and even (implicitly) the Lord Himself.

This Adamic plague of avoiding responsibility is widespread in our own day. Just listen to the responses of our civil leaders who are caught in some personal failure or even serious crime. Have you ever heard one of them simply say, "I was wrong. I sinned. There is no excuse for my behavior. I will make restitution. I ask your forgiveness"? No. Instead they minimize the wrong, blame others, change the subject—and take comfort in the latest polls that show the public doesn't care about their character.

And indeed the public doesn't care. Because the "public" is made up of men who don't take responsibility either, and especially not in the home. For generations men have passed off to their wives primary responsibility for child rearing. They are passive, disinterested, and irritated when their wives attempt to draw them into the decision-making process. Many simply walk away from their families, never to return. Many of those who stay are absent emotionally, even if their bodies remain under the same roof as their families.

Whether you like it or not, you are the lord of your castle, the pilot of your ship. Consider a ship's captain and his crew. The captain delegates authority to those under him in the complex process of running his ship and delivering it safely to its destination. But the captain remains totally responsible at all times. If he is in his quarters sleeping when a Helmsman or Third Mate makes a mistake that runs the ship aground, the negligent underling may be disciplined for his error, but the captain is still accountable to his superiors and may lose his command. He delegates authority, but he remains responsible.

So it is with a father. He is totally accountable for everything that happens in his home. He is answerable to God for everything his wife and children do, or don't do. They bear their own personal responsibility for their actions, but the overall burden is always his. When, on the day of judgment, the Lord inquires about the conduct of the family and the training of the children, it will be the father who renders an account.

However passive a father may be in his home, the fact is that it is *his* home. He may sit on the sidelines and leave the running of things to his wife, but that does not mean that he is not the leader; it only means that he is a poor leader. Because a leader he is, for better or for worse. So we might as well exercise our leadership since we are going to be held accountable by God anyway!

Most of us have inherited a good bit of our original father's penchant for avoiding responsibility. However we will be no more successful than he was.

One of the most encouraging signs accompanying the home schooling movement and the Christian men's movement of recent years is the fact that many fathers have been drawn back toward taking responsibility for their families. But we have a long way to go. Let's not resist the burden of duty. Let's act like men and embrace it willingly—for the long haul. In the home, the buck stops here, with you and me.

The lessons of Genesis 1-3 are many, but take these three with you if you forget everything else.

First, beware of those who question the clear teachings of the Bible, and learn to identify the subtlety of their temptations: "Has God really said? Is that what the passage really means?" Don't allow others to create a cloud of confusion about scriptural teachings that are perfectly plain.

Second, it is perfectly plain in Scripture that God has established an order of authority in this world. Feminism is a lie straight from hell. Men are the God-ordained leaders, and they should act like it.

Third, this means you're a leader. So act like it!

We'll proceed to spell out the fundamental principles of that leadership in the chapters ahead, starting with a look at the original Patriarch, God Himself.

CHAPTER 4

Getting to Know God the Father

But now, O LORD, You are our Father; we are the clay,
and You our potter; and all we are the work of Your hand.
Isaiah 64:8

Imagine a boy who had never been to a baseball game or
watched one on TV, never seen any backyard batting practice,
never, in fact, even seen a baseball, a bat, or a glove. Now suppose
he were handed a bat, taken to home plate, and told to swing at
the ball when the pitcher threw it his way. How would he act?

He would be all befuddled. He might hold the bat on
the wrong end and use just one hand. He might raise it high,
straight above his head, as he stood right on the plate with his
body directly facing the pitcher. He might never hit the ball!

Now imagine he was allowed to watch several other boys
bat first. He would observe that they grasp the bat with both
hands at the narrow end, stand perpendicular to the pitcher,
and raise the bat over their shoulders, swinging smoothly as they

keep their eyes on the ball. Having witnessed how it is done, the boy would be far better prepared to take his turn at the plate. He would still need lots of training and practice, but at least he would have some models to follow.

This is the way people learn: they watch other people do something, and then they copy what they see. This method of learning is called apprenticeship, and it is the most effective way to teach almost anything. Children are natural apprentices and will mimic the behavior of their parents, whether it is washing the car, hammering a nail, or cuddling a baby.

Apprenticeship is also how we learn to perform our more important occupations in life, like fatherhood. We watch what our fathers say and do, and we learn from their example. We observe other fathers and learn from them, too. When we get married and have children, we put into practice what we have seen. Along the way we may read books on fatherhood or hear preachers and teachers address the topic, but by far the greatest influence is the model we have watched for years.

This, of course, brings up a problem for millions of men today. So many were raised without a father in the home at all, and countless others have had fathers who were poor examples. And let's face it, even the best of fathers fall short of modeling fatherhood in one way or another.

So what's a man to do? What are *you* supposed to do if you want to turn your heart toward your family and be the best father you can be, but you haven't had good models to follow? Maybe you feel as befuddled as that little boy at home plate, convinced that you, too, will never hit the ball.

The good news is that you, along with every other Christian man, actually have a perfect Father whose example you can follow as you seek to become a better father yourself.

Here is the astounding truth that needs to lie at the heart of a return to biblical manhood and fatherhood: *God Himself is a Father!* Throughout Scripture, that is how He is revealed. He called Himself a Father. Jesus called Him Father. He was a Father to Israel and is a Father to believers in Christ. He is the original Father, he is our Father, and he is the example of fatherhood that we need to copy. We can apprentice ourselves to Him as we learn to be men and to turn our hearts toward our families.

Most of us have a dim image of God the Father. Perhaps we utter the words at church, "Our Father in heaven…," but we don't really comprehend what the words mean. We spend a lot of time thinking and talking about Jesus, as we should. In recent years many of us have even spent a lot of time thinking and talking about the Holy Spirit—a less scriptural practice since the Spirit wants to give glory not to Himself but to the Son (Jn. 15:26; 16:14), and the Son to the Father (17:4). Every spiritual thought and exercise leads back to the Father. So why does the Father occupy so comparatively little attention in our private, family, and corporate devotion and study? When is the last time you heard a sermon about God the Father?

It is time to return to God our Father. One of the greatest needs for Christian men in our generation is to get to know our Father in heaven once again. As we do, we will understand what it means to be a man and how we can fulfill the calling of fatherhood.

THE ARCH-PATRIARCH

Bear with me as we take a closer look at some important words. The word "father" in the Greek is *pater*. From that word is derived a similar word, *patria*, which denotes the results of fatherhood, those who come from a common father, thus, a family or descendants.

With this in mind read these two verses: "For this reason I bow my knees to the Father [*pater*] of our Lord Jesus Christ, from whom the whole family [*patria*] in heaven and earth is named..." (Eph. 3:14,15). My interlinear Greek New Testament translates verse 15 (literally) like this: "of whom every *fatherhood* in heavens and on earth is named."

In the original language the linguistic connection between "Father" in verse 14 and "fatherhood" or "family" in verse 15 is quite evident, and whether the word is translated "fatherhood" or "family," the meaning of the verse is the same: *God the Father is the great prototype of the fatherly relationship wherever it is found.* All fatherhood comes from God the Father.

We noted in the first chapter that "patriarch" (Greek: *patriarches*) is derived from *patria* and *arche* (beginning, first in origin, to rule). It means the first father in a family line, or a family ruler. While the term "patriarch" itself is not often used in Scripture, its meaning certainly applies to God the Father. He is the first Father, the prototypical Father of all fathers; and He is the ruler of His whole family, of every person He has created (His fatherhood of all creation) and of every person He has saved from sin (His fatherhood of the redeemed).

The harsh and perhaps uncomfortable truth is this: Those, like the feminists, who hate biblical patriarchy hate God, whether they realize it or not, because God is the Arch-Patriarch, the archetype of fatherhood. He is the source, pattern, and goal of all manhood.

God is Masculine

God is masculine. He is not feminine. He is not an androgyny, a mixture of masculine and feminine. God is a "he," not a "she" or an "it," as every scriptural reference to "him" testifies.

When we hear the statement, "God is masculine," we are inclined to hear it as saying that God is somehow like his male creatures. Not at all. When I say that God is masculine, I mean that God's own nature and actions are the very essence and definition of the masculine principle. He is the great Original; he is not defined by anything outside of Himself. The creature can only slightly comprehend God's nature, but what we can comprehend, as taught by God Himself in Scripture, is that whatever else He may be, He is masculine, in and of Himself.

What does it mean that God is masculine? Since we cannot fathom His very nature, we learn about Him through what He reveals to us about His nature and through how He acts. What we learn is that God's masculine attributes are displayed in this way: *He initiates action and sustains it toward a goal.*

He is the one who makes things happen; He takes the lead and gets things started by acting upon His creation. Then God sustains the work He began. He follows through by providing the ongoing care and protection needed to uphold what He has made. And all this action is aimed toward a great purpose that God is going to fulfill: namely, the glory of God in the exaltation of Christ.

The Eastern conception of the cosmos views masculinity and femininity as equally ultimate principles of the universe (with no personal creator). The Christian conception is that the transcendent God is the masculine principle of reality: the active, generative, and sustaining (personal) force. The creation is feminine in relationship to God: it is acted upon; it is receptive to His actions and fruitful in response to His care.

Again, the essence of masculinity as revealed in God is this: He *initiates* action and *sustains* it toward a *goal*. To learn about God as Father and to understand His masculine characteristics, we want to spend some time in Genesis again, because there we find the foundational revelation about God. What we discover is that His Fatherhood is expressed in three primary roles: leader, provider, and protector.

GOD THE FATHER IS A LEADER

"In the beginning God created the heavens and the earth" (Gen. 1:1). The opening words of the Bible reveal a God who takes the *initiative*. For all eternity there was only God Himself: Father, Son, and Holy Spirit. There would be no universe, no earth, no life upon the earth, no human race if God had not decided to create and then, having made His plan, taken the initiative to actually create all things.

His eternal counsel lay behind His decision to create the world. "The counsel of the LORD stands forever, the plans of

His heart to all generations" (Ps. 33:11). God did not begin His creative work without a *purpose* or *goal* and a plan to meet that goal. Ephesians 1:11 makes reference to "the purpose of Him (the "Father," v. 2) who works all things according to the counsel of His will." We catch a glimpse of the consultation among the persons of the Trinity when God says, "Let Us make man in Our image, according to Our likeness…" (Gen. 1:26).

God's ultimate purpose is increasingly revealed through the pages of Scripture until it becomes explicit in the New Testament. Paul writes of God's "having made known to us the mystery of His will, according to His good pleasure which He purposed in Himself, that in the dispensation of the fullness of the times He might gather together in one all things in Christ, both which are in heaven and which are on earth—in Him" (Eph. 1:9,10). God's plan for the earth was to use it as a stage upon which to exalt His Son, who through His becoming man and winning redemption for a fallen humanity, would reconcile all things and offer them back to the eternal praise and glory of God the Father (cf. John 17:4,5; 1 Cor. 15:24). Everything that happens in the creation is for the ultimate glory of God (1 Cor. 10:31).

Constantly throughout the early chapters of Genesis we see a display of God's leadership and initiative. He creates the world in six days. He evaluates His work and pronounces it "very good" (1:31). He institutes the Sabbath Day as a day of ceasing from work and enjoying the works of God (2:2,3). In chapter 2 He makes man out of the dust of the ground; plants a garden and places the man there, giving him the instruction to take care of it; establishes His authority by setting limits on Adam and speaking the law about the trees in the garden; decides that Adam should not be alone; brings the animals before Adam; takes a rib from his side and creates a woman, then brings her to him.

The pattern continues in chapter 3 where, after the sin of Adam and Eve, God takes the initiative to seek them out and holds them accountable for their violation of His commandment. He then pronounces a punishment for their sins and enforces his sanctions by driving them out of the garden. He sees their need and gives them decent clothes of skin to replace their leaf garments.

We could go on through the Bible to Revelation 22, but I don't want to belabor the obvious. God our Father is a leader who takes initiative and makes things happen, both in regard to the physical creation and to the persons He made in His image. Nor are His actions just to pass the time of day. He is going somewhere. He has a plan and a purpose, and everything He does is calculated toward the achievement of that goal: his own glory through the work of Christ.

Isaiah 64:8 records a very personal response to God's work as the Creator and sanctifier of His redeemed people, and it contains a striking picture of the role of the Father. "But now, O LORD, You are our Father; we are the clay, and You our potter; and all we are the work of Your hand." The Father is a potter. He sculpts people. We are clay in His hands. Thank God for His loving initiative and power directed toward our growth into His image! May He sculpt us to be the men He created us to be.

In later chapters we will be fleshing out in detail how to follow the example of the Father and act like men, but don't wait until then to begin to apply some of these truths. If you want to be a man, you have to be a leader, and to be a leader you must have a plan and then take action toward a goal.

Initiative. Purposeful action. That's leadership. That's the Father's way.

GOD THE FATHER IS A PROVIDER

These three primary roles of God the Father are not airtight categories, as if you can look at an action of God and declare it an act of leadership, or of provision, or of protection. They are just aids to our understanding and by no means adequate or exhaustive when it comes to setting forth the glorious character and works of our God. He exercises leadership in His acts of providing for His creatures and in His protecting them; in fact, in everything He does.

Having said that, as we reflected on God's leadership, we emphasized His initiative and His operating for a purpose. As we look at His roles of provider and protector, we will be emphasizing his ongoing work of *sustaining* that which He began through creation and the new creation in Christ. These roles have to do with His providence—His ongoing care for His creation. As we proceed, keep the main idea in mind: God the Father initiates action and sustains it toward a goal.

In the early chapters of Genesis we see God's provision for His creatures in several ways. Throughout the first six days of creation, right up to the creation of man, God is working to provide a suitable *home* for mankind. A world with light and darkness, cycling days and seasons, water and earth, and varieties of plants and animals—this becomes the perfect environment for mankind, who would be made in His image and who would take dominion over the earth for His glory. Then within this perfect world the Father creates a special home. "The LORD God planted a garden eastward in Eden, and there He put the man whom He had formed" (2:8).

God not only provides a home, he provides *food*. As soon as He created them, "God said, 'See, I have given you every herb that yields seed which is on the face of all the earth, and every tree whose fruit yields seed; to you it shall be for food'" (1:29). God cares for His creatures and sees that they have what they need to eat, or to produce food for themselves. "He causes the grass to grow for the cattle, and vegetation for the service of man, that he may bring forth food from the earth, and wine that makes glad the heart of man, oil to make his face shine, and bread which strengthens man's heart" (Ps. 104:14,15).

God is not merely utilitarian in His provision. He supplies extravagantly for all His creatures, meeting not only their bare nutritional needs but feeding their spirits as well with the *beauty* of what He provides. "And out of the ground the LORD God made every tree grow that is pleasant to the sight and good for food" (Gen. 2:9). The awesome splendor and variety of what God has made leads us to worship His infinite power and beauty, even as we partake of our daily bread.

In chapter 3, verse 21, we find the Lord producing clothes for Adam and Eve. "Also for Adam and his wife the LORD God made tunics of skin, and clothed them." These tunics were long garments that would serve as *shelter* against the elements as the first couple were exiled from the perfect garden into a world that would not now always be friendly to them as it brings forth thorns (3:18) and becomes marked by generally harsh living conditions. Even after their sin, God cared for His creatures.

One of the greatest gifts of God to Adam was the provision of a *spouse* (2:22). The Creator never intended the man to be alone in his new home, but He first helped Adam see his need of companionship and help by naming the animals and recognizing that none of them was a suitable partner (2:20). Then God performed the first surgical procedure, fashioned the woman from Adam's rib, and brought her to him. His ecstatic and poetic declaration (v. 23) is proof of the blessing God had given him:

> This is now bone of my bones
> And flesh of my flesh;
> She shall be called Woman,
> Because she was taken out of Man.

The very best gift of the Father, once Adam rebelled against Him, was the provision of a *Savior* who would defeat sin, Satan, and death and reconcile man to God. Even as he pronounced the curse against Satan, God signaled that He would be sending a Redeemer, the descendant ("seed") of the woman, the Lord Jesus Christ (3:15). Thus God gives, from the very beginning, a glimpse of His ultimate purpose in Christ.

The ample supply of gifts to mankind at the commencement of life on the earth was just the first display of the ever-gracious heart of the Father who cares thoroughly for those He has made. "Every good gift and every perfect gift is from above, and comes down from the Father of lights, with whom there is no variation or shadow of turning" (Jas. 1:17). God never varies: He is always a loving Father who gives what His children need to live. "If you then, being evil, know how to give good gifts to your children, how much more will your Father who is in heaven give good things to those who ask Him!" (Matt. 7:11). Provision is at the heart of fatherhood.

God the Father is a Protector

The Father's sustaining work also includes protecting His family from danger. There would be no need for protection in a perfect world. This defensive role is now necessary due to the entry into the world of Satan, sin, and the curse that sin brought.

Defensiveness does not suggest passivity or a merely reactionary posture toward evil. The Father again shows His initiative when He warns Adam about the danger of sin and its consequences: "And the LORD God commanded the man, saying, 'Of every tree of the garden you may freely eat; but of the tree of the knowledge of good and evil you shall not eat, for in the day that you eat of it you shall surely die'" (2:16,17). A leader does not wait to act until evil rears its head. He thinks ahead with an active defense strategy.

Notice that the form of the Lord's protection was a commandment. Issuing moral directives is one of the most important and effective ways (if the mandate is obeyed) of guarding against the dangers of this world. "Thus says the LORD, your Redeemer, The Holy One of Israel: 'I am the LORD your God, Who teaches you to profit, Who leads you by the way you should go. Oh, that you had heeded My commandments! Then your peace would have been like a river, And your righteousness like the waves of the sea'" (Is. 48:17,18). Leaders give commandments to protect those they love.

When the Protector's commandments are disobeyed, He becomes the disciplinarian. Genesis 3 records the curses pronounced upon Adam and Eve (as well as the serpent). She was cursed in her womanly calling of bearing children: she would have greatly increased pain. Also, she would experience a disrupted relationship with her husband: she would try to control him, but he would dominate her in return (v. 16). Adam's punishment took the form of God's curse on the ground and what it produced (vv. 17,18). Since the man's calling was to take dominion over the earth, his trial would be dealing with the thorns and thistles and having to work very hard to make a living.

Sin has consequences, and the Father protects His children by bringing sanctions against them for breaking His moral law. "You should know in your heart that as a man chastens his son, so the LORD your God chastens you" (Deut. 8:5). The Lord assured David that his son would benefit from God's loving chastisement: "I will be his Father, and he shall be My son. If he commits iniquity, I will chasten him with the rod of men and with the blows of the sons of men" (2 Sam. 7:14).

A father who does not discipline his child does not love him. "My son, do not despise the chastening of the LORD, nor be discouraged when you are rebuked by Him; for whom the LORD loves He chastens, and scourges every son whom He receives. If you endure chastening, God deals with you as with sons; for what son is there whom a father does not chasten?" (Heb. 12:5-7). Far from being a sign that God has withdrawn His care for His people, His discipline is the surest evidence of His love. It shows that He still regards them as His children and is determined to protect them from evil and its destructive consequences.

Modern men consider the exercise of judgment to be a harsh thing and incompatible with mercy. This is because they don't know God the Father. The dispensing of punishment for sin is a merciful action designed to give men a fear of God and a fear of sinning that will protect them from greater punishment. "And if you call on the Father, who without partiality judges according to each one's work, conduct yourselves throughout the time of your stay here in fear" (1 Pet. 1:17). Sin, death, and hell are fearful things! The Father wants to keep His children far from them all, so He sometimes acts as a dispenser of discipline.

We have already noted the fact that the Lord provided coverings for Adam and Eve to protect them from the harsh elements (Gen. 3:21). This act was a token of the countless acts of fatherly protection that God would perform for His children after that. "The angel of the LORD encamps all around those who fear Him, and delivers them" (Ps. 34:7). When necessary, God even becomes a "Man of War," fighting on behalf of His people and destroying their enemies (Exod. 15:3). But most of his acts of protection are far quieter. When admonishing His disciples not to fear men, Jesus said, "Are not two sparrows sold for a copper coin? And not one of them falls to the ground apart from your Father's will. But the very hairs of your head are all numbered. Do not fear therefore; you are of more value than many sparrows" (Matt. 10:29-31). The Father who defends the smallest of His creatures will not fail to defend His own dear children through Jesus Christ.

So the Father exercises His leadership over His children not only by taking the initiative in their relationship, but also by His ongoing care demonstrated in His providing for their needs and protecting them from danger. This is the nutshell version of what God's fatherhood is all about. Before leaving the subject, let's notice how this understanding of God's fatherhood is confirmed by two other well-known passages of Scripture.

THE FATHER IN PSALM 23

1 The LORD is my shepherd; I shall not want.

2 He makes me to lie down in green pastures; He leads me beside the still waters.

3 He restores my soul; He leads me in the paths of righteousness For His name's sake.

4 Yea, though I walk through the valley of the shadow of death, I will fear no evil; For You are with me; Your rod and Your staff, they comfort me.

5 You prepare a table before me in the presence of my enemies; You anoint my head with oil; My cup runs over.

6 Surely goodness and mercy shall follow me All the days of my life; And I will dwell in the house of the LORD Forever.

These familiar words have been a source of comfort and encouragement to believers for about three thousand years. The imagery of a shepherd caring for his sheep and the simple beauty of the poetry have assured it a place in the hearts of every generation of God's people.

What I want you to notice now is how the fatherhood of God, the Shepherd, is evident in the psalm. It is actually the poetic presentation of the Father's leadership, provision, and protection that gives this portion of God's word the power to comfort and support the faithful.

As our Shepherd, the Lord is the leader of His flock. "He makes me lie down… He leads me beside still waters… He leads me in paths of righteousness." Eventually, He leads me to the eternal house of the Lord.

The Shepherd provides for His sheep by taking them to green pastures and still waters. His provision is just what they need, not brown fields and rough waters. He prepares them a table with food and fills their cups to overflowing, delighting them also with oil on the head for refreshment and healing. His goodness and mercy are their constant source of blessing throughout their lives.

Finally, the Shepherd protects His sheep. Even in the shadow of death they need not fear since the Shepherd is there with them, defending them with His rod and guiding with His staff their every step through dangerous ground. They are so well guarded that He even spreads out a banquet table for them in the presence of their enemies, who are no threat with the Shepherd around.

So while this psalm conjures up pastoral images associated with the great Shepherd, it is actually God the Father in His roles of leader, provider, and protector who is presented here, and that is what has made this psalm such a source of comfort to the saints of all ages.

THE FATHER IN THE LORD'S PRAYER

Our Father in heaven,
Hallowed be Your name.
Your kingdom come.
Your will be done
On earth as it is in heaven.
Give us this day our daily bread.
And forgive us our debts,
As we forgive our debtors.
And do not lead us into temptation,
But deliver us from the evil one.
For Yours is the kingdom and the power and the glory
forever. Amen.
  Matthew 6:9-13

Christians by the millions worldwide utter the words of this prayer weekly in their worship services. The prayer, taught by the Son of God to His disciples, is addressed to "Our Father in heaven." It is one of the premier affirmations of the fatherly nature of God in the scriptures.

The first petition is noteworthy in the context of our present study. It is a cry that God's name would be hallowed or made holy, that is, set apart from profane to holy uses in our lives and in the world. And what is His holy name? There are dozens of names applied to God in the Bible, but the nearest one here, and the one Jesus chose in teaching us to approach God in prayer, is "Father." So the very first thing we pray for in the Lord's Prayer is that God's name would be set apart and honored by us and by the world. What better way to do that than to learn about His fatherhood and live it out as his image-bearers in the world!

The remaining petitions follow the outline of the fatherly roles we have already seen elsewhere in Scripture. First is leadership. "Your kingdom come. Your will be done on earth as it is in heaven." This is a recognition of God's sovereign leadership and control of all things. It is a request that the King of the universe would implement the kingdom of His Son on this earth so that His holy will is done here just as it is in heaven.

"Give us this day our daily bread." This petition is asking the Father to exercise His role of provider toward His people by giving them each day what they need for physical survival. By implication, it would include whatever is needed for their spiritual welfare as well.

"And forgive us our debts, as we forgive our debtors. And do not lead us into temptation, but deliver us from the evil one." Asking forgiveness and desiring a forgiving heart is a recognition of sin and of the need to be freed from its power. To ask God for these things is to acknowledge His role as the protector who also judges and disciplines His people for their good. Following is a petition that asks for protection in temptation and for deliverance from the enemy of God and man, Satan.

The concluding statement is a final affirmation of God's absolute leadership and control of all things, with His ultimate purpose being His own glory. "For Yours is the kingdom and the power and the glory forever. Amen."

So we can see that, whenever we pray the Lord's Prayer, we are addressing God the Father in terms of His three primary roles.

We have chosen Psalm 23 and the Lord's Prayer because they are among the most familiar passages of Scripture, and we wanted to show that the picture of God's nature and activities is consistent throughout the Bible. He is the Father who leads, provides for, and protects His own.

We should note before leaving this subject that while God is a Father in all His dealings with His creation, we realize that there is a qualitative difference between how He expresses His fatherhood toward the creation in general, including fallen mankind, and how He expresses His fatherhood to His redeemed children in Christ. The "Father in heaven... makes His sun rise on the evil and on the good, and sends rain on the just and on the unjust" (Matt. 5:45). But only those who are His reconciled, spiritual children through Christ have the right to be called the "children of God" (Jn. 1:12) and receive the special blessings of redemption. So in one sense God is a Father to all, but since sin separated man from God, that designation is reserved for the redeemed in Christ.

GETTING BACK TO THE FATHER

Manhood is in retreat in our day. Fatherhood is a mystery to most men. What does it mean to be a man? What is at the heart of fatherhood? Since the prevailing ideas and images of our culture are provided by feminism, it is no wonder that Christian men have lost their way.

We need to go back home, back to our original Father. He must become the object of our study and meditation so that we can begin to be like Him. However lacking or poor the examples of fatherhood in our own lives, we have Someone to study and to model ourselves after. We can apprentice ourselves to Him and, by His grace, become more like Him.

As you read your Bible, become conscious of God the Father: what He is like and how He acts. Then pray for wisdom to pattern your life and behavior after Him. Since it was God's idea to turn the hearts of fathers to their children, you can be certain that there is no prayer He will be happier to answer.

We will explore the callings of fatherhood more in later chapters. At this point you should carry with you the broad strokes of what masculinity and fatherhood are all about. A father initiates action and sustains it toward a goal. He makes things happen; he is the leader of his family. What he starts he continues; he sustains his family by providing for and protecting those under his leadership. And all this is done for one overriding purpose: to bring glory to God by offering Him a wife and children who know, love, and obey Jesus Christ.

Of course, to do that, a man must know the Father's Son, Jesus Christ, and model his behavior after the perfect Servant-Leader. A man's leadership must be shaped by the cross. That's the theme we will consider next.

CHAPTER 5

Manhood Under
the Cross

Whoever desires to become great among you, let him be
your servant..., just as the Son of Man did not come to be
served, but to serve, and to give His life a ransom for many.
Matthew 20:26-28

It was the first time I ever called a radio talk show to make a
comment. It was back in the mid-1970s, and I was a twenty-
something seminary student in St. Louis at the time. KMOX
radio, a flagship talk radio station, had as its guests Letha
Scanzoni and Nancy Hardesty. These two women had authored
the book *All We're Meant to Be*, one of the earliest works of the
"evangelical feminism" movement. After they conversed for
a few minutes with the host of the program, the phone lines
were opened.

My on-air moment of glory went something like this: "The
Bible teaches the essential equality of men and women, but it
also teaches role differences: the husband is given the job to lead

and his wife is called to submit to his leadership. Can you agree that having different roles does not necessarily mean that the persons are unequal before God?"

I don't remember which of the authors answered, but her answer was brief and revealed that, apparently, I was from Mars and these ladies were from Venus: we didn't seem to be communicating. Her answer amounted to this: "Unequal roles means they are unequal."

I can still recall my frustration at their inability to grasp this vital piece of biblical truth: essential equality and role differences are not incompatible.

Although "evangelical feminists" are driven by an ideological bias that blinds them to certain Bible doctrines, I have come to be more patient with the inability of most people to comprehend this truth. After all, in our day of gender confusion, there are not many examples of what this looks like in practice.

Nor is it easy (to take a related concept) to explain the meaning of "servant-leadership." This is one of the chief doctrines of the Christian men's movement: the man is supposed to be the servant-leader of his home. It sounds good, but what exactly does it mean?

I recall hearing a comment by Patricia Ireland, President of the National Organization for Women (NOW), back in 1997. She was remarking on Promise Keepers and its teaching about male leadership when she said, "I've never seen a master who was also a servant."

I don't suppose there is anything we can do to convince hardcore feminists that servant-leadership is possible, but I'm more interested in convincing the ordinary Christian man and woman. And for them, the problem is often the same as what the NOW leader expressed: they haven't seen many examples of a leader who was also a servant.

Happily there is a somewhere to turn to see such an example: our Lord Jesus Christ is the very embodiment of the Servant-Leader. In studying Him we also learn more about what God the Father is like and what it means to be a godly man and father.

In this chapter we will consider how the Son teaches us about the Father and fatherhood, we will consider the roles or "offices" fulfilled by Jesus and which every man is called to fill, and we will look closely at this business of whether a master can indeed be a servant.

JESUS SHOWS US THE FATHER

In our last chapter we looked at God the Father and the ways that He manifests His masculinity and thus models perfect fatherhood. Now we want to consider the Father's Son, because we can learn about manhood and fatherhood from Him as well.

This is because the Son of God is a perfect reflection of God the Father and shares His attributes. "He is the image of the invisible God" (Col. 1:15). Just as human sons reflect their earthly fathers, so the second person of the Trinity reflects the first.

Mankind could know a great deal about the nature of God even if He had not sent His Son. "For since the creation of the world His invisible attributes are clearly seen, being understood by the things that are made, even His eternal power and Godhead, so that they are without excuse" (Rom. 1:20). No man can claim he does not know God since "the heavens declare the glory of God" (Ps. 19:1). All men should bow before the Creator whose power and wisdom are obvious in what He has made.

The creation, however, offers a limited revelation of God. We could not know him intimately as a Father apart from the revelation of His grace and truth through His Son, who is the Word become flesh in the person of Jesus Christ (Jn. 1:14, 17). Only the Son has seen the Father, but He came to earth to make Him known to all mankind. "No one has seen God at any time. The only begotten Son, who is in the bosom of the Father, He has declared Him" (Jn. 1:18).

When we look at Jesus, His character and works, we see the Father. "Jesus said to him, 'Have I been with you so long, and yet you have not known Me, Philip? He who has seen Me has seen the Father; so how can you say, "Show us the Father"?'" (Jn. 14:9). Although the Father and the Son are distinct persons in the Godhead, the Son is so like the Father in His nature—and so completely carries out His will—that you see the one in the other.

The Son is not the Father, and the Father is not the Son, yet in reflecting His Father the Son Himself acts like a father. Have you ever wondered about this familiar verse heard each Christmas season: "For unto us a Child is born, unto us a Son is given… and His name will be called Wonderful, Counselor, Mighty God, Everlasting Father, Prince of Peace" (Isaiah 9:6)?

Having the name "Everlasting Father" does not mean the Son is the Father; it means that the Son acts like a father eternally to His redeemed people.

So there is a family resemblance between God the Father and God the Son, but Christ's perfect reflection of the Father goes beyond that. During His earthly ministry Jesus was fixated upon His Father. Listen to His own words from the Gospel of John:

> Then Jesus answered and said to them, "Most assuredly, I say to you, the Son can do nothing of Himself, but what He sees the Father do; for whatever He does, the Son also does in like manner. For the Father loves the Son, and shows Him all things that He Himself does; and He will show Him greater works than these, that you may marvel." (5:19,20)

Jesus concentrated upon His Father's will and sought to carry it out completely: "For I have come down from heaven, not to do My own will, but the will of Him who sent Me" (6: 38). His teaching was the teaching of His Father: "My doctrine is not Mine, but His who sent Me" (7:16; cf. 8:28). He made statements like this over and over. "All things that the Father has are Mine" (16:15). I have counted approximately one hundred such references to the Father in John's Gospel alone. This final example is a good summary of them all: "Do you not believe that I am in the Father, and the Father in Me? The words that I speak to you I do not speak on My own authority; but the Father who dwells in Me does the works" (14:10). Jesus manifested

His Father because His every word and work was guided by the Father.

One of the most significant things we learn from the example of Jesus is the importance of absolute submission to the Father. If the Son of God owes Him this kind of surrender, how much more do we! Just after His resurrection, Jesus sent this message to his disciples, "I am ascending to My Father and your Father, and to My God and your God" (20:17). Jesus' Father is also our Father. What an encouragement this is to follow Jesus' example!

We will return to the importance of submission later in this chapter, but let's first pause to consider how Jesus is the Ideal Man and thus sets a pattern for Christian men to follow.

KING, PROPHET, AND PRIEST

Did you know that there are two Adams in the Bible? We have already spent a good bit of time in this book with the first one, the Adam in Genesis. But there is also an Adam in the New Testament. In Paul's great chapter on the resurrection we read, "And so it is written, 'The first man Adam became a living being.' The last Adam became a life-giving spirit" (1 Cor. 15: 45). Jesus Christ is the "last" or second Adam.

Romans 5:14 says that Adam was "a type" of Christ. A type is something (or someone) that foreshadowed Christ by being like him in some significant ways. Some Old Testament types of Christ include Moses, David, the temple, the sacrificial lamb, the priests, and the prophets. Adam was a type of Christ, in that both were the head of the human family. Jesus became the second head of the human race so that he could bring salvation to the world.

As the second Adam, Jesus is the Ideal Man. He is what Adam should have been, and he is, therefore, a model for every man. As we consider the roles Jesus played as the Messiah, we also learn the roles fathers need to perform in their homes. For now we will look at the "offices" of Jesus (to use the term theologians use). Later we will spend a chapter each applying these roles to ourselves.

Jesus is a King

The eternal Son of God, of course, shares with the Father His dominion over the whole universe and all creatures. Our focus, however, as we look at each of these offices is the work of the Son made man, Jesus Christ.

As Jesus began His ministry He declared, "The time is fulfilled, and the kingdom of God is at hand. Repent, and believe in the gospel" (Mk. 1:15). Since the Messiah was a king, the kingdom of God was present wherever He was. While His primary mission was to gather a redeemed people, His kingship was not limited to the spiritual plane. He demonstrated His sovereignty over both the material and the spiritual creation through His miracles, as he changed water to wine, calmed the wind and sea, healed the sick, and raised the dead. As He himself said, "But if I cast out demons by the Spirit of God, surely the kingdom of God has come upon you" (Matt. 12:28).

The Father granted Christ dominion over the entire universe as a result of his sacrifice on the Cross. That is why Jesus could say, "All authority has been given to Me in heaven and on earth" (Matt. 28:20). Though He rules all things, His leadership is expressed especially in the church. "And [the Father] put all things under [Christ's] feet, and gave Him to be head over all things to the church, which is His body, the fullness of Him who fills all in all" (Eph. 1:22, 23).

It is in His kingly function that Jesus reflects His Father's works as leader, provider, and protector. As a leader He called His disciples, He sent them out to preach, and He set His face like flint toward Jerusalem despite what He knew would happen. As a provider He fed the multitudes, healed the sick, and arranged for His mother's care even as He was dying. As a protector He calmed the storm, delivered those oppressed by the devil, and told the adulteress to sin no more.

Jesus is a Prophet

A prophet was a mouthpiece for God. In this capacity, he would reveal the secret things of God and predict the future. But his primary ministry was to teach the people God's truth and call them to follow the Lord.

The Gospels are full of the teachings of Jesus, and these are expressions of His prophetic office. He had the special anointing of the Holy Spirit for this ministry: "The Spirit of the LORD is upon Me, because He has anointed Me to preach the gospel..." (Luke 4:18). His uniqueness as a teacher was recognized wherever He went. "[T]he people were astonished at His teaching, for He taught them as one having authority, and not as the scribes" (Matt. 7:28,29).

Jesus' prophetic ministry continued after He ascended into heaven. "But the Helper, the Holy Spirit, whom the Father will send in My name, He will teach you all things, and bring to your remembrance all things that I said to you" (Jn. 14:26). "I still have many things to say to you, but you cannot bear them now. However, when He, the Spirit of truth, has come, He will guide you into all truth; for He will not speak on His own authority, but whatever He hears He will speak; and He will tell you things to come" (16:12,13).

As a prophet, Jesus is the teacher of God's people even today.

Jesus is a Priest

If a prophet was God's representative with the people, a priest was man's representative with God. He had the privilege of approaching God with the worship of the congregation. In particular, he offered their sacrifices and offerings.

The book of Hebrews is replete with references to Christ's priesthood (5:1-10; 7:1-28; 9:11-15; etc.), and while He is not called a priest elsewhere in the New Testament, His priestly work is evidenced in many places. Any reference to His sacrificial work on the cross is a reference to His priesthood since it was as priest that He offered Himself as a sacrifice for the sins of the world. He is "the lamb of God" (Jn. 1:29) who died for sinners. "But God demonstrates His own love toward us, in that while we were still sinners, Christ died for us" (Rom. 5:8). "[He] Himself bore our sins in His own body on the tree, that we, having died to sins, might live for righteousness—by whose stripes you were healed" (1 Pet. 2:24).

As priest, Christ also prays for His people. His intercessory prayer for His disciples in John 17 gives us a glimpse into how He prays. His sacrifice makes His prayers effective with the Father as He pleads its merits on behalf of the saints. "For Christ has not entered the holy places made with hands, which are copies of the true, but into heaven itself, now to appear in the presence of God for us" (Heb. 9:24). This dimension of His priestly ministry will continue forever. "Therefore He is also able to save to the uttermost those who come to God through Him, since He always lives to make intercession for them" (Heb. 7:25).

Whole books have been written on the offices of Christ. Our purpose here is simply to identify these roles, make note of their essential characteristics, and keep them in mind as a model for manhood. Since Christ is a king, a prophet, and a priest, men who are made to reflect God and carry on the work of Christ should function in similar ways. We will return to these themes later in the book.

Jesus Isn't Power Hungry

Patriarchy has a black eye because men are sinners. It's not the system of male headship that is defective; it's the men who fill the positions. Let's acknowledge that men have often abused their office of leadership and have thus made themselves, and patriarchy, an easy target to attack—even apart from feminist propaganda.

Some of you may have traveled in third world countries where the police and other public officials are corrupt. Life can be precarious in such places since the security of the population— and even visitors—is subject to the whims of lawless men. The solution, of course, is not to do away with policemen and public officials, but to get better men in the positions of leadership.

So it is with male leadership in our homes and society. If men abuse their trust, the answer is better men, not the abandonment of God's order.

Underlying much of the failure of Christian men to lead effectively is a misunderstanding of the nature of godly leadership. As we return to *biblical* patriarchy, nothing is more important than that we define leadership the way Jesus does.

After the disciples had contended among themselves regarding who would be the greatest, Jesus proceeded to overturn their understanding of greatness:

> But Jesus called them to Himself and said, "You know that the rulers of the Gentiles lord it over them, and those who are great exercise authority over them. Yet it shall not be so among you; but whoever desires to become great among you, let him be your servant. And whoever desires to be first among you, let him be your slave—just as the Son of Man did not come to be served, but to serve, and to give His life a ransom for many." (Matt. 20:25-28)

The world's concept of authority is expressed in the phrase "lord it over." The one with authority wields power over his subjects—he controls them. Leadership is about the will of the leader. He is in command and implements his will over those he rules. Worldly definitions of authority center around the power that the leader exerts over others by the dominance of his will over theirs. Whoever holds the reins of power gets to have his way. Leadership is about *control* above all else.

Jesus rejects this model of leadership for His disciples. The heart of Christian leadership is not about asserting one's will over others; it is about serving them. Serving someone is the very opposite of imposing one's will upon them. A slave yields his will in order to serve his master. A Christ-like leader will yield his will in order to serve those under his authority. Jesus demonstrated this style of leadership as he gave His life for the sake of those He came to lead back to the Father.

No one can argue that Jesus Christ wasn't an effective leader. People literally followed him everywhere He went, and He established the most influential movement the world has ever seen. What was the key to His greatness? Paul tells us in Philippians, chapter 2. He took upon Himself "the form of a bondservant," and "He humbled Himself and became obedient to the point of death, even the death of the cross." As a result God also has highly exalted Him and given Him the name which is above every name (vv. 7-9). Jesus' greatness as a leader lay in His act of yielding His will to God in the service of the people He led.

Christian leadership is more a matter of *influence* than control. God's kingdom advances in this world not by God's external control of people but by His changing people from within, making them want to obey Him. Jesus could have established His kingdom by the exercise of raw power, demanding obedience and enforcing it with the sword. Instead He chose to serve those over whom He was Lord and to cause them to want to submit to Him. His leadership is not primarily an external application of power. It is an internal influence, leading His followers to obey Him willingly.

We need to be clear about something. Jesus did not give up His *position* of authority nor let go of His power when He took the form of a servant. He is indeed King of kings and Lord of lords, and His subjects owe Him their obedience. He has the authority and the power to make His subjects obey Him. The point is that He does not make use of His power to lord it over His subjects. He prefers to exercise His power through the means of winsome influence.

The character of Jesus' leadership and the nature of His kingdom are well expressed in a poem entitled "A Battle Hymn," by Charles H. Spurgeon.[12] Notice how martial imagery is used to describe how King Jesus wields the sword of the Spirit, the Word of God, to turn His enemies into His friends. He applies His power not to overwhelm in order to destroy, but to overwhelm through love in order to save.

A Battle Hymn

Forth to the battle rides our King; He climbs His conquering car;
He fits His arrows to the string, and hurls His bolts afar.
Convictions pierce the stoutest hearts,
    they smart, they bleed, they die;
Slain by Immanuel's well-aimed darts, in helpless heaps they lie.

Behold, He bares His two-edged sword, and deals almighty blows;
His all-revealing, killing Word 'twixt joints and marrow goes.
Who can resist Him in the fight? He cuts through coats of mail.
Before the terror of His might the hearts of rebels fail.

Anon, arrayed in robes of grace, He rides the trampled plain,
With pity beaming in His face, and mercy in His train.
Mighty to save He now appears, mighty to raise the dead,
Mighty to staunch the bleeding wound, and lift the fallen head.

Victor alike in love and arms, myriads around Him bend;
Each captive owns His matchless charms,
    each foe becomes His friend.
They crown Him on the battle-field, they press to kiss His feet;
Their hands, their hearts, their all they yield:
    His conquest is complete.

None love Him more than those He slew;
    His love their hate has slain;
Henceforth their souls are all on fire to spread His gentle reign.

Charles H. Spurgeon

This "gentle reign" is a pattern for all Christian men. It shows us how power is to be used in Christ's kingdom.

DEATH TO LEADERS!

The man who wants to lead like Jesus needs to die like Jesus. Jesus' disciples had to learn this secret, and so do we. The path to greatness in any calling, especially a leadership calling, is a yielding of the will, a humbling of oneself, a voluntary taking on the role of a servant. "Then He said to them all, 'If anyone desires to come after Me, let him deny himself, and take up his cross daily, and follow Me. For whoever desires to save his life will lose it, but whoever loses his life for My sake will save it'" (Luke 9:23). Self-denial, not self-will—that is the key to victory in Jesus' army. Taking up one's cross means a daily dying to self, yielding the will to God, and serving other people. Jesus expressed the attitude in the garden of Gethsemane where He prayed to His Father just before His death, "Not as I will, but as You will" (Matt. 26:39).

Not all that goes by the name "patriarchy" is the real thing. At least it's not all *biblical* patriarchy. I have been distressed upon occasion to run across a man who seems to have grasped only half of the biblical patriarchy message. Usually he is very clear about the part that says the man is the head of his family, that he rules the home, and that his wife and children are required to submit to his authority. Perhaps you remember me quoting earlier, with approval: "A patriarch is a family ruler. He is the man in charge."

But that seems to be all some men understand about male leadership. What many men don't grasp is the *nature* of the leadership they have been given and *how* it should be exercised. The result is a distorted form of leadership that can be damaging to a man's family and especially to his relationship with his wife. These men think that they are leading effectively just because they insist on having their way in the home, when in fact they are simply being self-willed tyrants, lording it over their little kingdoms. Pity the poor wife and children who are cursed with such a man!

Christian men need to bring their leadership under the cross of Jesus Christ before they can effectively lead as Christian *husbands and fathers.*

The application of this truth is as obvious to state as it is hard to practice. Men have the position of leadership within their homes. Their authority and power are real, and they come from God. Their wives and children owe them obedience and respect. But the Christian family head will not lord it over his family. He will not harshly assert his will and demand his right to control them. He will instead seek to lead by service, by dying to his own will as he seeks their welfare. The subtle and winsome working of influence will characterize his leadership, not the raw exercise of power. Yet he will not abdicate his position of authority and his responsibility to direct the family.

If the perfect God-Man chose this humble approach to leadership, how much more must sinful fathers who themselves live under God's mercy! The realization of his own weakness and sinfulness—and of God's great mercy toward him—should cause a man to wear his authority with humility, not pride, and with gentleness, not harshness.

THE ANGRY MAN

A pattern of anger is one of the signs that a man is lording it over his family instead of leading them in a Christ-like manner. A tyrant gets angry when his will is not obeyed, when his subjects don't submit to his control. The tyrannical husband gets angry a lot because his self-will is always near the surface of his heart and because anger is itself a device to control others through intimidation. When there is a conflict with his wife, for example, he tries to solve the problem by the assertion of his will and the display of his temper. If he wins this battle of wills, he will have lost the heart of his wife, and his family will be worse off for his "leadership."

A mature Christian husband and father, in contrast, doesn't take it personally when his will is crossed. His aim is to guide his family in *God's* ways, and he is more grieved than angered when his authority is not respected (cf. Matt. 23:37). If he believes his wife has failed to submit to his leadership, he is able to look beyond the offense (real or imagined) and continue to care for her. Out of love for her, and with a heart of service, he will gently carry on a discussion. He will grant that he may not be seeing everything correctly himself and will be genuinely open to his wife's opinion and insights. If the disagreement persists, at least the relationship will not be broken. He will be communicating love and a willingness to yield to his wife where possible, but he will stand on principle when he needs to do so. His wife may disagree with him, but she will know he is not being self-willed and that he truly cares for her.

Husbands need to pay close attention to the admonition found in James 1:19-20: "So then, my beloved brethren, let every man be swift to hear, slow to speak, slow to wrath; for the wrath of man does not produce the righteousness of God." In any conflict we should listen carefully to our wives. This in itself shows that we have regard for them in love, but we may also learn what is motivating their concerns and may discover some blind spots in ourselves. We also should be slow to speak. We should not be too quick to pronounce judgment on the wife's behavior or attitude; we should instead be very careful to give her the benefit of the doubt. Being slow to speak may also protect us from bursting forth with angry words that we will later regret. Finally, we should always be doubtful about the righteousness of our anger. It may be possible to be angry and not sin if we are sharing God's anger at some sin or injustice, but the self-willed anger of a man does not accomplish God's righteous purposes in the life of a family. The vast majority of the time, our anger is a sign of a failure of leadership and an indication that we are not submitting to God.

THE SUBMISSIVE MAN

For the Christian man every relationship in life is mediated through the Lord Jesus Christ. The realities of His cross and His lordship shape the nature of every encounter we have. As Paul wrote, "For to me, to live is Christ" (Phil. 1:21). And again, "I have been crucified with Christ; it is no longer I who live, but Christ lives in me; and the life which I now live in the flesh I live by faith in the Son of God, who loved me and gave Himself for me" (Gal. 2:20). The husband and father should say, "For to me, to lead is Christ." That means his leadership will be exercised in submission to Christ and His Word.

Submission lies at the root of godliness. The most basic statement of faith is that there is one God. This one living and true God made us and He demands and deserves our worship and obedience. That is why the first of the Ten Commandments is that we must not have any other gods before the Lord (Exod. 20:3). That is why the greatest commandment, according to Jesus, is to love the Lord with all of our heart, soul, mind, and strength (Matt. 22:37,38). More fundamental than God's love or holiness or any other characteristic is that He is utterly unique—He alone is God. Therefore He is a "jealous" God who demands our absolute loyalty and submission (Deut. 5:8). The fact that we as Christians are "bought at a price" and therefore are not our own (1 Cor. 6:19,20) only accentuates the total demand of God upon our lives.

The father's authority in the home is a delegated authority; he is a steward (which means "household manager") acting on behalf of God who is the true Lord of the home. So to properly carry out his role as vice-lord he must be in a proper relationship with his superior. If he doesn't know how to follow his Master, he won't be very good at getting others to follow his leadership. Indeed, he will not be worthy of leadership, and he will either fail to lead or will revert to lording it over his family.

In order to follow the Master a man must be receiving his orders from the Master. This suggests the value of a habit of daily personal Bible reading and prayer. As we have observed already, the purpose for reading the Bible for a Christian father is not just to get some spiritual or sentimental lift for the day; it is to get concrete direction for living his life and leading his family. The purpose of his prayer is not to fulfill some religious obligation; it is to pour out his heart and seek God's blessing upon those under his care. A time of personal worship is a vital foundation of family leadership. It gets the father himself back under authority.

King Saul is an example of a man who failed to remain under the authority of God. The Lord made him king over the nation of Israel. He began to enjoy the reins of leadership and soon forgot who had placed them in his hands. On two occasions he disobeyed the Lord (first, by offering a sacrifice that only the priest was authorized to offer; second, by not destroying all of the plunder from a victorious battle, as God had commanded—1 Sam. 13,15). Each time he felt justified in stepping outside the bounds God had prescribed for him—after all, he was king! But the Lord removed him from his position of authority. Saul heard these words from Samuel the prophet: "Behold, to obey is better than sacrifice... For rebellion is as the sin of witchcraft... Because you have rejected the word of the LORD, He also has rejected you from being king" (1 Sam. 15:22,23). God replaced self-willed Saul with David, "a man after God's own heart."

A man's home *is* his castle, his kingdom, by God's decree and appointment. But it is *not* his own personal kingdom to do with as he pleases—he leads on behalf of the Lord. God will not use a self-willed man. He is looking for men whose hearts are fully yielded to Him so that He might strengthen them and make them successful (2 Chron. 16:9).

SUBMITTING TO AUTHORITY

A submissive man is one who willingly and joyfully submits to authority in his life. Of course he submits to the Lord. But he must also submit to any others whom the Lord has placed over him. He must submit to his employer and work for him as for the Lord (Eph. 6:5). He must submit to civil authorities, even when they are not exemplary men themselves, because God has placed them in authority (Rom. 13:1). He must submit to the leaders of his church and expect

God to work through them in his life (Heb. 13:17).

The man who dishonors his boss and cuts corners at work, the man who speaks disrespectfully of elected officials and ignores their lawful demands, the man who sneers at church authority and leaves a church rather than yield to correction— such a man is living in a state of anarchy. He cannot expect to successfully hold the position of authority in his home. A man who lives in rebellion himself will tend to create a home characterized by either tyranny or anarchy. A man who submits to others where he ought has taken the most important step to being a leader himself.

The importance of church authority deserves special emphasis. For the Christian man the church is his spiritual family. It is the primary arena in which he can practice the virtue of submission on the human level. As he is trying to learn how to lead his family it is essential that he is also learning how to yield to his fathers and brothers in the Lord within the local assembly. Peter challenges us with these words: "Likewise you younger people, submit yourselves to your elders. Yes, all of you be submissive to one another, and be clothed with humility, for 'God resists the proud, but gives grace to the humble'" (1 Pet. 5:5).

I'm sure this is a problem with many others, but I'm familiar with one group in particular. Too many home schooling fathers have developed an independent streak that undermines their ability to be good leaders. This independence is not surprising actually: home schoolers are by nature a very independent lot, or they wouldn't be doing what they are doing. Add to this the fact that many of them feel out of place in churches that do not understand or accept the choices they are making, and you have the ingredients for an understandable, but nevertheless dangerous, declaration of spiritual independence. Many families do not even worship with a church anymore, choosing rather to worship as a family on the Lord's Day. Except for an exceptional transitional situation, such independence from spiritual authority is a form of anarchy. A man's devotion to the body of Christ is no more optional than his devotion to his family (Rom. 12:10; Heb. 10:24).

Yielding Self for the Good of the Family

The submissive man, then, must submit directly to God on a daily basis, living a "crucified life" in which he says, "not my will, but yours be done." He must also submit to those in his life who have been given authority over him. But there is more. The submissive man must put aside his own will in order to do what is best for those under him, for his family.

What we mean is that while he sets the pace and directs the affairs of his household, the godly father will do so in a way that places the family's welfare above his own comfort and convenience. He must often sacrifice for their benefit, saying no to his own desires. This is part of the dying to self we discussed above.

When Dad comes home tired after a long day he might like to relax, read the paper, or take a nap. Instead, however, his wife may need to tell about her frustration with the children's behavior. She may need him to tighten the railing on the basement steps before one of the kids takes a tumble. The children will, no doubt, want Dad to play or talk or help them with their projects. In other words, the man will have a choice: Serve himself or meet the needs of his family. His role as family leader will be better achieved by serving the family.

The essence of leadership is dying to himself and saying to his Master, "Not my will, but yours be done." Sometimes that will mean being forceful and aggressive and leading where even his wife may not want to go and he himself may prefer not to go. It will involve taking initiative every day to guide and guard his little flock. But it will also involve countless decisions to yield his own will for the sake of the others in the home. Being a leader is not about being served, but serving, and giving one's life for others. The expression "servant leadership" is a good one and captures the nature of true Christian leadership in any sphere, especially in the home.

MASTERS WHO ARE SERVANTS

What Jesus shows us about the Father is that He is characterized not only by authority but also by love—not only by truth but also by mercy. "All the paths of the LORD are mercy and truth, to such as keep His covenant and His testimonies" (Ps. 25:10; cf. 89:14). God is not an austere authority, demanding and removed. God is love (1 John 4:8). The heart of our Father in heaven is mercy—but not mercy divorced from truth. There is no contradiction between absolute authority and absolute love. "Mercy and truth have met together; righteousness and peace have kissed" (Ps. 85:10). Mercy is married to truth, love to authority, peace to righteousness, relationship to law. What is found in the heart of God will also characterize His people gathered under His reign in Christ: "For the kingdom of God is not eating and drinking, but righteousness and peace and joy in the Holy Spirit" (Rom. 14:7).

Fathers are called to reflect God by displaying both qualities in the exercise of their home leadership. "Let not mercy and truth forsake you; bind them around your neck, write them on the tablet of your heart" (Prov. 3:3). We can't compromise on the truth that we are the heads of our families and accountable to God for those we lead. Nor can we lead our homes apart from the spirit of mercy that comes from dying to self and living under the cross of Jesus. It is vitally important that we plant these principles in our heads and engraft them in our hearts.

Sarah was commended by God for calling her husband, Abraham, her "lord" (1 Pet. 3:6). A man is the master of his house. This is a truth that our society will need to recover if it wants to return to the path of God's blessing. But this is hard—even impossible—for most people to swallow in our egalitarian age.

Perhaps it will be easier if they come to see more and more examples of the other truth about a father's calling—that he is the servant of his house. Ms. Ireland said she'd never seen a master who was also a servant. Maybe not. We need to provide her and other doubters many examples of such men and of such homes. In other words, the world needs to see Christ-like men and God-centered homes—homes where the cross tempers the exercise of real authority.

CHAPTER 6

Turning Hearts
Toward Home

And you, fathers, do not provoke your children to wrath, but
bring them up in the training and admonition of the Lord.
    Ephesians 6:4

"Dads, be sure to hug your kids today—and don't get
a divorce!"

I could have made those admonitions the main themes of
this study of fatherhood—if I believed that all that was needed
to fix families in our day was to keep Dad married to Mom and
get him a little more involved with the kids.

But I don't believe that. I'm all for staying married and hugging
the kids, of course; but the problem is far more deep-seated than
that. It involves, as we have seen, a serious lack of knowledge about
the Bible's teachings on manhood combined with the brainwashing
effects of our culture's devotion to the anti-biblical ideology of
feminism. The result is that most Christian men are confused, if
not actually committed to an unholy alliance of truth and error.

We have been over some pretty demanding terrain in the first few chapters, but I believe that material is essential if we are to see a deep and lasting family renewal based on the restoration of Christian manhood.

Men need to rediscover what it means to be a man instead of a woman. We need to re-learn how to be a father like the Father. Adding psychological band-aids to the disease of emasculated manhood will not be enough. Prescribing a list of behavior modifications for fathers to employ in the home will not bring the healing our families and nation need.

Central to our whole project is the matter of fathers turning their hearts toward their children. In the first chapter we noted the hopeful signs of home education and the Christian men's movement. Both seem to have moved many men in the direction of making the home a higher priority. But we also noted the need for these initial movements back home to become well grounded in the Bible.

Unless Christian men self-consciously ground their behavior on the Bible's view of their identity and their callings, there will be no long-term family renewal. This will involve study, and it will involve a costly commitment to a new way of life.

The heart of this way of life is expressed in fathers turning their hearts to their children. Let's now consider what that means. We'll start by thinking about why this is such a big deal anyway.

Good Fathers in God's Plan

One of the central relationships in the universe is the relationship between the Father and His Son. Before the world was created, this relationship existed in the eternal Godhead: God the Father and God the Son. When Christ came to earth, He acknowledged His dependence on His Father, "Then Jesus answered and said to them, 'Most assuredly, I say to you, the Son can do nothing of Himself, but what He sees the Father do; for whatever He does, the Son also does in like manner'" (Jn. 5:19).

Thus the father's position is foundational. The role that he plays in shaping the lives of his sons and his daughters is critical—not only for the welfare of the children themselves, but for the general well-being of the family, the health of the church, the welfare of civil society, the strength of the economy, the moral climate of the civilization, the prosperity of the kingdom of God in history, and the future of the world. Everything depends upon what is happening between fathers and their children in their homes. Such is the central place of the family in God's plan, and such is the pivotal role of fathers in that foundational institution. (It is to be understood that a mother's relationship with the children is similarly pivotal. What we say about fathers applies to mothers as well, excepting only those matters that apply to the father's leadership role.)

The home is the original society in which each person is placed by God at birth. It is, for better or worse, the place where people are shaped—their intellect, their values, their character, their aspirations. All that a person later becomes depends upon the factors that forged him in his youth, and the home is the primary shaper of young human beings.

Over the family stand the parents. And of the parents, it is the father who has the calling and the position to be the primary molder of the family. He may abdicate his role or do a poor job, but that, too, shapes the family. There is no escaping his influence—for better or worse. The central role of fathers in the foundational institution of the family is simply an inescapable fact of life.

We have God's word on it. One of the most surprising findings when one studies Scripture concerning fathers is the prominent place given to them in connection with the progress of God's saving plan in Christ, the kingdom of God. The crucial part played by fathers is highlighted at the very close of the Old Testament and the very opening of the New, as we saw in chapter 1. Let's look a little more at those fascinating portions of Scripture.

The prophet Malachi, the last mouthpiece of God to speak in the Old Testament era, ended his oracle with a forward look toward the "Day of the Lord." After calling for the people of God to "remember the law" of God given through Moses (Mal. 4:4) and thus continue the life of holiness that marks them as His people, the Lord then speaks of His plan to send "Elijah the prophet before the coming of the great and dreadful day of the LORD" (v. 5). This is followed by the very last words God's people would hear from Him for over four centuries: "And he will turn the hearts of the fathers to the children, and the hearts of the children to their fathers, lest I come and strike the earth with a curse" (v. 6).

Preparatory to sending the Messiah, God would send one who would be empowered with the same measure of the Spirit as the greatest prophet Israel had ever known, Elijah.

And what would be the definition of his mission? How did God characterize this, the highest calling of any prophet, the assignment preparatory for Messiah's appearance? He will turn the hearts of fathers and children toward one another.

About 430 years later the Lord breaks His silence to announce the arrival of the prophet He had promised. The angel Gabriel appeared to the priest Zechariah to tell him of the coming birth of his son, John, who would be "Elijah who is to come" (Matt. 11:14). Here is how the angel described his mission: "And he will turn many of the children of Israel to the Lord their God. He will also go before Him in the spirit and power of Elijah, 'to turn the hearts of the fathers to the children,' and the disobedient to the wisdom of the just, to make ready a people prepared for the Lord" (Luke 1:16,17).

This inaugural revelation of the New Testament age repeats the definition of the prophet's assignment as a turning of fathers' hearts toward their children. Like Malachi's message, this one also stresses the need for holiness among God's people: the disobedient will need to repent and turn to the wisdom of the righteous. And both these conditions, holiness of life and fathers being good fathers, are presented as vital elements of preparing God's people for the Messiah. These conditions describe the kind of people who are ready, "prepared for the Lord" to be used in Messiah's work on earth. Malachi had said the same thing in a negative way when he warned of God's visiting the land with a curse. God's people will either be fit and ready to serve his purposes—or they will come under his discipline.

Holiness of life we can understand. God cannot use corrupt instruments to perform His work. But what is so important about fathers and children? How does this condition rank as so vital to the success of God's plan in Christ? What is so critical about fathers turning their hearts to their children?

The short answer would seem to be that the family is central to God's plan to advance the gospel and kingdom of Jesus, and the turning of hearts is simply a way of describing a healthy family that is useful for God's purposes. We will soon proceed to explore exactly what it means for fathers to turn their hearts to their children, but let's first be sure we understand that families are in fact the foundation of God's redemptive plan for this world.

THE FAMILY IS THE FOUNDATION

The home has always been the foundation and center of true faith in the world. God's original fellowship with man was with a family unit in the Garden. God entered into covenants with men and their families (Noah, Abraham, Isaac, Jacob, David). The Old Testament people of God, the Israelites, were one huge family. Families were prominent in the New Testament as the church met in the homes of Christian families and as whole households came to Christ.

Throughout the ages the family has been the nursery of faith for each new generation, the primary place in which Christian discipleship has occurred. The future is shaped, generation-by-generation, in homes. Other institutions come and go, but the family remains a constant part of life in this world and of

God's plan for the ages. Even the New Testament church itself is modeled on the family and copies its patterns of life among its members.

The home is the primary arena for living out the Christian life. In the home sin, hurt, reconciliation, and healing occur daily. In the home the ignorant are taught, the rebellious disciplined, the repentant restored, the hungry fed, the naked clothed, the sick healed. In the home the relationship of Christ and His bride, the church, is exhibited in the relationship of husband and wife. The home is the place where proper roles and relationships are learned and practiced. The Christian home is a sanctuary, an oasis of holiness, sanity, and beauty in the midst of an evil, insane, and ugly world.

For God's plan for families, and thus for His world, to proceed, He must get hold of fathers. Marriage and family commitments are the chief way men learn to redirect their natural energies to truly productive purposes. Someone has suggested that most men would be barbarians but for the domesticating influence of women and children. This may be essentially correct. Family duties moderate the natural tendency of men to pursue selfish ambitions and pleasures and to focus on merely temporal concerns. For the Christian man especially, the duties of family call him to higher, even eternal, concerns.

The benefits of a man turning his heart toward home go beyond the welfare of the rest of his family. The rigors of family life also develop the man himself by providing a training ground, thus preparing him for his larger dominion tasks in this world. A man must prove his skills as a family shepherd before he is considered ready to become a shepherd of God's sheep, an elder in the church (1 Tim. 3:5). Certainly the same prerequisite would apply to a role of leadership in civil government and other larger domains of responsibility.

So families are at the center of God's plan, and fathers are crucial to the welfare of families. That is why He is so interested in fathers turning their hearts to their children.

DOMESTICATED MEN?

With all this talk of men turning their hearts toward home, someone might ask: Doesn't the Bible teach that the home is the woman's primary sphere of operation and the man is to go out of the home and take dominion in the world? Good question. Is our solution to the problem of families, in effect, to feminize the men by bringing them home to the wife's domain?

I stand by the viewpoint that men are indeed supposed to be home-centered—but not in the same way as women. To understand the difference, let's pay another visit to the early part of Genesis.

When God created man he made the male first (Gen. 2: 7), gave him a job to do (v. 15), and provided him with the moral guidance he needed to get the job done (vv. 16-17). Adam's occupation was to take care of the garden the Lord had planted in Eden. This was a specific application of the general job description God had given to man upon his creation: to rule, or take dominion over, the whole earth (1:26,28). The calling of the man was clearly an all-encompassing, world-changing, outward-oriented task. He was to reflect the universal dominion of his Creator-King by being a steward of this planet, re-creating and ruling this earthly domain to the glory of God.

But his task was not one he could do very well by himself. So the Lord God made a woman out of the man to be his companion-helper (2:22). Eve was, like him, in the image of God (1:27) and was to be his partner in carrying out the dominion mandate. But her role was a subordinate one—she was to assist Adam in carrying out the task God had given him before she was even created.

The heart of her role can be discerned in the other part of the dominion mandate: beyond ruling the earth, the man and woman were to "be fruitful and multiply" (1:28). The creation of woman made this fruitfulness possible. Adam could have ruled the earth to some small degree without a wife, but he could not have borne children! The woman's role was thus focused upon her husband, first of all, and then upon the children she would bear him to enable him to fulfill his calling as ruler over the earth. In this way the woman becomes a joint-ruler with the man, but subordinate to him and with a different focus.

The woman focuses on her husband and her home, while the man focuses on his dominion tasks with the whole world in view. This understanding of their respective roles is confirmed by noting that, after they sinned, the curse on the woman involved her children and her husband (3:16) while the curse on the man involved the ground (vv. 17-19), the earth over which he was to exercise dominion. Man is outward-oriented and woman is home-centered.

The rest of Scripture supports this understanding. The virtuous wife of Proverbs 31 is totally focused upon her husband, her children, and her household, while her husband in out in the city gates (v. 23). Similarly, Titus 2 presents a picture of a godly woman who is a "home-worker" and whose calling is absorbed with her husband and children—"that the word of God may not be blasphemed" (vv. 4,5). Men are tentmakers, fishermen, carpenters, and church and community leaders, carrying out their masculine callings in a myriad of ways.

We should note that although fulfillment of the dominion mandate has been complicated by sin, God has never suspended it. Rather, he has provided in the cross of Christ the remedy that makes its fulfillment possible. So now we preach the gospel in order to make disciples of all nations, disciples who obey everything God has commanded, including the original command to rule the earth to the glory of God (Matt. 28: 18-20). The Great Commission is the means to fulfilling the Dominion Mandate of Genesis.

Defining "Home-Centered"

While men are outward-oriented in their life callings, the Bible also clearly shows that men are to be home-centered. Now, they are to be so in a way that is different from their wives, but they are to be so nonetheless. Let's summarize the point first and then look at the biblical data.

A wife is home-centered in the sense that the *scope* of her particular calling as a woman begins and ends in the home. As we have seen, she is properly preoccupied with matters that relate to her husband, her children, and her household. As the family ministers to extended family, church, and community, she will have contact with many other people and her influence will spread. As she helps to offer hospitality and stands by her husband in his various callings, she will have an effect on many other people (even "in the gates" of the city, Prov. 31:31). But all of her influence results from her role as the helper of her husband. God did not intend her to have an independent influence. She does have a vital part to play in taking dominion over the earth, but it is a part that is expressed in her home-centered functions.

A husband, on the other hand, is home-centered in the sense that the *foundation* of his particular calling as a man is in the home. His calling by no means ends in the home—it extends to every physical element, every person, every institution on the earth, all of which he is to offer to the glory of God through Jesus Christ. But his calling most certainly does *begin* in the home. The family is the most important sphere in which any man exercises his God-given dominion, and he cannot effectively serve God in other spheres unless he serves well first at home. A man should be home-centered in the sense that he makes his family the first priority in his life. Out of that commitment will grow effective dominion over the whole earth.

The home-centered calling of a man is seen, first of all, in the biblical injunction for a man to love his wife, to cherish her, to live with her as a joint heir of the grace of life (Eph. 5: 25,28,29,33; 1 Pet. 3:7). She who was made from his own body, and is thus bone of his bones and flesh of his flesh, is the most important person in a man's life. She is his partner, his lover, his best counselor, his friend. In marriage he enters into a covenant with her to love her faithfully as long as they both live (Mal. 2: 14). At the emotional center of any home stands the woman, and it is her husband's devotion to her that makes her a radiant wife (Eph. 5:27), a channel of blessing to every member of the household and all who come into contact with it. The second way in which the Bible reveals the home-centered calling of a man is in its emphasis upon his duty to raise his children for God. Out of the one-flesh union of the man and his wife comes the blessing of children. The multiplication of godly offspring is one of God's chief purposes for marriage (Mal. 2:15), and the man is blessed of God whose quiver is full of child-arrows with which he can fight the battle for godly dominion (Ps. 127:3-5). Merely having children is not enough; the Lord wants *godly* offspring, well-wrought arrows. Fathers are commanded to bring up their children "in the training and admonition of the Lord" (Eph. 6:4).

Turning his heart toward his wife and children is both the highest temporal duty of a man and the most effective way to fulfill his manly duty of taking dominion over the earth and making disciples for Jesus Christ. As he devotes himself to shaping his children as disciple-arrows, and they in turn shape their children in the next generation, and so on, the earth becomes filled with godly seed. The children of the man who fears the Lord will indeed "be mighty on earth" (Ps. 112: 2). *Being home-centered is the most potent way for a man to be outward-oriented.*

A home-centered focus is also necessary in order for a man to be effective in the other spheres in which God has called him to serve: church, community affairs, civil government, business, etc. The Holy Spirit makes clear through Paul that a man is not even fit to lead in the church if he is not first leading his own family in a godly manner (1 Tim. 3:4-5). Faithfulness in the smaller sphere is necessary before a man can be entrusted with stewardship of a larger sphere (Matt. 25:21). A man who has not learned to manage his own family well has not developed the character necessary to take dominion in the other areas of life. Conversely, if he succeeds in the home, he is primed for success elsewhere. Real men are trained for their larger dominion tasks by the faithful fulfillment of their home duties.

So men are indeed supposed to be home-centered—but that does not mean they are feminized. Quite the contrary. They are most masculine when they recognize that their family calling is the absolutely essential foundation for successfully carrying out their larger, outward-oriented dominion tasks.

Now that we have assured ourselves that it is indeed a good thing to do, we're finally ready to explore what it means to "turn the fathers' hearts to their children."

THE 'HEART' OF THE MATTER

Obviously our answer must begin with an understanding of the word "heart." In modern usage "heart" connotes primarily matters of the emotions or affections, and while that is a part of the biblical definition, it is not at all the whole picture.

The word "heart" in both testaments generally refers to the whole of man's soul and all of its faculties as they are focused together upon something, whether good or evil. It is this usage that is in view in Proverbs 4:23 when it says, "Keep your heart with all diligence, for out of it spring the issues of life." The heart is here viewed as the source from which the whole of a man's life flows. Similarly, Jesus says, "A good man out of the good treasure of his heart brings forth good; and an evil man out of the evil treasure of his heart brings forth evil. For out of the abundance of the heart his mouth speaks" (Luke 6:45; cf. Matt. 15:18; Rom. 10:10). This truth is why God repeatedly admonished His people to give him their whole hearts (Deut. 6:5; Ps. 119:2; Jer. 29:13; Matt. 22:37). The heart is the person at his core, the seat of all his faculties.

Sometimes the word "heart" refers to a particular faculty considered as distinct: the mind, the affections, or the will. Most commonly it encompasses all of these. Jerry Bridges writes, "The mind as it reasons, discerns, and judges; the emotions as they like or dislike; the conscience as it determines and warns; and the will as it chooses or refuses—are all together called the heart."[13]

We may conclude, then, that for a father to have his heart turned to his children he must be wholly oriented toward them, focusing his mind, will, and affections upon them. Such a man will use his *mind* to study God's perspective on his children, to learn of God's purpose for them, the means of their training, and their needs. He will seek to understand his particular children so that he can apply God's wisdom to their personal needs and circumstances. He will take responsibility before God by exercising his *will* to act on what he comes to understand concerning his children. He will set his *affections* upon them, cherishing them, expressing his love for them. In short, his children will be a top priority in his life; he will be absorbed in his God-given duties toward them.

So now we must ask: How specifically does a man make his children a top priority? In what particular ways is he to be absorbed in them? What exactly does it mean to turn his heart toward his children?

In Ephesians 6:4 we find the Bible's most pointed and specific command addressed to fathers concerning their duty to the children God has given them: "And you, fathers, do not provoke your children to wrath, but bring them up in the training and admonition of the Lord." Two primary duties are presented in this verse. Taken in reverse order they are: *godly training* and a *loving relationship*. Let's look at these in turn.

GODLY TRAINING

"The training and admonition of the Lord" encompasses a lot. As the father exercises his roles of king, prophet, and priest within the home, godly training occurs. We will be exploring each of these offices of a father in detail in the following chapters. For now, we'll mention some of the key elements of training, and then we will spend more space on what a loving relationship is like, since that dimension of the father's role is not covered in detail elsewhere in our study.

To properly train a child a father must first deal with sin in his child in a biblical manner. He must *discipline* rebellion with the rod. "Foolishness is bound up in the heart of a child; the rod of correction will drive it far from him" (Prov. 22:15). "Foolishness" here is not just silliness, it is willful disobedience. If a father does not use the rod for rebellion, no other training will have much effect.

Training also includes *positive instruction and admonition*. The scope of the curriculum here is great, covering character development, equipping in life skills, vocational training, and preparation for future roles as father/husband and wife/mother and as churchmen and citizens.

Psalm 78:1-8 describes the process of fathers passing on a godly heritage through the generations. The two main components of that heritage, the content of a father's teaching of his children, are these: the *works of God* and the *Word of God*. God's mighty works include creation and redemption and His whole plan for history as it unfolds in fulfillment of His purpose. To study the works of God is thus to explore science, history, literature, art, music, language, etc.—all that He has made and all that He has done through history and culture. The Bible itself, of course, must also be at the center of a father's teaching plan—its content, its doctrine, and its application to every area of life. The Bible must be the foundation of all other learning.

The method the Bible prescribes for this training and admonition is what we call *discipleship*. It is the pattern provided by Jesus as His disciples apprenticed with Him for over three years. Jesus was with them all the time so that He could be both their teacher and a model of what He taught. This pattern is also suggested in the language of Deuteronomy 6, which says, "And these words which I command you today shall be in your heart. You shall teach them diligently to your children, and shall talk of them when you sit in your house, when you walk by the way, when you lie down, and when you rise up" (vv. 6,7).

How does the truth of God make its way from the heart of a father to the hearts of his children? Through an intimate discipleship relationship, a relationship that continues at all times (from rising up to lying down) and in all places (at home and along the way). This, by the way, is "home education," which the Bible presents as the way to provide godly training for the next generation. Having mentioned the discipleship process which is essential to godly training, we have already touched on the second duty of fathers, the second way in which they are to make their children a top priority, the second means by which they should turn their hearts to their children: fathers must create a loving relationship with their children.

A LOVING RELATIONSHIP

Whenever the Bible gives us a negative command we should sit up and take special notice. "Thou shalt not"—so begin most of the Ten Commandments. It is sin to fail to obey the positive command to "love your neighbor," but it is worse to disobey the command "thou shalt not murder!"

Ephesians 6:4 presents a negative command for fathers: "And you, fathers, do not provoke your children to wrath." To disobey this command brings devastating results. The parallel text in Colossians 3:21 does not include the positive words about providing training at all. It says simply, "Fathers, do not provoke your children, lest they become discouraged."

God has made children so that they are naturally inclined to respond to their father's initiatives. Malachi mentioned fathers' hearts being turned to the children and the response of children who would turn their hearts to their fathers. This is the natural order. If fathers treat their children right, they will win their hearts. If not, the children may lose heart, and their hearts may be lost to their fathers.

So how do fathers win the hearts of their children and avoid "provoking" them? They do so by maintaining a loving relationship with them. Without this heart relationship, all the efforts at providing godly training can come to naught. So what does a loving relationship look like?

A loving relationship exhibits *justice*. There is no quicker way for a father to provoke his children than to be inconsistent in his standards, unjust in his discipline, or to show favoritism. The God-fearing man of Psalm 112 is one who "will guide his affairs with justice" (v. 5). That is certainly also a description of a father. Jacob was unjust toward his sons, showing favoritism toward Joseph. This embittered the other sons, alienating their affections from their father, and led to their mistreatment of Joseph (Gen. 37:3,4ff).

A loving relationship is also characterized by *sacrifice and service*. Jesus showed the full extent of His love for His disciples by washing their feet (Jn. 13:1ff). A father must wash the feet of his children. He must set aside his will in order to do what is best for them. He must sacrifice his desires, his comfort, and his self-pleasing agenda in order to meet their needs. Such sacrifice may display itself in everything from taking the time to teach them himself, to giving up his plans for an evening in order to have family time, to yielding his desire for a new computer for his home office in favor of his children's desire for a new camper for family trips. Children will become exasperated by a self-centered father who fails to yield his time and resources to serve his family.

A loving relationship is further characterized by demonstrations of *compassion and tenderness*. "As a father pities his children, so the LORD pities those who fear Him" (Ps. 103: 13). Our heavenly Father has modeled the gentleness that is a manly virtue.

It is tempting for men who may not have a natural inclination to demonstrate tenderness to define their fatherly roles purely in terms of training, decision-making, and such. But we must not miss the essential quality of demonstrated love and affection which are so necessary to reach the heart of a child. Observe what Paul wrote to those who were his children in the faith: "But we were gentle among you, just as a nursing mother cherishes her own children. So, affectionately longing for you, we were well pleased to impart to you not only the gospel of God, but also our own lives, because you had become dear to us" (1 Thess. 2:7,8). Men have a lot to learn from women. There is nothing more winsome than genuine compassion tenderly expressed. It is a key to winning the hearts of children. Imagine what it did for their relationship when the prodigal son was nearing home and "his father saw him and had compassion, and ran and fell on his neck and kissed him" (Luke 15:20).

A loving relationship is demonstrated by *heartfelt encouragement*. In the same passage from 1 Thessalonians we quoted above, Paul continues further on, "…as you know how we exhorted, and comforted, and charged every one of you, as a father does his own children, that you would walk worthy of God who calls you into His own kingdom and glory" (2:11,12). The heart bond between men and their children is strengthened by the manly exercise of exhortation.

Hear the cry of the father in Proverbs: "My son, give me your heart" (23:26). A godly father does not merely present truth and duty to his children; he appeals to them earnestly to believe and obey! He urges them. He encourages them. He entreats them. He lets his children see his own passion for the Lord, and he invites them to share in that passion.

Jesus said in John 10:14, "I am the good shepherd; and I know My sheep, and am known by My own." An effective leader has a transparent relationship with his followers in which his life is open to them and theirs to him. Family shepherds need to be open about their faith and their fears; they need to confess their sins. Their fear of God, their love for God, and their trust in God—these must all be on display. They need to live the total Christian life in full view of their families.

All this assumes, of course, that the father himself has turned his own heart to the Lord so that his life is a model for his family. The command of Deuteronomy 6 began: "And these words which I command you today shall be in your heart" (v. 6). It is impossible to pass on to children a heart for the Lord and His Word if the father himself is not truly walking with God.

Finally, fathers must be known by their little flock, but they also must know the condition of their flocks. Perhaps the most important characteristic of a loving father is that he makes it a point to *understand* his children, their heart condition, their character, and their walk with God. "Counsel in the heart of man is like deep water, but a man of understanding will draw it out" (Prov. 20:5). It takes a great deal of time to discover what is in the heart of a child, but fathers must make it their business to know. Only then can they give the encouragement that will be most helpful to the child.

Good Fruit

The parent-child bond is one of the strongest relationships God has created, and He created it to assure the success of His great plan for history, namely, to create a people for Himself in Christ.

God said to Abraham, "I will... be God to you and your descendants after you" (Gen. 17:7). But how did God plan to pass the heritage of the true faith from generation to generation so that this promise could be fulfilled? The answer is in what the Lord Himself said about Abraham in the next chapter of Genesis: "For I have known him, in order that he may command his children and his household after him, that they keep the way of the LORD, to do righteousness and justice, that the LORD may bring to Abraham what He has spoken to him" (18:19). As Abraham fulfilled the assignment for which God chose him, as he turned his heart to his children in godly training and in a loving relationship, they would follow in his faith and the Lord would fulfill His promise to be the God of each succeeding generation.

You see, the concept that the prophet Malachi and the angel Gabriel presented—the heart bond between fathers and their children—has been God's plan from the start. It has always been God's "secret weapon" for changing the world. And whenever men have faithfully employed it, they have seen good fruit.

It is just as the Lord promised in Proverbs 22:6: "Train up a child in the way he should go, and when he is old he will not depart from it." Why? Because once a father's heart is turned to his child and that child's heart is turned to his father, there is no breaking the bond that is created!

Faith of Our Fathers, Living Still

One of the saddest facts of history is that godly men lose their children to the devil. The book of Judges records one such time. The generation of Joshua had witnessed God's miraculous hand in the crossing of the Jordan River on dry ground and in the defeat of their enemies as God gave them the Promised Land. But then we read this sad record:

> When all that generation had been gathered to their fathers, another generation arose after them who did not know the LORD nor the work which He had done for Israel. Then the children of Israel did evil in the sight of the LORD, and served the Baals; and they forsook the LORD God of their fathers, who had brought them out of the land of Egypt; and they followed other gods from among the gods of the people who were all around them,

and they bowed down to them; and they provoked the
LORD to anger. (Jud. 2:10-12)

One generation has an experiential encounter with the
living God and walks with him; the next generation hears the
stories but has no direct experience of God, so they lose their
faith. Is there no remedy for this course of affairs?

According to Scripture there is, and it is nothing other than
the heart bond between fathers and their children which we have
been considering. This is what preserves a living faith in the living
God. Each generation may not have the opportunity to witness
the crossing of the Jordan River on dry ground or the felling of
the walls of Jericho, but each generation has the opportunity to
experience the living God in a way that will preserve their faith.

As fathers open their hearts, love and train their children,
walk with God openly before their families, and urge their
children to follow the Lord with them—then the children come
to experience the God of their fathers, not as memory and story
only, but as living reality in their own lives. *The parent-child heart
channel becomes the means for each generation to have an encounter
with God that assures their continuance in the faith.*

As children come to walk with God as they walk with their
parents, they will create their own history of divine encounters.
Sin confessed, God's discipline received, forgiveness experienced,
prayers answered, guidance gained from Scripture—all these
create a personal history of God's dealing with the child that
assure the genuineness, depth, and perseverance of his faith. The
faith of the fathers thus becomes the faith of the next generation
and the next.

GENERATIONS OF WORLD-CHANGERS

When the hearts of fathers (and mothers) and their children are bound together, God works to spread His gospel and His kingdom through the generations. Such families are "ready... prepared for the Lord" (Luke 1:17). From this kind of family will come what God needs to carry out His world-changing plan in Christ. Not only will the family itself multiply the number of godly people in the earth as time goes on, but each new generation of saints will provide leaders for the church, state, and every sphere of life in this world. "Blessed is the man who fears the LORD, who delights greatly in his commandments. His descendants will be mighty on earth; the generation of the upright will be blessed" (Ps. 112:1,2).

In 1900 A.E. Winship made a study of the descendants of Jonathan and Sarah Edwards. It turns out that Jonathan was not only effective as a preacher during the Great Awakening, he was also effective in populating the world with godly offspring. Over the following 150 years, this one marriage produced: thirteen college presidents, sixty-five professors, one hundred lawyers, thirty judges, sixty-six physicians, three U.S. Senators, three mayors of large cities, three state governors, and a Vice President of the United States. Edwards' descendants authored 135 books and edited eighteen journals and periodicals. Scores entered the ministry, and at least one hundred served as missionaries overseas. Other descendants were leaders in industry and commerce (banking, insurance, mining, oil, etc.). And this is just the public fruit. More important is the unrecorded heritage of quiet faith and holy life that multiplied in hundreds of family units, and spread then to others under their influence. Beyond all his other reasons for fame, Jonathan Edwards' greatest work was his work as a father.

Do you see the potential for godly influence when just one man turns his heart to his children? We must elevate our vision beyond just "surviving" the process of child rearing. Our goal must be loftier than to have children who merely profess Christian faith in their adulthood. We must pass on this multi-generational vision of what God can do when fathers do their job in the home.

God's plan is so simple, and yet so comprehensive! He puts the tools for shaping the world and advancing the kingdom of God into the hands of every man. The truly great men are the fathers. History books record the stories of those who gained notoriety through position, power, or wealth; but the true shapers of history are men in their humble houses, in their shops, and in their fields, with their children by their sides. Each man is privileged by God to be the molder of the future in the form of the children God has given him.

Fathers, stop looking for greatness only in your work, in what your hands and mind produce, in some passing status or prestige, or in the wealth you accumulate. Your greatest mission is the hearts of your children. In them lies your potential for true greatness. In them lies your greatest opportunity to bring glory to God.

We end up where we began. After his relationship with his wife, a father's relationship with his children is the most important in his life. It is God's humble yet effective means for assuring the spread of His kingdom.

So, by all means, stay married and hug your kids. Just remember that God's plan for families involves much more than that.

CHAPTER 7

A Father is a King: Leader, Provider, and Protector

And if it seems evil to you to serve the LORD, choose for yourselves this day whom you will serve... But as for me and my house, we will serve the LORD.

Joshua 24:15

Have you seen this picture? An American pioneer family is standing together, fixing their eyes on the unseen horizon. Their homespun clothes are worn from previous travels, their faces hardened by wind and sun but full of light as they expectantly view a distant place and time.

Father and mother are side by side, each leaning slightly toward the other. With one hand the man is pointing in the direction of their mutual gaze. With the other he supports the muzzle end of his flintlock rifle, the stock resting between his feet. Over his shoulder he has flung the skin of an animal. Mother is holding a baby, and several more children crowd around. The boy in front is holding, in prominent view, the family Bible.

It is a picture that exemplifies the spirit and strength of the pioneers who fanned out westward through this great land and made it what it is today. The values of another era can be seen in this portrait; values like family solidarity, risk-taking, and religious faith.

For our present purposes the picture also teaches something of value for men. It portrays the roles a father plays as the leader of his family. The extended pointing hand speaks of his directing his family toward a goal; the Bible also suggests direction of a spiritual sort. The animal skin suggests his role as the provider for his loved ones. The rifle tells of his role as the protector of his household.

Leadership, provision, and protection—these are what every family needs from a father, whether a pioneer family of yesteryear or a suburban family of today.

All three responsibilities reflect the masculine works of God the Father, as we saw in chapter 4. These tasks are also performed by Jesus Christ in His role as King. A king leads his people, provides for their needs, and protects them from evil.

A father is a king. He reflects the masculine qualities of the Father and the Son, chief among which is their sovereign leadership and care for their creation and their redeemed family in Christ.

THE KINGMAKER

Psalm 8 speaks of the glory of man as the ruler of the earth (cf. Gen. 1:26):

> What is man that You are mindful of him, And the son of man that You visit him? For You have made him a little

lower than the angels, And You have crowned him with glory and honor. You have made him to have dominion over the works of Your hands; You have put all things under his feet... (vv. 4-6)

These verses are quoted by the writer of Hebrews in chapter 2 in reference to Jesus:

"You have put all things in subjection under his feet." For in that He put all in subjection under him, He left nothing that is not put under him. But now we do not yet see all things put under him. But we see Jesus, who was made a little lower than the angels, for the suffering of death crowned with glory and honor, that He, by the grace of God, might taste death for everyone. (vv. 8, 9)

Jesus is not only God—He is fully human. And as a man He has reclaimed the dominion over the earth that God originally gave to mankind. Adam, in effect, gave over his rule of the earth to Satan whom he obeyed. Jesus has restored sovereignty to man. He is the Ideal Man who perfectly fulfills what man was created to be (and more), serves therefore as a model for all men, and actually restores men to their calling to rule the earth for the glory of God. Jesus enables men to be kings.

A Christian man fills the same offices held by Christ, chief of which is that of king. The domain of a father is his household, his family, and it is there that God calls him to reign with gentle but sure authority. As we have seen, a man's dominion extends beyond the home, but it begins there.

EMBARRASSED BY AUTHORITY?

I may not have attended any Promise Keepers rallies, but I have read the literature of the Christian men's movement. I have been struck by one consistent trait of the dozens of such books I have read: they almost always hedge in their discussions of the father's role as leader.

One of the better writers, in my opinion, and one who identifies a man as a king, begins his description of him this way: "The heart of the king is a provisionary heart. The king looks ahead, watches over, and provides order, mercy, and justice. He is authority. He is leader."[14] All very true! But what exactly is the nature and extent of his authority, his leadership? I couldn't find any answers. Later on he writes concerning headship: "It is leadership with an emphasis upon responsibility, duty, and sacrifice. Not rank or domination. No 'I'm the boss' assertion. Most people who have to insist they are the leader, usually aren't."[15] Of course he is right on target that leadership is not domination, if he means the self-willed "lording it over" we addressed earlier. But what exactly is "leadership"? And why does he mention "rank" along with "domination"? Does leadership not contain the component of rank? Is acknowledging rank a form of domination?

Most authors recognize the leadership role of a father, but that acknowledgement is almost always paired with some qualifier that obscures one of the core meanings of male "leadership": that the man is the ruler of his family. Christ-like leadership must indeed be servant-leadership, but leadership is not just service. It also contains the elements of authority, rank, and control. These concepts are almost never discussed. They seem to be an embarrassment even to the modern teachers of men. It's as if the existence of authority is the awkward family secret that we Christians don't want to discuss.

It might make sense to downplay authority and stress service if we lived in a culture where authority structures were already understood and honored. Or perhaps leaning hard on the servant side of servant-leadership would be necessary if we lived in a day when men were generally authoritarian in their homes. But this is far from the case. Our generation doesn't have a clue anymore about the importance and nature of God's order of authority. And the scourge of the American home is not the bossy husband—it's the passive, disconnected male.

I believe that the inability or unwillingness to provide a strong, dare I say masculine, definition of leadership shows two things about the Christian men's movement: 1) a lack of a rock-solid understanding of the Bible's teaching on authority; and 2) an unwillingness to stand up to feminism and say right in its face, "You're wrong. The man is in charge. He is the ruler of his family." Yes, we need to clarify the concept of leadership by describing its servant nature, but we also need to be plain about what is being clarified!

We are caught in a momentous cultural battle for the future of manhood, families, and our civilization. As Charles Colson has observed, "Unprincipled men and women, disdainful of their moral heritage and skeptical of Truth itself, are destroying our civilization by weakening the very pillars upon which it rests."[16] It will do no good, in the face of this onslaught, to speak in euphemistic generalities about the nature of masculine authority.

The Christian men's movement needs to make a choice. Will it stand firmly on the biblical definitions of masculinity and family structure, or will it blunt its message in an effort not to offend the ruling ideologies? The choice we face is evident in this statement by an observer of the men's movement:

> The Promise Keepers certainly aren't perfect. Some of them *do* speak as if they want to re-establish the old patriarchy. But the more serious among them understand that is unacceptable and recognize the need to be clear and consistent about their goal, which is to restore strong, loving families where husband and wife *serve* each other.[17]

Notice the choice. Either you are not to be taken seriously because you want to bring back the "unacceptable," "old patriarchy," or you are to be taken seriously because you recognize that we have progressed to the enlightened stage of human development where husbands and wives relate to each other as mutual servants. In other words, Promise Keepers and the like are acceptable as long as they follow the cultural dogma of egalitarianism and renounce the old idea that a man rules his home.

Our choice is to either be men like King Jesus, who calls men to be kings, or to be some kind of gender-blended almost-man who wears the mantle of an empty authority. A lot is at stake, for our families and our culture. As the first writer I quoted above also says, "When men are not men, a civilization falls. When men let their masculinity drift with the winds of culture, everyone loses. When a culture is castrated, it dies."[18]

Our culture and our homes are castrated because men are embarrassed to be kings.

RULER OF THE HOME

When you hear the word "government," what comes to mind? Almost certainly you thought about the federal government centered in Washington, D.C., or that of your state or city. In other words, you thought of civil government.

But this is not the only government, nor even the most important. The foundational governmental unit in society is the family, and in times past people understood the concept of "family government." Today the idea is almost unheard of. The church is another government created by God, along with the family and the state. These three are the governmental spheres recognized in Scripture.

It is beyond the scope of this book to launch into a teaching on the three spheres of government, but suffice it to say that each sphere has someone in charge (headship), a law to operate by (the Word of God as addressed to that sphere), and the power to reward or punish (the rod for fathers, excommunication for church elders, and physical punishment, including execution, for civil rulers). These are the essential elements of government.

The importance of respecting governments and submitting to those in authority is taught in Romans 13: "Let every soul be subject to the governing authorities. For there is no authority except from God, and the authorities that exist are appointed by God. Therefore whoever resists the authority resists the ordinance of God, and those who resist will bring judgment on themselves" (vv. 1,2). While this passage proceeds to use the illustration of a civil ruler, these first two verses speak about any of the governmental structures established by God. Submission to governments is submission to God since He appointed those who rule in each sphere.

The father is the ruler of the sphere of government known as the family. He is the head of his wife who must submit to his authority (Eph. 5:22,23). We explored this concept of headship in depth in chapter 3. Since he is head of the woman, she shares his authority over the children, such that they owe obedience to both their parents (6:1). While children must obey both, the father is the one addressed specifically concerning the oversight of the children (6:4; cf. Col. 3:20,21). The father is also the one who is instructed by God to discipline the children for their good (Heb. 12:9).

His authority is such that God speaks of a father "commanding" his family. "For I have known him, in order that he may command his children and his household after him, that they keep the way of the LORD, to do righteousness and justice, that the LORD may bring to Abraham what He has spoken to him" (Gen. 18:19). God expected Abraham to direct his household to follow the Lord. It was his to command, and the father's leadership would determine whether the family received the blessings God had promised.

Joshua 24:15 is another verse that depicts a father in his leadership role over his family. "And if it seems evil to you to serve the LORD, choose for yourselves this day whom you will serve... But as for me and my house, we will serve the LORD" (Josh. 24:15). Joshua didn't know what choices others might make, but he knew what he and his family were going to do because he was planning to take the lead and see that they followed the Lord.

Remember that God the Father is portrayed in Isaiah as a potter, one who shapes His people as "the work of [His] hands" (64:8). Fathers are responsible to be the potters of their households, shaping their wives and children to be vessels of honor that bring glory to God (cf. Rom. 9:23).

A father is the head of his house, its lord, its master, its ruler. Yes, this leadership is indeed softened by love and made merciful by the cross, but it is true authority. It is the power to command and direct. It carries with it the responsibility for the course of the home. Truly the buck stops with fathers since they are in charge. They make the final decisions in the household. This is what the term "leadership" means.

The author we quoted at the beginning of this discussion shied away from the idea of "rank" in the context of describing headship. While it is true that rank is not what a husband is going to *emphasize* with his wife (I've never brought it up with mine), it is essential that they both *understand* that rank does exist and that this is a factor in how they relate to each other (my wife already understands this). As her head, the husband outranks his wife, just as Christ outranks the man and the Father outranks Christ (1 Cor. 11:3). It's a chain of authority, which is a chain of command. In this order of authority God the Father is Christ's superior and Christ is man's superior. Also, man is woman's superior—not superior in value, dignity, or ability, but superior in authority.

Abraham's wife, Sarah, understood rank and thus had a rightly patriarchal view of her relationship with her husband. "For in this manner, in former times, the holy women who trusted in God also adorned themselves, being submissive to their own husbands, as Sarah obeyed Abraham, calling him lord, whose daughters you are if you do good and are not afraid with any terror" (1 Pet. 3:5,6). Sarah called her husband "my lord" (Gen. 18:2), a word that means "supreme in authority; controller." It is the same word used of the "Lord" Jesus. As Jesus is Lord over His kingdom, so a husband is lord over his household. That is why Sarah "obeyed" her husband. It is also why the old form of the marriage vow for the bride had her promise "to love, honor, and obey" her husband. That's when they understood family government and were not embarrassed by authority and the order it creates.

This biblical language sounds strange, even offensive, to our modern ears accustomed as we are to hearing the leveling language of egalitarianism. Abraham commanded his family and Sarah obeyed him as her lord. Modern men and women talk about husbands and wives serving each other, and no more.

If you think I am reverting to barbarianism in this chapter, I just ask you to do two things. Test what we are saying by Scripture—"Test all things; hold fast what is good" (1 Thess. 5: 21). And go back and read the chapter on manhood under the cross. We haven't forgotten that the man is a servant-leader. We just want to bring a proper balance to the term. "Servant" is the modifier. "Leader" is the main word.

STEWARDS

Man is the ruler, the lord of his home because he is a man under authority. Let's expand on the notion from a previous chapter—that fathers must be submissive to God—by applying this principle to the specific issue of family government. We already looked at Romans 13, which says, "there is no authority except from God, and the authorities that exist are appointed by God" (v. 1). Everyone who holds a position of authority in this world is in a position that God has established, and God has put each one in the place of leadership he holds.

This means that he is answerable to God for his service as a government head. Three times in the verses that follow Paul describes rulers as "ministers of God" (vv. 4,6). They serve on His behalf in whatever domain they rule. When discussing church leaders elsewhere, Paul describes them as "those who must give account" to God for their work (Heb. 13:17).

A ruler is a steward of God. A steward is a man who is put in charge of an estate by the owner. The steward rules the household, but he does so only by the will of the owner, and the steward must give account of his stewardship whenever the owner demands it. Joseph was a steward of Pharaoh's house, which amounted to the whole kingdom of Egypt.

Luke 12:42 reveals clearly what the role of a steward is, "And the Lord said, 'Who then is that faithful and wise steward, whom his master will make ruler over his household, to give them their portion of food in due season?'" The accountability of the steward comes through in Luke 16:2: "So he called him and said to him, 'What is this I hear about you? Give an account of your stewardship, for you can no longer be steward.'" The owner trusts the steward, who must prove faithful to his charge. "Moreover it is required in stewards that one be found faithful" (1 Cor. 4:2).

God owns the family and he has appointed the father the steward of the family. God delegates His authority to the father to govern on His behalf. Toward God, the father is a steward. Toward his wife and children, the father is the head of the household; its ruler or governor.

The father's authority is revealed symbolically and effectively in his right to wield the rod of discipline against rebellion in his children. God has given all rulers some means to enforce their authority.

The law he enforces in the home is the law of God, and he himself is subject to that law. This means that the father's authority, though very broad, is also limited by the revealed will of God. A man does not, for example, have the power of life and death over his wife and children. If he abuses them physically, he is violating his duty to protect them and has become the opposite: a threat to their safety. If a father abuses his authority, he can be punished for that misuse of his office by church and civil authorities. He could even lose his right to rule his family if the abuse is extreme or continuous. The reach of a father's authority is extensive, but it is limited by the law of God.

Psalm 127 begins: "Unless the LORD builds the house, they labor in vain who build it." A Christian family cannot be built by the efforts of a mere man, and certainly not by a man who sees himself as the dictator of the home. A father needs to see himself as God's representative, acting on His behalf and according to His revealed will in the Bible. Only then is it safe for him to be the master of the household.

The Essence of Leadership

"Lead, follow, or get out of the way." I'm sure you've seen the signs with that message. It was probably originally written by a man who had a lot of drive and who got frustrated watching groups of people ooze along with no leadership. I know it comes to my mind when I'm in a situation where no one seems to be in charge, or the person who is supposed to be in charge won't take the reins and direct the group. "If you're supposed to lead, lead! If not, then follow somebody who will. But don't just sit there doing nothing."

There is an energy to leadership that is not easy to define with precision. We made a start when looking at God the Father. Our statement describing His masculine energy was this: He *initiates action and sustains it toward a goal.* We also saw that God acts consistently as a leader, provider, and protector, with the leadership function encompassing the other two.

A leader is someone who provides direction to whatever outfit he heads. He takes the initiative to move the group toward the goal. Being made in God's image in their masculinity, men are task-oriented creatures. They are made to take dominion, to rule. They like having a job to do and working to see it accomplished. They thrive on having a mission with an objective to be reached. Fathers have a mission: "as for me and my house, we will serve the Lord."

Let's take a look at how a father should give direction to the outfit called his family.

Modern families, Christian families included, need men who are willing to stand up and point the way and expect the others to follow their direction. Unfortunately, most families flounder about like rudderless ships with no sense of overarching mission or purpose and no clear guidance for day-to-day life. In place of purpose they substitute frantic busyness, trying to mask their lack of direction with their endless activities.

To be an effective family leader a father needs first to *develop goals*. His overarching goal is to see Christ formed in his family members and Christ proclaimed through their words and works— to the glory of God. But to achieve this high purpose he needs to break it down into some smaller objectives. He must decide what his goals are for his children's education and vocation, for their character development, for their financial situation when he releases them, and for their future spouses. He must set goals for the running of his household year-by-year, week-by-week, and day-by-day. He is the one who is designed to stand before his family with his finger pointing out the direction they all need to go.

Second, a father needs to *take initiative*. Most men tend to be reactive rather than proactive. We will solve a problem if our wives set it in our laps. We should instead be the ones looking ahead for problems and planning what is best for the family welfare. A leader makes things happen, he doesn't wait for them to happen. Perhaps we should think of our family life as one big game of Follow the Leader, and we are the ones out front — except that it is no game, and the stakes are very high indeed.

Third, to be an effective family leader, a father must *accept the burden of making decisions.* Taking responsibility is painful for most men, just as it was for our first father, Adam (who, you will recall, blamed his wife for his cowardly choice to disobey God). Making decisions he can be held accountable for may be distasteful to a father, but it is the essence of leadership. He is the one who must make decisions about education, friendships, courtship, allowances, entertainment, church, and a seemingly endless list of other major and minor issues that confront a family. And what he delegates to his wife will be his decision still (again, look at Adam and Eve).

My own passivity and unwillingness to make decisions was revealed early on in our marriage in a comical way. When I would take the family on a camping trip and we would arrive at the campground, we would drive around the whole park—more than once—trying to be sure we got just the right campsite. "That one is too near the road. That one is too far from the bathhouse. That one is not quite level." The real problem was not the imperfection of the campsites, it was my fear of making a decision that might prove imperfect or be questioned by my wife or kids. If I had trouble making a decision in the small things, how do you think I did in the big things?

Finally, a godly father needs to *enlist the strengths of his family* as he leads them. The origin of the word "husband" suggests stewardship and prudent management. A "husbandman" is one who cultivates land. The wise husband-father will cultivate his wife and fully utilize her gifts and wisdom in reaching his decisions. He will also consult his children as they grow in wisdom. Those who are led should enjoy the experience of being taken seriously as fellow-heirs of God's grace, even as they rest in the security of being directed by a wise and firm leader.

Godly leadership is not defined as tyrannically making independent decisions without regard to the opinions and needs of others. Quite the opposite. True masculine leadership mobilizes the strengths of others in carrying out its mandates. A wise husband will view his wife as his best counselor; he will seek out her opinions and cherish her perspectives; he will consider her needs and do what he believes is best for her and the children. It was right for me to consider the opinion of my wife and children as to which campsite to choose—but seeking consultation can also be a cover for not having the courage to make a decision.

A godly father will not defer to his wife in a way that effectively transfers to her the decision-making process in the home. She must help *him* reach *his* decisions and then submit to them and seek to carry out his will to the best of her ability. It's good to practice that pattern even when it comes to choosing campsites.

THE FAMILY POLICYMAKER

A large part of the direction a father provides to his household will come through the policies he enacts. These policies will direct his family as they walk through their days, even when he is not around.

My online *Merriam Webster's Collegiate Dictionary* defines the word "policy" this way: 1) "a definite course or method of action selected from among alternatives and in light of given conditions to guide and determine present and future decisions;" and 2) "a high-level overall plan embracing the general goals and acceptable procedures especially of a governmental body."

As we have seen, the foundational governmental body in this world is the family unit. At its head God has placed the man. As head he is responsible to establish the policies by which the family operates. *He articulates the overall plan, the general goals, and the acceptable procedures that provide the family with a definite course of action and guide their decision-making.*

Here is a passage from Proverbs that describes how policymaking works:

> My son, keep your father's command, and do not forsake the law of your mother. Bind them continually upon your heart; tie them around your neck. When you roam, they will lead you; when you sleep, they will keep you; and when you awake, they will speak with you. For the commandment is a lamp, and the law a light; reproofs of instruction are the way of life. (Prov. 6:20-23)

Verse 20 speaks of the "father's command" and the "law of your mother." Verse 23 then creates the picture of these commands being a lamp and these laws a light. As the lamp the father's commands are the source of guidance for the family. The wife's job is to draw from the father's general guidance and illuminate the family with the particular application of his commands. He pronounces the policies, and she applies them to the details of home life.

Obviously a godly man is not going to create family policies out of his own imagination. He is himself going to be guided by the Word of God which is called "a lamp to my feet and a light to my path" (Psalm 119:105). His commands will be rooted in the commands of his God.

Very few homes today, even among Christians, have any clearly defined policies by which the family operates. Most are simply swept along by the current of whatever values are popular among the families with whom they associate and by the sheer busyness that substitutes for any real plan of action for family life. It is a lot easier to go with the flow than to step back and set goals based on biblical priorities and establish plans and procedures to reach those goals.

There is often an amazing contrast between the way a man functions at his place of employment and how he conducts himself at home. On the job he may be engaged in a process of "management by objectives," subjecting every facet of his work to careful assessment, planning based on those assessments, rational implementation procedures, and follow-up evaluations of the whole process. Yet at home he may act like he hasn't a clue as to the direction the family ought to take; he waits for things to happen and then reacts, making *ad hoc* decisions (if he makes any at all) by which he "leads" the family.

If fathers want to fulfill their leadership calling at home, they must learn to view their family headship as the most important vocation they have. They must make the family their highest priority and apply their very best energies to effective leadership there.

As he begins to function as the family policymaker there are several key areas that he ought to address: personal and institutional relationships, education, use of time, use of money, and family convictions. In each of these areas the father is responsible to establish the overall plan and procedures for his household. He should make the decisions that will shape his family's life.

Relationships

Relationships are the content of life. Beyond our relationship with our Creator, we have contact continuously with people individually or grouped into a variety of institutions (family, church, school, club, ministry group, political action group, etc.). These relationships are the source of the greatest influences upon us and our loved ones, and they are the arena in which we can have the most influence upon others.

The father must decide what relationships his family will have. Which church will they attend? What friends will they have? Will his children participate in any clubs? If so, which ones? Will he or any members of his family be involved in pro-life activities? With which ministry?

What rules will govern the children in playing with neighbor children? Are there any restrictions as to whom they can associate with? Any restricted activities? Can they visit neighbor homes to play with friends? Which ones? What are they allowed to do there?

As the primary gatekeeper for his home, it is the father's job to control who has access to his wife and children and to regulate who they come into contact with and for what purposes. To not make decisions in this area is to decide to allow others to control the influences on the family.

Education

There is a general tendency in our culture for decisions related to the children to be made by Mom. But here is a perfect opportunity for Dad to reclaim his headship.

A father must take charge of his children's education: which curriculum to use, whether to co-op with another family, what daily and annual schedules the family follows, etc.—these are all policy issues that he must settle.

The day-to-day implementation of these policies can be delegated to his wife, but she ought to have the foundation of his general guidance as a basis for her own decisions. He speaks the "commandments" for the household, she uses these to frame its "laws."

My wife and I used to go to many curriculum fairs for home schoolers, representing a particular company. I don't know how many times I had this experience: a woman would stand across the table talking to us about her children, her home school program, her plans for the year. Once I decided to actually ask, "Are you married?" When I did, the lady (who was married) responded with a blank look that said in effect, "What's that got to do with home schooling?"

A huge portion of a child's life is spent in an educational context. If fathers don't set the policies for this part of family life, they are failing to control one of the greatest influences on their children.

Use of Time

In too many Christian homes today there is no rational control of the schedule. Families are tyrannized by the urgent demands of school, church, youth groups, sports teams, fieldtrips, birthday parties, part-time jobs, and on and on it goes. It is common for families to be so busy with seemingly good activities that they have no time left for the best: quiet family times for conversation, reading, worship, play—the stuff of which memories are made and by which unbreakable bonds of love are woven.

The policymaker in the home can have some of his greatest influence by taking charge of the family schedule. He should determine when the members of the family arise in the morning and when they retire at night, at least until the children are nearing adulthood. He should decide when they worship together and when they eat. He should lay down the rules that will determine in which of the out-of-home activities the children can participate.

Above all else he must guard against the insane busyness that characterizes modern family life. If things are out of control and the family members simply meet each other coming and going, he is the one who must call a halt to the rat race and establish time priorities that will build rather than fragment his family.

Use of Money

One sign of a well-ordered home is that the man takes charge of the finances. This does not mean necessarily that he has to maintain the checkbook, but he must create the policies for the family concerning spending, tithing, saving, and debt, as well as the policy for children's allowances or pay for work.

Will the family live on a budget? If so, he should draw it up. What are the spending priorities? Does the family tithe? Where does the tithe go? How much of income is saved? For what can savings be spent? Will the family ever go into debt? If so, for what purposes? Do the children get an allowance or are they paid for work, or neither?

The wife should know the boundaries within which she is free to spend money on a week-to-week basis. Some men try to assuage a guilty conscience brought on by a lack of family leadership by allowing their wives to become shopping addicts. She should be able to find her joy in a husband who cares enough to carefully manage the family finances rather than in the cheap thrill of impulse spending.

On the other hand, some wives are thrifty to a fault and hate to spend any money. Such women may need to be encouraged to go ahead and buy that new sewing machine rather than fiddling with the barely running one they have.

Family Convictions

There are many issues of belief and practice that have no clear biblical mandate attached to them. Whether matters of doctrine or lifestyle, it will be the father who must determine where his family will stand on the issues.

What do we believe about eternal security, about spiritual gifts, about the end times? Father, as the family teacher and the one who will give an account for the rest of his household, must shape the convictions of his family on doctrinal points.

To what kind of music do we listen? What sort of movies or videos will we watch? Do we go shopping on the Lord's Day? What are our standards for modest attire?

Of course many of the questions that pertain to relationships, education, time, and money are also questions of conviction: Do I want my children in peer-oriented youth groups? Is home education God's best for my family? Is family worship an essential part of each day's schedule? Should my family get completely out of debt, or is a home mortgage acceptable?

These and many other lifestyle issues we could name are matters of personal conviction that must become matters of family conviction under the leadership of the head of the home.

HANDS-ON LEADERSHIP

You have probably seen the picture many times before. Some prominent person, usually a politician or statesman, is standing before the podium of some university adorned in full academic regalia. He is addressing the graduates and guests, having himself just been awarded an honorary degree. Not a bad deal: show up and give a speech, and forever after you get to be called "Dr." so-and-so. None of the rigors of academic study, but you get the title anyway. (I realize that the purpose of these degrees is to honor the life achievements of the recipient, and they are usually well-deserved.)

I am afraid that too often we men act as if we have been awarded an honorary title called "Family Leader." Very few of us would question that the title belongs to us by God's design, and it does. We nod appreciatively whenever we hear a speaker mention the fact that a man is in charge of his home. We enjoy the trappings of the office, like sitting at the head of the table or being the primary driver of the family vehicle. But family leadership is more than titles and cultural perks. If we want to wear the title with integrity, we will not be content to accept it as if it were an unearned degree; we will earn it through the hard work of actually leading our families.

A father needs to do more than set general policy for his home. He must also act as a program director for the family. The concept of program director suggests immediacy. It is a "hands-on" title. A program director is the one who actually sees that a program is carried out. He receives his orders from a board or an executive, but he is the one on the frontline assuring that the plan is executed. Others may plan the work, but he works the plan. In the case of a father it is the Lord who is his superior, his Chief Executive, his Head (1 Cor. 11:3), and the Lord has appointed the father as the program director for the family.

It may seem at first thought that if the man is the policymaker (under the Lord), then the wife must be the program director. After all, her role is to carry out her husband's plans for the home. This is true, but we must not view the man's role as simply setting up guidelines for family operation and then stepping back and letting his wife take over. He must maintain a day-by-day oversight of the actual execution of the policies he sets forth. He must be an involved leader. Yes, his wife assists him by carrying out his plans; but she is his assistant, his helper (Gen. 2:18), and that certainly suggests that he is also involved in the process. She is the *assistant* program director.

The great challenge to implementing the concept of the father as the hands-on leader in the home is the fact that most fathers are absent from the home for the greater part of most days. His occupation generally requires him to be gone about ten hours a day. On top of this, he may have other commitments like church ministries that take him away from the family all evening once or twice or even more each week.

We meet here the heart of the challenge of modern family life. How do we restore a well-integrated family life, with fathers and mothers each doing their part, when so much of life is lived outside the home? Those who home school their children have brought part of life back home, but Dad is usually still gone most of the day. The process of home education cries out for the restoration of the leadership role of the father at a moment in history in which fathers are not there to do the job. Fathers need to consider making changes that enable them to better lead their families. This may mean eliminating those evening commitments to the church or the political action group. A father has no business pouring his energy and time into other callings until he has maximized his contribution to his own family.

He may even need to change occupations. If the job requires fourteen hours a day on a consistent basis, thus eliminating the possibility of his directing the affairs of his household effectively, then there is only one solution: he should find another job that permits him to do his most important job. Surely God is able and willing to give a man employment that allows him to be obedient in his family calling.

Just getting the father home more is, of course, no guarantee that he is going to actually become the program director of his family. Whether home a little or a lot he may not be much good to the family if he is *emotionally absent* from the home. The emotionally absent father is characterized by a lack of interest in what is going on in the home and with the children. He may be distracted by his vocation, his ministry, his hobbies, or by that champion motivation-destroyer, the television. He may be passive about the conduct of the household and hoping his wife will take care of whatever problems arise. He may be lazy and without the desire to exert himself by getting involved in the day-to-day hassles of family life.

Such a man needs a good dose of repentance. It is a sin to neglect his role in the home, and no excuses about a lack of role models or a lack of energy can cover up his basic need to get serious about his most important responsibility. If a man is lacking the motivation to lead his family, he needs to pray for his Father in heaven to share some of His Father's heart, to give him an affection and love for his wife and children that will drive him toward involvement. He needs to ask God to turn his heart toward his children, and then begin to take action as that turning is accomplished.

ASSIGNMENT AND REPORT

Now let's get down to some practical application of all these principles. One way in which a man can begin to act like the program director in his home is through a daily assignment and report system. This is especially important for the man who must leave home for the better part of the day to work.

In the morning before he leaves for work (or the night before if his morning departure is too early) the father takes a few minutes with his wife (and optionally the children) to go over the *assignment* for the day. This would include especially the school schedule, including specific lessons for the children. However it would also encompass household chores, family projects, and other activities planned for the day. The purpose is to have a common understanding between husband and wife. He is announcing his plan for his household for the day; she is affirming the plan and her intention to carry it out.

When he returns in the evening he takes a few minutes once again. This time he checks in with both his wife and children to get a *report* on how the plan was carried out during his absence. His wife reports on the school lessons and the other activities, making special note of the attitude of the children through the day. Dad looks at some of the schoolwork and asks the children about their day. What is happening here is that he is holding both Mom and the children accountable for their work while he was gone. He in turn is getting the information he needs to be accountable to his heavenly Boss concerning his little domain.

This simple system has the great benefit of keeping the focus on the father as the leader. By verifying the plan before the day starts and checking up on it after the fact, he is at least twice daily functioning in his leadership role. This is good for him as it keeps him involved and responsible. It is good for the children as they realize who is in charge and respect their father as a genuine authority in the home. But this system is especially good for Mom, who is relieved of a great burden God never meant her to bear. She was created to help her husband and carry out his decisions. She was not meant to make the big decisions and enforce them on the children.

Now during the day her role is simply that of carrying out the father's program. The children view her in a different light than if the dad were not involved. She is not the slave driver who is making the children finish their math or the spoilsport who insists that they practice their piano for a full half-hour when they have other things they would rather do. Now she is their helper, the one who assists them in meeting Father's expectations. And if they are wise they will accept her help. She need not get into a big fight with them about doing their work and keeping a good attitude. The power play is not between her and the children; it is between Father and the children.

She is relieved of being the stand-in head of the family as the focus is back where it belongs: on Dad. She can blossom in her nurturing and supportive role when she does not have imposed upon her the alien role of director and enforcer. This does not mean that she does not give directions and enforce them during the day, but the focus has changed. *She represents a higher authority* to whom the children will give an account at the end of the day.

This assignment and report process is a simple way for the uninvolved father to begin to exercise hands-on leadership in his home. Even if the wife is still doing most of the day-to-day planning, he can at least find out about her plan and give it his stamp of approval at the start of each day. It then becomes *his* plan. We've got to start somewhere!

At this moment in history most of us fathers may need to be physically absent from the home during the day, but that does not mean that we cannot be directing the affairs of our home all day long. It just takes a little more forethought and planning. But then, isn't that what leadership is all about?

Having spent a lot of time on the father's general leadership role, now let's look at the two other ways that a father acts as the king in his family.

God delegates authority for a reason, and the reason he has given the man authority in the home is not to make him feel superior. "The head rules his household and expects submission, but he rules the household so that he can care for its members."[19] And this care takes the form of providing for their needs and protecting them from danger.

PROVISION

God our Father is the source of every blessing we enjoy in this life and in eternity. "Every good gift and every perfect gift is from above, and comes down from the Father of lights..." (Jas. 1:17). Even the rich blessings of salvation that are mediated through the Son and the Spirit come to us from the Father, the one whose plan was carried out at the cross.

Following the example of our heavenly Father, we must give good gifts to our family. In the Sermon on the Mount Jesus speaks of children asking their fathers for bread and fish and expecting the blessing of a meal (Matt. 7:9,10). As God provides for us, so a man ought to provide for his wife and children.

We must be careful as we consider each of these roles to remember that the human father only fulfills them in a derivative sense. God the Father remains the ultimate Provider (and Protector); we copy his ways and become providers and protectors in our God-given spheres, but only as channels of *His* blessings. Unless the Lord builds the house, its builders labor in vain (Ps. 127:1); unless the Lord provides for my family, my work as provider will produce nothing.

A man's provision must be both physical and spiritual. In the realm of the *physical* it is his job to see that the family has what it needs to live and thrive. He sees that they have food, clothing, and shelter.

This does not mean that we should embrace the stereotypical idea of the husband as "the breadwinner." That term has come to imply that it is his job to get out there in the world, earn some money and buy the things the family needs. Meanwhile, the wife (and children) sit at home essentially unemployed and gratefully receive his provision.

In the fully functioning historical household (in contrast to our contemporary urbanized version) the wife and children were very much employed in the tasks that provided for the family. They helped with planting and harvesting the garden; they canned food, cared for livestock, and made clothing. In short, they were essential to the household economy and played a crucial role in the provision for its physical needs. However, it was the father's job to provide them with tools to use so that, through their work, they could help the family provide for itself. Everybody had a part to play, but he was responsible for the whole process. Also, because of his physical strength, he had the most physically demanding jobs, like breaking the soil and pulling the stumps, and thus served a role that could not be filled by his wife or children. He was the provider, but he had a lot of help.

Today, whether in an urban apartment or a rural homestead, men must embrace the role of physical provision for the family. The Mr. Mom household in which the woman works to support the family and the man runs the household and cares for the kids is a perversion of God's order. How is the man reflecting the fatherhood of God by acting like a mother? No, it is *his* calling to provide. Better a family lives poorly on the father's lean wages than that the gifted wife supplant him in his role.

More important than physical provision is the father's responsibility to provide for his family *spiritually*. Without physical food his wife and children will die; but without spiritual food, they will die eternally.

He is the family shepherd. He is the one who must see that they are led to the green pastures and still waters of God's Word. He must lead the family in the worship of God. He must instruct them from the Bible. He must lead them in hiding the scriptures in their hearts. This is his task both in scheduled family times and as he walks along the way with them. As a child may expect his father to give him bread, so he may expect his father to give him the bread of life as well.

One of the greatest tragedies in Christian homes today is the spiritual malnutrition of wives and children. When a person is starving physically we can see it in their gaunt faces and swollen bellies. If we were to put on our "spiritual glasses" we would see that the children in many a Christian man's home look like those in a "Feed the Children" documercial—they are starving for spiritual food. (We will deal more with spiritual provision when we look at the father's roles of prophet and priest.)

It is a God-like calling to provide for a family, and in a day that has emasculated men and denied them their proper roles, we must return to the notion that the husband and father is the provider for the household.

Protection

God is a Protector. That is another expression of His fatherhood. He protects those under His care, those in special need of protection. Indeed, the angel of the Lord encamps around all those who fear Him, and He rescues them (Ps. 34:7).

Since evil was introduced into this world there has been a need for protection. Evil is threatening and must be counteracted by righteous action. A failure of defense can mean the destruction of those who are vulnerable.

The man is the protector of his family. Again we must emphasize that his role is derivative and that it is God's protection that is worked through his efforts; but a defender he must be. And once again this role has both a physical and a spiritual dimension.

For most of us the days are past when we are called upon to bolt our loved ones in the cabin and face down that grizzly bear with our muzzleloader. Yet that urge to protect is still part of men who are in touch with their maleness, and it must be carried out in ways appropriate to the modern condition.

In terms of *physical* protection the following examples come to mind. A father must determine where his family will live and if they are safe there from the attacks of evil men. He must see that his house is a safe place to live through careful maintenance. He must keep up the family car to protect his dear ones from the dangers of worn tires and leaking brakes. He must defend his home against intruders, with force if necessary. He must set limits for the children in play: how far can they go, how high can they climb?

He must keep a constant eye out for danger and take steps to defend his wife and children when necessary. The cry of men on the sinking *Titanic*, "Women and children first," appropriately expresses godly priorities. It is a man's job to pay any price necessary, including his own life, to defend women and children, especially his own household.

More subtle than physical dangers are the *spiritual* threats to a man's family. Scripture warns that the real battles for Christians are those that involve spiritual forces (Eph. 6:12). Many a man's family who live in physical safety are defenseless against some serious threats to their souls.

These threats come by means of evil influences that the man allows to act upon his home and its members. One such threat is that of evil companions, whether neighbor kids, schoolteachers and classmates, or even members of the extended family. Another is evil in the form of print or electronic media, including television and videos. As the family gatekeeper, it is Dad's job to decide who and what has access to his little flock and to bar exposure to that which could draw them away from the Lord.

Just as tragic as spiritually malnourished children is the spectacle of spiritually vulnerable children whose fathers leave them exposed to soul-destroying influences. Surely no man could stand idly by if his kids were being threatened by a hungry predator with a taste for human blood. How is it that so many Christian men can allow their children to be devoured by the offspring of that roaring lion, the devil? Christian children by the millions are slaughtered in schools that have godless teachers and immoral peers, they are consumed by the deadly jaws of MTV and its kin on the tube, and their chastity is destroyed by the reckless and immoral patterns of the modern dating game. Why are Christian children being left so vulnerable? Where are the fathers?

Whether it is fixing a tire, buying a gun, restricting TV, or interviewing a daughter's prospective spouse, the many ways a man can protect his family are each a part of his calling to reflect the one who is our Protector.

How Vulnerable Are Your Kids?

Most of us have seen the card-pack form of advertising in which we receive a bundle of postcard-sized ads related by some common theme like family life, church ministry, or home schooling. A pack that I received some time back was devoted to youth ministries in the church—and was it ever an eye-opener!

Bear in mind that these ads are directed at youth workers in Christian churches (words in quotation marks are directly from the ads):

Item—There is a deal for a series of videos with titles that promise edifying themes: "AIDS Among Teens"… "Shattered"… "How Far is Too Far?" The videos are touted as "changing the way thousands of youth ministers communicate with their teens." ("Their teens"? Since when did youth ministers take over the raising of our youth?)

Item—"Your kids have seen MTV. Now take them to the edge." This ad is promoting a quarterly video magazine for kids. (*Whose* kids have seen MTV?)

Item—Another video, with the eye-catching headline, "It's Killing Our Kids." This one is about alcoholism.

Item—Here is another resource on AIDS, a book. This one is headlined: "Why AIDS is Exploding and No Teen is Safe!" It continues: "Just being a Christian doesn't keep teens or church members safe from AIDS! … No youth pastor, health professional, or thought leader should be without these new facts!"

Item—Finally, a youth group resource is introduced with these comforting words: "You know teenagers face some tough decisions—sex, drugs, the occult. Television and popular music won't help them make Christian choices. They need guidance from the Bible, but the old teaching methods just don't work anymore with this new generation."

You see, the depressing assumptions exhibited in all of these and similar ads are these: 1) Christian young people are exposed to the basest evils around. They watch MTV, pair off and get involved physically, have contact with alcohol and drugs or those who do, and consider suicide because life is so depressing. In other words, Christian children are not distinguishable from the world's children. 2) It is the job of the church, and in particular the youth pastor (often young, inexperienced, and single), to guide our children through this difficult period. 3) The "old" ways of training children don't work; we need new methods to match a new generation.

Has it really come to this? Is this really the way it is in America's homes and churches? Well, no wonder our nation is in trouble. No wonder the church is so ineffective. No wonder teens rebel against parents and depart from the faith.

A failure to protect our children in this day of suffocating evil almost guarantees a victory for the enemy.

But there is nothing inevitable about all this. We make choices and live with the consequences. We fathers control how our children are brought up, for better or for worse. We are the potters. Our children are the clay, and we have a mandate to shape them for God. "But as for me and my house, we will serve the LORD."

Surely our goal is not just to have children who manage to reach adulthood without being pregnant out of wedlock or addicted to drugs. That's a pretty low goal for a Christian father to have for his sons and daughters. Let's aim higher. Let's aim to produce young adults who are radiant examples of faith and holiness, who are unstained by the world, and who are ready to serve the Lord Jesus all through their lives while they pass on this heritage to their children's children. It can and will happen, by God's grace, when we fathers apply ourselves to our kingly duty to lead, provide for, and protect our households.

CHAPTER 8

A Father is a Prophet: Moral Teacher and Enforcer

Come, you children, listen to me; I will teach you the fear of the LORD.

Ps. 34:11

You know how we exhorted, and comforted, and charged every one of you, as a father does his own children.

1 Thess. 2:11

K ing David's failure to give moral training to his son nearly cost him his kingdom. Adonijah, son of David's wife Haggith, sought to topple his father from power. We read in 1 Kings 1:5,6:

> Then Adonijah the son of Haggith exalted himself, saying, "I will be king"; and he prepared for himself chariots and horsemen, and fifty men to run before him. (And his father had not rebuked him at any time by saying, "Why have you done so?" He was also very good-looking. His mother had borne him after Absalom.)

This attempted *coup* was short-lived, and David eventually succeeded in passing his kingdom along to his intended heir, Solomon. But what is interesting for our present purposes is the parenthetical note in the verses above. By way of explanation for Adonijah's shocking and rebellious behavior, the text adds, "And his father had not rebuked him at any time by saying, 'Why have you done so?'" In other words, David was reaping the bad fruit of bad parenting. He had allowed his son to do whatever he pleased, without ever challenging his behavior or rebuking him when he did wrong. So the untrained young man had no internal restraints to prevent his pursuing his evil ambitions.

The text also adds the comment that Adonijah was "very good looking." This could help explain some of David's neglect. Adonijah's appearance would have invited an affection from his father (and mother) that made it more difficult to oppose him: "Surely this good-looking boy will turn out alright. We'll just give him time to mature." And mature he did—into a handsome rebel.

You need to be more than a king in your household to be a successful father. You also need to be a teacher and moral trainer, and failure in this role can be devastating.

We are addressing now the office of prophet. Earlier we looked at the prophetic role of Jesus and saw that a prophet is a mouthpiece for God, a man who represents God to the people. His fundamental mission is to teach people God's truth and call them to follow Him. He is a teacher with a moral focus.

Jesus is a prophet and he calls men to fulfill this office as well. Nowhere is the need for the faithful practice of the prophetic role more important than in the home, where children are shaped into adults before they are launched into the world.

The prophetic office includes the roles of teacher and exhorter, and we will consider these now. We will also be considering the father's job as the disciplinarian of the home, even though this is more an expression of the kingly office. The prophet exhorts people to obey God; the king enforces the law of God. As we have stated previously, these roles are not airtight categories without overlap. It is, after all, the same man fulfilling all the roles, and he often functions in more than one role at a time. Prophetic exhortation often becomes kingly enforcement in the sense of chastisement. So for simplicity sake, we will cover discipline under our discussion of the father as prophet.

God's Ordained Teachers

When most of us hear the word "teacher" today we think first of a schoolteacher or some person who fills the position of instructor in another setting, like a Sunday School teacher. In the Bible God makes no mention of schoolteachers, Sunday School or otherwise, but he does talk a lot about teachers.

Whenever the reference is to children, it is the parents who are identified as the instructors, and the father in particular. God said of Abraham, "For I have known him, in order that he may command his children and his household after him, that they keep the way of the LORD, to do righteousness and justice, that the LORD may bring to Abraham what He has spoken to him" (Gen. 18:19). Abraham was responsible to instruct his household in the way of the Lord, to teach them how to live righteously and justly. Nearly two thousand years later Paul gave this guidance under the Holy Spirit's inspiration: "And you, fathers, do not provoke your children to wrath, but bring them up in the training and admonition of the Lord" (Eph. 6:4).

Of course, as the man's helper, his wife is also a teacher of the children. "My son, hear the instruction of your father, and do not forsake the law of your mother" (Prov. 1:8; cf. 6:20). Even the grandparents are to share in the teaching task: speaking of God's commandments, Moses said to God's people, "And teach them to your children and your grandchildren" (Deut. 4:9).

Teaching and training by the parents is highlighted at the very summit of Old Testament revelation. Israel has just heard Moses pronounce the sacred Name: "Hear, O Israel: The LORD our God, the LORD is one!" (Deut. 6:4). This is followed immediately by the commandment which Jesus called the "greatest commandment" (Matt. 22:38): "You shall love the LORD your God with all your heart, with all your soul, and with all your strength" (Deut. 6:5). Then comes the climactic charge to the people: "And these words which I command you today shall be in your heart. You shall teach them diligently to your children, and shall talk of them when you sit in your house, when you walk by the way, when you lie down, and when you rise up" (6:6,7). The teaching role of parents is central to the fulfillment of God's plan to create a people who are fully devoted to Him.

The mandate for parents to teach their offspring is a perpetual one. "For He established a testimony in Jacob, and appointed a law in Israel, which He commanded our fathers, that they should make them known to their children; that the generation to come might know them, the children who would be born, that they may arise and declare them to their children" (Ps. 78:5,6). Each generation should be raised with the expectation of teaching the next. "Tell your children about it, let your children tell their children, and their children another generation" (Joel 1:3). Fathers teach sons, who teach their sons, and so on.

The priests and Levites had a teaching role in the holy community; but they did not teach children directly apart from the parents. They taught "the men and women and those who could understand" when gathered as a group (Neh. 8:3,7,8).

The Bible, through command and example, presents the father, and his wife beside him, as the teachers of children.

A husband also has a teaching role toward his wife. Following the example of Christ, he is supposed to "sanctify and cleanse her with the washing of water by the word" (Eph. 5: 26). He is responsible for her spiritual growth, and teaching the Word of God is central to the fulfillment of this shepherding task. Another evidence that a man is the primary teacher of his wife is found in this verse: "And if [the women] want to learn something, let them ask their own husbands at home; for it is shameful for women to speak in church" (1 Cor. 14:35). A wife should look first to her husband as her Bible teacher.

THE GOAL OF EDUCATION

A prophet-teacher always has in mind the relationship between the people he is teaching and the Lord. The verse we read earlier did not just say to train your children any old way, it said to "bring them up in the training and admonition *of the Lord*" (Eph. 6:4). This echoes the perspective of the psalm writer: "Come, you children, listen to me; I will teach you the fear of the LORD" (Ps. 34:11). The fear of the Lord is the beginning of wisdom and knowledge (Ps. 1:7; 9:10) and must be the heart and goal of a father's instruction to his family.

All teaching is moral teaching, and God's goal for us is to raise children who fear God and who know, love, and obey Jesus Christ. The aim of teaching is a part of the great aim of this age: to "go… and make disciples of all the nations" (Matt. 28:19). For a father, the discipleship mandate begins in the home. He must make disciples of his own wife and children.

Education ought not to be seen as an end in itself. Nor should it be viewed in terms of mere academic or social preparation for life. Knowledge, by itself, is nothing and leads only to pride ("Knowledge puffs up," 1 Cor. 8:1). We could give our children the very best academic preparation in the world and only end up making them more effective instruments in the devil's hands. No, God has something higher in mind.

God did not say: "Train a child in what he should know, and when he is old he will not forget it." He said, "Train up a child in the way he should go, and when he is old he will not depart from it" (Prov. 22:6). Education is not just about what a child knows; it is primarily about how he lives.

Understood in its broadest terms, teaching is character training. God is in the business of transforming people; and He is creating a people who have a living relationship with Himself.

The beginning of the process is simply to take God seriously in everything—the fear of the Lord. The end of the process is mature people who know God, and who, knowing Him, love Him; and who, loving Him, obey Him in all things.

Christian fathers should desire for their children what Paul, imitating the heavenly Father's own yearnings, wanted for his children in the faith: "My little children, for whom I labor in birth again until Christ is formed in you…" (Gal. 4:19). The great objective of all instruction must be Christ-like men and women.

The Method: Reaching the Heart

Scripture does not even use the word "education" to describe the process of training children for adulthood. That word, as we use it, is freighted with connotations of schooling, academics, and training of the mind—a very narrow Greek and Western concept of training (rationalism views man's mind as his supreme faculty).

Those who are informed by a biblical and Hebraic perspective would say that true "education" is discipleship. It is a process of training the whole person, not just the mind. The goal is not a mind stuffed with facts; the goal is a changed person.

The heart is the most important part of a person "for out of it spring the issues of life" (Prov. 4:23). The purpose of life is to love God with the whole heart (Deut. 6:5); and this purpose is realized in children as parents have God's Word engrafted in their own hearts and then impress that Word on their children (6:6,7). Fathers are to say to their sons, "Let your heart retain my words; keep my commands, and live" (Prov. 4:4).

God's method of teaching is revealed in Deuteronomy 6: 7-9. Notice what it says about God's commandments and how to teach them: "You shall teach them diligently to your children, and shall talk of them when you sit in your house, when you walk by the way, when you lie down, and when you rise up. You shall bind them as a sign on your hand, and they shall be as frontlets between your eyes. You shall write them on the doorposts of your house and on your gates." True education occurs anyplace (at home and along the way) and anytime (from rising to lying down). The parents are to be the constant companions of their children, teaching them God's view of life at every opportunity. Every child of a godly family should live continuously in an environment that is saturated by God's Word, and his parents should be overseeing that environment.

Since the purpose of education is to love God with the whole heart and to have His commandments lodged in the heart, the method must be one that reaches the heart. Discipleship—along-the-way living with the two people to whom the child is closest (his parents)—is God's method for reaching the heart of children.

The method is seen also in Jesus' relationship with the Twelve. He did not enroll his disciples in a classroom course and address only their minds. He chose them "that they might be with Him" (Mk. 3:14); and they talked, worked, walked, ate, and slept together for over three years. They were His apprentices. They learned by watching, listening, and doing as Jesus taught them about, and modeled for them, the life God wanted them to live.

Jesus said, "A disciple is not above his teacher, but everyone who is perfectly trained will be like his teacher" (Luke 6:40). That is the discipleship method: on-the-job, real-life training until the student is like the teacher. And that is the only method of education that results in the changed lives that God is seeking.

Biblical education through discipleship cannot be accomplished within the mere confines of a classroom, which is a contrived environment designed to teach the mind, usually in the narrow social context of a child's age-mates. Biblical discipleship requires involvement in the real world, with a variety of people, doing real things. It requires doing work and ministry. It demands character training and learning life skills. It requires spontaneity as well as structure. Training the intellect can occur in a school, but biblical education can only occur in the context of day-to-day living which, practically applied, is home schooling.

Our educational method must reflect a biblical understanding of truth and life. The Greco-Western worldview sees truth as ideas that can be reduced to printed pages and considered in abstraction in a classroom. In the biblical Hebraic worldview truth is personal (Jesus said, "I am... the truth" John 14:6); and while it can be expressed in the statements of Scripture, it is always connected to life and conduct ("speaking the truth in love," Eph. 4:15). Truth is not only something we can know, it is also something we can and must do or "practice" (1 John 1:6). God's truth is only communicated truly in the context of relationship. God did not just give us the written

Word of truth, he gave us His Son and fills us with Himself: "Whoever confesses that Jesus is the Son of God, God abides in him, and he in God" (1 John 4:15).

God wants truth to fill our children's minds, but He wants much more. He wants the one whose name is Truth to fill their hearts and shape their lives. That is what discipleship is all about.

In a thoroughly biblical approach to teaching, the method is as important as the content.

THE CONTENT OF TEACHING

Most discussions about teaching and education dwell upon the content of the curriculum. Whereas the importance of method is often minimized, we should not, in our attempt to balance the discussion, minimize content. It is absolutely critical. Truth has content, and part of a father's job is to transfer that content to his children.

What exactly is the content of education for Christian children? Psalm 78 puts it this way: "We will not hide them from their children, telling to the generation to come the praises of the LORD, and His strength and His wonderful works that He has done. For He established a testimony in Jacob, and appointed a law in Israel, which He commanded our fathers, that they should make them known to their children" (vv. 4,5). The Word of God ("testimony" and "law") and the works of God ("His wonderful works") are the content of a godly education.

All education should focus upon the Lord God: who he is, what he has said, and what he has done. Again, Christian training is not supposed to be the instruction of the world or of mere men, but "of the Lord" (Eph. 6:4).

Study of the Word of God itself is the foundation for all learning since the Word is the source of all wisdom. That is why parents are given the task of impressing God's commandments on their children at every opportunity (Deut. 6:7-9). In Psalm 78 fathers are commanded to teach God's "law" to their children, referring again to the written Word. Fathers should teach diligently and systematically the very words and passages of Scripture and the history and doctrine they contain. But that is not the only use of the scriptures. Psalm 119:105 presents one of the broader purposes of the Bible: "Your word is a lamp to my feet and a light to my path." God's Word is intended to illuminate the world we live in so that we can walk in a way that is pleasing to God. The purpose of a light is to shine on an object so that it can be discerned more clearly. Similarly, the Bible is meant to "shine" on anything we encounter in the world so that we can understand it from God's perspective. This means that, beyond studying the Bible itself, we should use the Bible as our lens through which to view any other subject in life.

The second component of study in a godly education is what Psalm 78 calls "His wonderful works that He has done" (v. 4). To study these works of God we must, of course, begin with the Bible itself which reveals His mighty works of creation and redemption. But this study will lead us beyond the pages of Scripture to the whole wide world that God made and sustains by His power. History, science, geography, law, art, music, mathematics, language--any subject area is a study of the works of God since it is He who created this world and guides the history of men in their scientific, cultural, and civil endeavors.

Each of these subject areas must be approached in the "light" of the Word, if it is to be properly understood. The Bible should not only be a subject in the curriculum—its truths should permeate every other area of study, providing God's perspective on every subject.

Also, each field of study must be viewed in relationship to the others since creation and history are a seamless fabric of overlapping influences—all under God's sovereign control. Life in God's world does not unfold in neat categories. The traditional approach to education that presents a student with a collection of unrelated disciplines is a mere caricature of the real world. All realms of study find their unity in our Creator and Savior. The best education will present any particular subject in its relationship to other subjects and to the God of truth who gives them all meaning.

Ideally, children should engage in academic study in the same manner in which they experience the rest of the world—encountering the connectedness of the various elements of life. Such an approach not only respects the nature of the content of education, it is also the most compatible with the discipleship method of teaching.

HOME EDUCATION

For your method of education to reach the heart, for the content of the teaching to demonstrate its biblical foundation and relevance in every area of real life as it is encountered along the way every day, home education is the practical application. All the elements of the Bible's plan for child-training combine to achieve the goal of producing Christ-like men and women; and each ingredient of the plan is important to the outcome.

If you replace the parents with other people, even godly fellow believers, as the primary teachers of your children, you disrupt the parent-child bond that is God's chosen channel of grace and influence toward a child. Remember God wants to turn the hearts of fathers (and mothers) to their children, and children to their parents.

If you choose a sterile classroom full of peers instead of the rich home-based community environment with its natural variety of ages and conditions; if you choose mass teaching focused on the mind instead of face-to-face discipleship along the path of real life experiences—then you will bypass God's chosen means of reaching the heart of a child.

If you choose teaching which presents academic subject areas in isolation without a biblical reference point instead of the unity of all truth based on the God of truth and His Word, then you eliminate the means of providing a coherent Christian worldview from which the child can engage the false ideas of the day.

Tamper with any of the facets of God's revealed plan, and you cannot expect that your children will turn out to be godly men and women. Scripture gives us a promise in Proverbs 22:6: our children will not depart from God's way if we faithfully raise them according to the way they should go. Modern Christians have come to doubt the truth of this verse because they are seeing their children fall off the path in such great numbers. But the problem is not God's plan or His faithfulness. The problem is that we have departed from His plan in so many ways.

The path of safety and blessing is always that which adheres most closely to the revealed will of God. Home education as it is practiced today may fall short of the perfect pattern set forth in the scriptures, but it is the biblical way to carry out a father's teaching mandate. It turns the hearts of parents and children toward each other and encourages fathers to assume, once again, the role of head teacher of their sons and daughters.

WHEN WORDS AREN'T ENOUGH

Sometimes a father's teaching and exhortation of his children prove inadequate: his kids fail to honor God by obeying their parents. This is the time for the father to do more than talk—he needs to act. He must correct and restrain their bad behavior. His prophetic role leads a father to become the enforcer of God's moral standards in his home.

One of the saddest stories in the Bible is that of Eli and his sons (1 Samuel 2-4). Eli was the chief priest of Israel in the generation before King Saul. It was he to whom the boy Samuel was entrusted by his mother Hannah, to be raised in the priestly family. Eli's sons, Hophni and Phinehas, served as priests under the direction of their father during the time Samuel was being brought up.

Startlingly, the scriptures record, "Now the sons of Eli were corrupt; they did not know the LORD" (2:12). What? The sons of Eli, the man who tenderly taught Samuel to recognize the

Lord's voice (3:1ff), did not know the Lord? The priests of Israel were corrupt?

Yes, and their corruption was not of a minor sort. We are told that they utterly disregarded the Lord's direction for how the sacrifices of the people were to be administered. God in His law carefully specified how the animals of sacrifice were to be killed, which parts were to be burned, and which part the priests were to receive as their share. However, the sons of Eli totally ignored God's law for the sake of personal appetite. They claimed the best parts of the sacrificial meat for themselves, and if the one making the offering objected, they would simply threaten to take the meat by force. "Therefore the sin of the young men was very great before the LORD, for men abhorred the offering of the LORD" (2:17). As if this were not enough, Eli's sons "lay with the women who assembled at the door of the tabernacle of meeting" (2:22). The sin of these priests was notorious. Instead of urging the people toward holiness, they were actively engaged in corrupting them.

So what was Eli's reaction when "he heard everything his sons did to all Israel" (2:22)? Here is the report: "So he said to them, 'Why do you do such things? No, my sons! For it is not a good report that I hear. You make the Lord's people transgress. If one man sins against another, God will judge him. But if a man sins against the LORD, who will intercede for him?'" (2: 23-25). This sounds like a righteous response. He rebuked his sons in a way that showed the seriousness of their offenses. But it wasn't enough. "Nevertheless they did not heed the voice of their father..." (2:25).

A few verses later we hear from a prophet that the Lord had sent to address Eli. He spoke the words of the Lord: "'Why do you kick at My sacrifices and My offerings which I have commanded in My dwelling place, and honor your sons more than Me, to make yourselves fat with the best of all the offerings of Israel My people?'" (v. 29). Obviously God was not pleased! He blamed Eli for his sons' behavior and accused him of honoring his sons more than God. How could this be? Eli had rebuked their sin in no uncertain terms. What more could he have done?

We learn the answer when we read the content of Samuel's first prophecy, which was a prophecy of doom on Eli and his household. "'For I have told him that I will judge his house forever for the iniquity which he knows, because his sons made themselves vile, and he did not restrain them'" (3:13). Apparently God regarded Eli's verbal rebuke of his sons as inadequate. Something more than scolding was called for.

The Lord expected this father to actually "restrain" his sons and put their offenses to an end. He was in the position of authority. His sons were under his control. His failure to get beyond scolding to actually demanding and obtaining a change of behavior was a sin sufficiently large to call for the most severe of judgments. "'I have sworn to the house of Eli that the iniquity of Eli's house shall not be atoned for by sacrifice or offering forever'" (3:14).

God takes seriously a father's duty to demand and to obtain proper behavior from his children.

But what could Eli have done? His sons ignored his rebuke. They were adults. Could he have taken them over his knee and spanked them? Would that have done any good? Of course it was too late for that. But that is precisely the lesson we need to learn from this story: a father must train his children to obey when they are young because it is too late when they are grown. Obviously Eli had been a permissive father and had not made demands on his sons. Oh, he apparently scolded them when they did wrong. But they learned that this meant nothing. They could go on and do what they pleased with no consequences.

Eli should have restrained his sons' behavior when they were growing up; then he wouldn't have had to deal with their outrageous offenses when they were older. Even then he should have dismissed them and, if necessary, called out the Levites who assisted in the temple work to remove his sons forcibly from their priestly service. He had the power to do that, and that is what the Lord expected of him. But he was not used to restraining his boys and stayed with the patterns that apparently he had long ago established: rebuke the sin, but don't actually put a physical restraint on the behavior.

The Rod: A Means of Grace

If we are not to repeat the sin of Eli we must learn how to train our children when they are young, and specifically, we must learn how to train them in a way that goes beyond scolding to enforcement of God's standards of right and wrong. But how is this done? What is God's method of enforcing proper behavior on our children? How do we "restrain" their actions, even to the extent of taking physical measures to assure results?

The solution offered in Scripture is the rod. "Do not withhold correction from a child, for if you beat him with a rod, he will not die. You shall beat him with a rod, and deliver his soul from hell" (Prov. 23:13,14). Fathers are given the tool of corporal punishment to shape the behavior of their children. The rod represents the father's authority (and hence the mother's as well, since she shares his authority as his helper). It is the parents' means of physically restraining the bad behavior of their children and bringing them into line with God's standards.

Beating with a rod is not acceptable to modern "child-raising experts" who think they know better than God. These false teachers view spanking as a form of violence, of child abuse. Well, it is indeed a mild, restrained use of force and pain (not violence); but it is not child abuse. It is a carefully administered dose of superficial injury that is designed to bring about repentance and a change of behavior. We know it is restrained since the proverb tells us that the child beaten with the rod "will not die." The aim is not serious injury. The aim is pain which results in a change of heart and of actions.

"Child abuse" would be defined from the biblical perspective as a *failure* to use the rod. Those who disdain its use do not love their children enough to save their souls from hell! Just as Eli's undisciplined sons grew into incorrigible rebels destined to the severest judgment, so any child from whom the rod is withheld is in danger of hell. That is why another proverb concludes: "He who spares his rod hates his son, but he who loves him disciplines him promptly" (13:24).

Proverbs presents parents with the choice: they can give their children a moment of physical hurt or an eternity of soul-tormenting pain. The rod is the means God has designed to transform children from rebellious to obedient. "Foolishness is bound up in the heart of a child; the rod of correction will drive it far from him" (Prov. 22:15). A fool in Proverbs is not a simpleton or a merely naive person; he is a rebel. So when the verse tells us that foolishness is bound up within the hearts of children, it is saying that they have a deep-rooted tendency toward rebellion. It is so deeply rooted that mere scolding will not dislodge it from the heart. More drastic measures are required. And God promises that bodily chastisement with the rod will have a beneficial effect: it will drive the rebellion out of the heart. If Eli had done this to his boys when they were young he would not have had such grief when they were older.

This is an amazing truth. In the rod we have a veritable means of grace, a measure that is part of what God uses to transform our children from rebellious offspring of Adam into obedient sons of God. There is no gospel grace in the rod itself, of course. The physical instrument of spanking does not have a direct effect on the soul, and many who by spanking in childhood have been shaped into decent, moral adults nevertheless have not yielded their wills to Christ as Lord and Savior.

Yet God uses the infliction of physical pain by the Christian parent as part of the process of opening the heart of a child to the Lord. How can a child who is stubbornly resisting his parent's authority possibly be open to the gospel of grace in Christ? Rebels don't bow before the cross. But as the heart is freed from its mutinous instincts through chastisement, the soul is opened to the further gracious influences of the Holy Spirit which lead a child to salvation.

Christian fathers will physically restrain their children from sin through the appropriate use of force. Feminized men will agonize over their right to do this and will be more concerned for the child's body than for his soul. One sure sign that fathers' hearts are being turned to their children will be when they give the rod its proper place within the home. And what these dads will find is that there is no surer way to win the hearts of their sons and daughters than to demand their obedience and enforce their authority through the loving use of corporal punishment.

Following the Lord's prescription for dealing with sin is often an act of faith. Our own confused sympathies for our children and the natural inertia that hampers any decisive action in most of us will make us hesitate to use the rod consistently. But as we keep the goal in view, we will be motivated to obedience in this area. Biblical discipline produces good fruit. "Now no chastening seems to be joyful for the present, but painful; nevertheless, afterward it yields the peaceable fruit of righteousness to those who have been trained by it" (Heb. 12:11).

Taught by the Lord

A prophet represents God to the people. As a prophet, a father communicates God's Word and God's standards to his family. Remember that a father is not acting in his own authority: he is a steward of God. And the authority by which he teaches and by which he disciplines is the authority of God Himself.

This truth suggests how important it is for a father to be in touch with his heavenly Father. He has to know what God wants to teach and he has to know God's standards of behavior so that he can exhort his wife and children to follow the Lord with him. A man can hardly be a prophet of God if he is not listening to God speak in His Word and seeking to apply that Word to his own life.

But if he is receiving his orders from his Father, a dad will be a channel of blessing to his family. After all, then it will be the Lord himself who is doing the teaching and chastising through him. Here is the promise of God for every father who dares to be a prophet in his household: "All your children shall be taught by the LORD, and great shall be the peace of your children" (Is. 54:13).

CHAPTER 9

The Father is a Priest: Intercessor and Worship Leader

…[H]e would rise early in the morning and offer burnt offerings according to the number of them all. For Job said, "It may be that my sons have sinned and cursed God in their hearts." Thus Job did regularly.

Job 1:5

On a spring afternoon in 1992 the enemy fired a two-ton missile at my family.

It was about one o'clock on a Friday afternoon as the children and I were loading up the car in preparation to go to the home schooling seminar and curriculum fair in the town where we lived at that time. (Pam, my wife, was in another state to visit some friends and attend a curriculum fair there.)

As my oldest son Drew (eleven at the time) and I were putting some supplies in the car, the other (then) four children were putting their things in order and gathering in the living room for our departure.

Just then my elderly neighbor lost control of her car, and it shot rapidly, in reverse, across my front yard. I'll not soon forget that eternal moment in which I saw the car, out of human control and yet aimed with a menacing intelligence, shoot right toward the room where my children were gathering.

It wasn't just idling along, either. It was accelerating, as if the lady had mistakenly stomped on the gas instead of the brake, and then had frozen in panic.

The full-sized car climbed the one step to the porch, another to floor level, then exploded through the living room wall right under the large picture window. Wood splintered, glass shattered, and metal screamed with the impact. The heavy oak bench seat in front of the window, loaded with boxes of books, was launched through the air, crashing into the cabinet on the opposite wall. Fragments of the bench and front wall were hurled through the living room, through the door into the kitchen, stopping only upon impacting the sink, twenty-five feet from where they sat a split-second before. An interior wall with a reinforced corner stopped the motion of the car several feet into the house.

The enemy seemed to have pulled out his big guns.

But "the angel of the LORD encamps all around those who fear Him, and delivers them" (Ps. 34:7).

Drew and I were in the driveway. Sarah (13) and Laura (8) had stepped back into their bedroom to get some things. Only Joanna and Seth (our two youngest at the time, 4 and 6) were actually in harm's way. But the Lord held their hands. Joanna ended up by the smashed bench with only a red ear from some impact. Seth was hit in the forehead (probably by part of the bench). Neither was really hurt, just scared. The only "injury" was a cut on my hand from climbing rather hastily and carelessly through the debris to find the cause of the piercing screams that had begun an instant after the impact.

I found four panicked children huddled in a collective embrace in the hallway just off the living room. When I saw that no one was hurt, I quickly assured them all that everything was all right—we could fix the house. (The driver was dazed but not hurt at all, though this incident did end her driving career.)

If the car had entered the house a foot or two over from where it did, it would not have stopped until it reached the kitchen, and one or two children would have been in its path. If all the children had been in the living room... If Drew or I had been entering or leaving the room... If... It doesn't really matter. There are no "ifs" with the Lord. He is in control; and He rescued us.

My first thought after calling the police ("I think we need some help") was to run and find the camera. We had quite a scene around the place for a while: several police cars, fire trucks, a rescue truck, and an ambulance, not to mention curious neighbors. I wanted to record the event on film so that my children would have a concrete "memorial" to God's gracious care for us. "Remember when the car came into our living room? Wasn't God good to protect us from harm!"

What struck me in this incident was just how real the attack is on our families, and how real the protection is that the Lord provides us.

In our church fellowship at that time we had seen many attacks in a short span of time: one family had a head-on collision in their car some months before (no serious injuries!); another had been to the emergency room three times in the past few months with injuries to children; another had children come within inches of being hit by a car while they were riding bikes, and this happened *twice* within a few minutes; another had a two-year-old wander out of the yard who was found twenty minutes later under the watchful eye of a caring neighbor (three or four blocks away!). What was striking in all of these incidents was how evident the Lord's protection had been. No one had been killed or permanently injured. In every case things could have been *much* worse. God had been our Protector.

We were soon to be reminded that the Lord, as Job discovered, does allow tragedies to occur for His own inscrutable purposes. Three months after the car violated our domestic tranquility, one of the members of our fellowship died in a one-car accident, leaving three children and a pregnant wife behind. Outside our church, but within our Christian home schooling circles, a mother of seven died of leukemia, and a father of four was killed while rock-climbing on vacation.

Of course, just as real as the physical dangers that our families face are the spiritual dangers. The latter are even more serious since they have eternal, not merely temporal, consequences. We should let the visible threats remind us of those that are not visible. Scripture tells us that our true battles are against spiritual powers, not against flesh and blood (Eph. 6:12), but our spiritual enemies often use temporal means in their effort to fight us.

Against both of these threats we fathers are especially called to take out stand. We are, on the human level, the guardians of our families. Just as we must protect them physically, so we must guard them spiritually.

One thing the near-tragedy with my family taught me was the importance of praying daily for the Lord to protect my family. It is my job as priest of my household to intercede on their behalf, as Jesus intercedes for all the redeemed (Heb. 7:25).

Here again we see the overlap in a father's roles. The work of intercessory prayer is part of his priestly function, yet it is also an act of protection and thus the work of a king.

Praying for a Hedge of Protection

Job is my favorite biblical example of a father who interceded with God for his family. We are told in Job 1:5, "So it was, when the days of feasting had run their course, that Job would send and sanctify them, and he would rise early in the morning and offer burnt offerings according to the number of them all. For Job said, 'It may be that my sons have sinned and cursed God in their hearts.' Thus Job did regularly." He interceded daily with the Lord on behalf of his family.

But his was no perfunctory prayer, "Bless my wife and kids. Amen." He took so seriously his role as family priest that he presumed to ask the Lord for forgiveness of his children's sins! We know that the children themselves must have asked for forgiveness in order to be right with God, but can we doubt that God was at work in the children of a man who so prayed to the Lord on their behalf?

Confirmation of God's acting in response to Job's prayers comes in verse 10 of the same chapter. Here we find Satan presenting himself before God and being directed to consider the righteous man Job. Satan's response is instructive: "Have You not made a hedge around him, around his household, and around all that he has on every side?" Indeed Job and his family were under God's special protection, and Satan could not harm them, because God himself had erected a wall against those devices Satan might use to attack them. Surely we are meant to see a connection between Job's faithful prayers for his loved ones and the Lord's hedge of protection around them.

The most important work a man can do to protect his family is to pray daily for the Lord to protect them all, guarding them physically as well as protecting them from the assaults of the devil who, like a "roaring lion" attacking a herd of deer, will often try to pick off the smallest and weakest in order to devour them (1 Pet. 5:8). What an encouragement to realize that Satan and his minions have no power over our families except what our God allows! But how sobering to realize that God's maintenance of His protecting hedge may be directly connected with our faithfulness in prayer!

The concept of "praying a hedge" finds its root in Scripture. Let's look at some of the biblical data. The term "hedge" itself simply means a wall or fence (Mk. 12:1), but this was often actually a thick hedge of vegetation, possibly thorns, that was placed to surround a vineyard or a sheepfold and served as an effective barrier against intruders. The term also is used metaphorically to refer to God's protection of His people: "And now, please let Me tell you what I will do to My vineyard: I will take away its hedge, and it shall be burned; and break down its wall, and it shall be trampled down" (Is. 5:5).

From the standpoint of the one intent on doing evil the hedge acts as a barrier to prevent his progress. Israel found her way blocked up "with thorns" so that she was not able to fulfill her (spiritually) adulterous plans and was driven back to her husband (i.e., the Lord; Hosea 2:5-7). Hedges block the progress of evil.

The agency of God's protecting hedge is often the work of angelic ministers. "The angel of the LORD encamps all around those who fear Him, and delivers them" (Ps. 34:7). It was an angel who shut the mouths of the lions to prevent their harming Daniel in the lions' den (Dan. 6:22). Speaking of the angels, the writer of Hebrews asks, "Are they not all ministering spirits sent forth to minister for those who will inherit salvation?" (Heb. 1:14).

No Incantations

In praying for a hedge of protection we must remember that God is doing the protecting, not our prayers. As the archangel Michael in his dispute with the devil said, "The Lord rebuke you!" (Jude 9). We do not control the spirits; God does. Another peril in this matter of praying a hedge is that we will come to see it as some kind of magical incantation. It is simply an exercise of a man's spiritual headship, as he appeals through his authority, the Lord Jesus Christ, to God for His protection. There is no "formula" to be used. God is not impressed with the outward form of our prayers; He is impressed with a man like Job who fears the Lord. More accurately, He is impressed with the intercession of Christ and the Holy Spirit on behalf of the man who prays (Rom. 8:26,27,34). We should simply entreat our Father with a genuine heart, knowing that He is pleased to hear and answer His children, whatever words they use.

In terms of the specific need for God's protection, we would do well to pray specifically that the name and the blood of Jesus would protect each family member. I believe I have prayed something similar to this every day since the day I was so vividly reminded of its importance by the runaway car. Nor do we ever set out on a long trip in the family vehicle without a prayer for the blessing of the Lord's protection. It is comforting to think of the angel of the Lord encamped around my home, or traveling with us down the highway.

In all our prayers we need to remember that God is sovereign and will do as He pleases. He is not a genie who, when summoned from the bottle, is obligated to give us three wishes. We are His servants; He is not our servant. Times will come when the Lord allows sickness, loss, and of course, death. So we need to pray for protection, not out of fear and a sense of bargaining with God, but out of a sense of complete rest in His disposition of our lives. We ask for protection and know He hears and answers. But when His answer is to allow trouble, like Job we should say: "The LORD gave, and the LORD has taken away; blessed be the name of the LORD" (Job 1:21). Our heavenly Father will see that all things work out for our good and the good of our families, in His own way.

I mentioned earlier the woman who died of leukemia and the man who was killed in a mountain-climbing accident—both unmitigated tragedies. Yet a couple of years later, Pam and I received a wedding invitation that surprised and delighted us: the widowed spouses, who had not known each other before their losses, had been drawn together and were getting married. Their combined family boasted eleven children at the time, and a twelfth soon followed! Truly God works in mysterious ways.

So act the part of the family priest and pray for the Lord to put up a hedge of protection to guard your family. Then rest assured that any harm He allows will be swallowed up in blessing later on, in eternity if not before.

How to Pray

The father is strategically placed at the head of his household to wage spiritual warfare on its behalf. Fathers are warrior-priests who, by God's design and grace, are equipped to protect their precious charges from spiritual danger. Prayer is powerful, especially when it comes from one in authority on behalf of those under his oversight.

A leader has a duty to pray for those entrusted to his care. Samuel, the priest and prophet who led the Israelites just prior to their having a king, said to them in his farewell address, "Moreover, as for me, far be it from me that I should sin against the LORD in ceasing to pray for you" (1 Samuel 12:23). It is a sin against God for a leader to fail to pray for those under his care. This certainly applies as well to the leader of a family.

How should you pray for your family? The Lord does not want you to be mystified by a simple and straightforward duty. Here are some suggestions for how to pray for your wife and children:

Establish a daily time for personal devotions, part of which is devoted to prayer for your family. Job got up early in the morning in order to give part of his day to specific spiritual exercises. We would do well to follow the example of his disciplined life. One of the chief reasons many men do not pray for their families with any regularity or specificity is that they don't have a set time in their schedule devoted to prayer. We always make room for the important things in life, like a meal or an appointment with the doctor. How much more important it is to meet regularly with our Master to fellowship with Him and plead His mercy on behalf of our families!

Use the prayers in Scripture. A man can do no better than to use as examples the words and thoughts of Scripture on behalf of those he loves. Jesus gave us a model prayer in Matthew 6: 9-13. We should learn to meditate on the petitions given there and use them to guide our prayers. Likewise, the apostles left us with several prayers that we can use to shape our requests for our families. Examples of these are Ephesians 1:16-19, 3:14-19, and Colossians 1:9-12.

Pray for the fruit of the Spirit and other specific character traits to grow in the lives of each member of your family (Galatians 5: 22,23). As you consider the specific needs you see in their lives, think of them in terms of the spiritual fruit required to meet the need. Much of the point of prayer is the transformation of people—ourselves and those for whom we pray. So let's pray that our loved ones are transformed into the image of Christ by taking on His character qualities.

Pray for a hedge of protection around your family members. Ask specifically that the name and the blood of Jesus Christ would protect each family member and that the angel of the Lord would encamp around your household (Psalm 34:7). Be sure to address both physical and spiritual dangers.

As we pray, we should do so with the humble acknowledgment of our sin and a hunger for holiness. As we come before the Father in the name of Jesus, the great High Priest, we have the assurance that He will hear and answer (Jn. 14:14). "The effective, fervent prayer of a righteous man avails much" (James 5:16).

The Family Priest

While a prophet represents God to His people, a priest is a man who represents the people to God. He offers up worship and prayer on their behalf and is heard because of his special position as a God-appointed mediator. The Old Testament priesthood, and in particular the High Priest, was a type of Christ, an imperfect picture of what He would be in fullness. So in reality, there is only one Priest, and that is Jesus Christ, who offered up Himself as a sacrifice to God the Father, and who thus continually intercedes for the saints.

But Jesus, the Ideal Man, enables every redeemed man to become a priest as well. Christ "has made us kings and priests to His God and Father" (Rev. 1:6). "But you are a chosen generation, a royal priesthood… that you may proclaim the praises of Him who called you out of darkness into His marvelous light" (1 Pet. 2:9). All Christians, male and female, are priests in the sense that each one has immediate access, through Christ, to the Father. There is no need for any other mediator besides Christ (1 Tim. 2:5).

However, since the Christian man holds the position of headship in the home, he expresses the general office of priesthood, which he shares with all the family members, through the unique office of family head. Thus he reflects the priesthood of Christ in a special sense: he not only has access to God for himself, he has a special representative role for those under his authority. We could state it formulaically like this: Priesthood plus family headship equals family priest. So while he is not a mediator between God and his wife and children, he does have a unique privilege of representing them before God in spiritual matters.

We have discussed at some length the father's ministry of intercessory prayer. Another important dimension of his priestly work is that of leading his family in worship. Since Christ has been sacrificed once for all, there is no more need of offering animal sacrifices. Instead Christians offer themselves as "a living sacrifice, holy, acceptable to God, which is your reasonable service" (Rom. 12:1). The Christian family is a priesthood chosen by God "to proclaim the praises" of God, and as the family head, the father is responsible to lead the family in their united proclamation of God's praises.

PRACTICAL HUMANISTS

You have probably heard the observation that when you point a finger at someone else you are, at the same time, pointing three fingers back at yourself. There is no doubt that this proverb is often quoted to stifle a well-deserved criticism. After all, ours is a day in which it not considered "nice" to pass judgment on someone else's behavior. But it occurs to me that the observation is quite apropos when considering a commonly heard condemnation made by Christian men during the last couple decades, namely, that our nation's spiritual heritage is under attack by those we call "secular humanists."

Certainly it is true that there is a godless element intent upon rewriting history so as to deny our Christian heritage and eradicate the last vestiges of Christian values from our culture. This element of our population deserves finger-pointing and the blame it communicates. Unfortunately, as we apply such fitting judgments to these obvious malefactors, we are implicating ourselves, as well. Three fingers are pointing back at Christian men—because while we correctly denounce the humanism of others, we fail to recognize that which lodges in our own hearts and in our families.

Yes, Christian men, even dedicated, family-centered men, are too often what we might call "practical humanists." This means we are humanists in effect, though not in profession. We affirm the reality of God with our mouths, but our lifestyle denies our confession. While we denounce the overt godlessness of others, we ourselves have been guilty of a quiet godlessness. If "humanism" is a denial of God, many Christian men are humanists in the fabric of their daily lives.

In the Bible we find a more reliably true proverb than that with which we began this section: "The fear of the LORD is the beginning of wisdom" (Prov. 9:10). What it means is this: taking God seriously is the foundation for right thinking and right living.

Applying this to our discussion, we must acknowledge that too many Christian men do not take God seriously in how they think and how they live. While professing faith in God, there is no evidence that God shapes their approach to major portions of their personal and family lives. In matters as diverse as business, recreation, dress, education, finances, and music, for example, there is no discernible difference between many Christian men and others who make no such claims to faith. I suggest that if so much of a man's life is unaffected by the God he claims to revere, he is not actually taking God very seriously. He does not truly fear God. He is, while a professing believer, a practicing humanist.

It is no surprise that wicked men act wickedly. What is disastrous is when good men fail to act righteously. The reason our nation is on the skids is not that godless humanists are out to eliminate public expressions of faith, which they surely are. The problem is rather that Christian men are too often guilty of voluntarily eliminating private expressions of faith. Our nation is being destroyed by the failure of Christian men to take God seriously in the way they live in the home and in the small circle of their daily experience.

In particular, one of the prime symptoms of our malady is the absence of family worship in Christian homes. Yes, this is one of the chief barometers of how much "the fear of the LORD" infects a generation of believers; and by that measure, our generation does not take God very seriously at all. When a family goes through a day without corporately acknowledging God, they are, for that day, living like humanists. They are saying that God is not present in their family, that He can be ignored without it making any difference to their lives.

The children of that household are being taught a subtle lesson: while we talk about God, He does not affect our daily lives. The children are being raised to be practical humanists. If God is really the God we claim He is—the majestic, all-powerful Creator; the gracious, all-merciful Redeemer—how can we ever live a day without acknowledging Him together in our homes? It just does not make sense.

Writing in the last century, James W. Alexander in *Thoughts on Family Worship* had this to say about children and the practice of (in his time, twice-daily!) family worship:

> The simple fact, that parents and offspring meet together every morning and evening, for the word of God and prayer, is a great fact in household annals. It is the inscribing of God's name over the lintel of the door. It is the setting up of God's altar. The dwelling is marked as a house of prayer. Religion is thus made a substantive and prominent part of the domestic plan. The day is opened and closed in the name of the Lord.
>
> From the very dawn of reason, each little one grows up with a feeling that God must be honored in every thing; that no business of life can proceed without Him; and that the

day's work, or study, would be unsheltered, disorderly, and in a manner profane, but for this consecration. When such a child comes, in later years, to mingle with families where there is no worship, there is an unavoidable shudder, as if among heathen or infidel companions. [20]

In too many Christian homes today, someone who truly fears God would shudder. God is acknowledged in words, but He is not "a substantive and prominent part of the domestic plan."

A Father's Chief Duty

As Alexander wrote, regular, even daily (or twice daily), family worship is simply an historical fact among godly families in all ages and places. This gathering of the whole family for the purpose of worship, Bible reading, and prayer is a conscious, corporate ritual. It is a specific, intentional gathering to acknowledge God together in addition to thanks offered at meals or bedside prayers. While the church gathers weekly to worship the Lord, the family assembles daily for that highest of all human endeavors.

Both Old and New Testaments contain abundant evidence that family devotion is assumed as the lifestyle of the godly. We see the pattern of domestic worship in the example of the patriarchs who so often gathered their families around their crude altars to offer thanks to God for His guidance and blessing (Gen. 8:20; 12:8; 13:4, etc.). The pattern is evident as well in the life of Cornelius about whom we read that he was "a devout man and one who feared God with all his household" (Acts 10:2); and he gathered his family to hear the gospel proclaimed (v. 24).

The fact that the early church met in homes testifies eloquently to the fact that faith and worship find their first manifestations in the household (Acts 2:46; Rom. 16:5,23; 1 Cor. 16:19, etc.).

From the early church to the Reformation times in Switzerland, France, Holland, Scotland, and elsewhere, to the colonial days in America, indeed, up to our own century, the institution of family worship is an ever-present evidence of a vital faith within the home. During times of spiritual health, family worship was the rule among Christian households, not the exception.

In 1647 the Church of Scotland, which was then in the full bloom of the Reformation, produced a *Directory for Family Worship*. In the introductory section the following guidelines were given to local church elders (called collectively a "session"):

> And, to the end that these directions may not be rendered ineffectual and unprofitable among some, through the usual neglect of the very substance of the duty of Family-worship, the Assembly doth further require and appoint ministers and ruling elders to make diligent search and inquiry, in the congregations committed to their charge respectively, whether there be among them any family or families which use to neglect this necessary duty; and if such family be found, the head of the family is to be first admonished privately to amend his fault; and, in case of his continuing therein, he is to be gravely and sadly reproved by the session; after which reproof, if he be found still to neglect Family-worship, let him be, for his obstinacy in such an offense, suspended and debarred from the Lord's supper, as being justly esteemed unworthy to communicate therein, till he amend.[21]

Back then you would come under severe church discipline for the habitual neglect of the "necessary duty" of family worship. Today it is too often regarded as optional for a family to have devotions, and if they do, it may frequently be the mother who leads them. But God's plan is clear: each man should lead his family regularly in the worship of God as a family. Worship is not just for the church. The family is the first form of the church on earth, and worship is a vital element of godly family life.

Men of God, no matter what our churches say (or neglect to say) about it, we can and must assure that at least in *our* homes God is taken seriously. It does not matter how far short of godliness the church and Christians in general have fallen today; we must say, "As for me and my house, we will serve the Lord!"

If my highest overall priority in life is God Himself, and if my highest temporal priority is my family, then it follows that the duty that rests at the intersection of these two greatest obligations is my paramount concern in life—and that duty is none other than family worship. It is here that my devotion to my God and my commitment to my family find their inevitable expression. I honor God best by leading and loving my family; I lead and love my family best by bringing them before God. Family worship is the most important obligation of a Christian father.

If you have been regular in this practice, keep up the good work! You show that you understand what it means to fear God, and He will bless you as you remain steadfast in your family leadership.

If you have not been regular in family worship, how do you go about developing this habit? Let's take a look now at how to get started with a habit of family worship.

Laying the Groundwork for Success

The first thing you must do is to *deal with your own relationship with the Lord.* Family spiritual leadership is simply an overflow of a man's own walk with God. In this regard, do two things. 1) If you are not already doing so, *establish the practice of daily personal worship* (devotions, or quiet time). Again, you must be walking with God yourself before you can lead your family in that walk together. Spend some part of every day (preferably first thing in the morning) reading God's Word, offering worship and thanksgiving, and engaging in intercessory prayer. 2) Go before God and *confess the sin of neglecting family worship.* Confess that you have been a humanist in practice and have encouraged your children to become practical humanists as well. It is only as you acknowledge sin that you will find the grace to develop new patterns in your home. Mere efforts at "reform," apart from repentance and grace, will not succeed in the long run.

Secondly, *deal with your relationship with your wife and children.* Don't just try to sneak up on them and get them to join you in family worship if you have not been in the habit. 1) Sit them down and *confess the sin* of failing to be the spiritual leader of the home. This is humbling and painful, but it is necessary. Great failings require great humility in acknowledging the fault. The most manly thing you will ever do will be to admit that you have failed in your manly calling. Your family needs to see that you recognize the gravity of the matter of your spiritual leadership. They need to see that you are serious about making the changes that are needed. Taking this humble posture before your flock will elevate you far higher in their esteem than if you kept silent on the point.

While you have the ears of your wife and children, 2) *ask their help* as you begin to do your job. Let them know you realize it will be hard to develop a new family habit, but that you are committed to God to do so and must have their support. Invite their ongoing counsel on the matter of how family worship is conducted in the home. Ask their commitment to cooperate with your efforts to lead, and ask them to pray for you as you seek to obey the Lord in this way. Family solidarity will go a long way toward assuring the success of your program.

The third step in laying the groundwork for your successful practice of family worship is to *establish it as a part of the family schedule.* This means selecting a time when you can daily gather the whole family together. Don't plan just once a week, or "whenever it works out." God deserves more honor than that! Plan a daily time to meet. The ideal time is early in the day since this is the best preparation for taking God seriously the rest of the day. For some, this will mean having the family rise earlier than they otherwise would. If it is simply not possible to worship in the morning, then plan a time in the evening, perhaps right after a family supper before everyone scatters. Whenever you decide to meet, stick with it and make the rest of your schedule bow to this priority.

Many families will need to de-clutter their hectic family schedule before they can establish a realistic, sustainable meeting time. But be clear about this: if your family is too busy to find a time to worship God together, you are busier than the Lord wants you to be. Don't allow so many good things in your family schedule that they crowd out the most essential family activity. Simplify your family life and learn to walk with God together.

A Pattern for Family Worship

If you have not led your family in worship before it may seem like a monumental undertaking as you anticipate getting started. Recognize that fear and acknowledge it, but don't allow it to prevent your diving right in. The fact is that once you have overcome the inertia of past neglect, have laid the groundwork outlined above, and are willing and ready to conduct family devotions, you have come 90% of the way toward success. The actual "how to" of leading worship is no big deal. That's the easy part.

Get over the feeling that there is some "right" way to lead that you have not yet learned. What your family needs is you, right now, just as you are. God has appointed you the spiritual leader of your little flock, and He will use you to lead them. See yourself as an adequate leader, because your Father does!

There are three basic elements to family worship: praise, Bible-reading, and prayer. There is no formula for how these should be incorporated; rather, there is an infinite variety of approaches. Here is the key thought behind the inclusion of each of these three elements:

1) *Praise* is simply the response of creatures to their Creator, of saints to their Savior, of children to their heavenly Father. It is acknowledging the greatness of God and the greatness of His works. Praise can be expressed in prayer, in the reading of a psalm, or in a hymn or chorus. Children especially enjoy singing, so having the family sing praise to God—even if it is literally a joyful "noise"—is a desirable part of any family worship plan.

2) *Bible reading* is God speaking to us. As the family gathers in His presence, this is the most natural of activities. The Bible reveals God, communicates wisdom, points us to the Savior, and tells us how to live. It is our spiritual food. Feasting on a portion of it each day is the best prescription for family health.

3) *Prayer* is our speaking to God. Through it we can express praise for who God is, thanksgiving for His blessings, confession for our sins, and supplication for God's help in our needs.

The simpler the plan for family worship the better. Just gather your household, read a chapter of the Bible, sing a hymn, and lead in prayer. As you get in the habit of doing this and feel comfortable, you can begin to experiment with other ideas. For now, the important thing is to get with the program.

Here are some of those other possibilities: You can have a discussion on the passage you read; practice Bible memory; read a devotional or doctrine book; hear insights each family member has gotten from their own personal devotions; develop a brief "service" with a call to worship, a hymn, confession of sin, a Bible lesson, intercessory prayer, another hymn, etc.; incorporate your wife and children in the reading and prayer; have some of the children provide "special music;" focus prayer on different topics on different days, like church families on Monday, missionaries on Tuesday, government leaders on Wednesday, etc. The key is to include the three basic elements of any family worship time.

When King David was bringing the Ark of the Covenant back to Jerusalem there was a mishap that caused him to leave it for a time at the house of a man named Obed-Edom. Scripture makes this report: "The ark of God remained with the family of Obed-Edom in his house three months. And the LORD blessed the house of Obed-Edom and all that he had" (1 Chron. 13:14). The Ark symbolized the presence of God among His people, and when God was thus present in the house of Obed-Edom, he and his family were mightily blessed!

God doesn't live in boxes or temples. He is present wherever two or three gather in his name (Matt. 18:20). When a family gathers in God's presence on a regular basis, God is in their midst in a special way. If you want to be blessed like the family of Obed-Edom, make the Lord a daily part of your family life.

Before leaving this vitally important subject of family worship, I will address some questions and problems.

QUESTIONS AND SPECIAL CHALLENGES

Q: *Is it necessary for the father himself to lead the family worship?*

A: Yes! Although leadership does not mean that he does everything. Dad should take the initiative to establish the practice and set the time; he should lead in gathering the family at the set time; he should take charge of the worship time itself. During worship, he may have others read or pray; he may even disciple an older son by letting him lead the whole worship at times; but the father should retain clear control of the family worship time. When the children are grown and away from home, their memories of their father should include hearing his voice reading the Bible to his gathered flock and lifting them all up to God in prayer.

Q: *What about those days when it just is not possible to have family worship?*

A: Let them be the exception to a very clear pattern. Urge each family member still to have their own devotions, acknowledge the unfortunate break in the family pattern, and let them know you plan to resume the practice at the next opportunity. Ask your wife to lead the family if you will be out of town (no need for them to abandon the Lord just because you cannot be there). If you are leaving home some day before you have been able to gather the household to worship, you can at least have them stand with you by the door to pray briefly before you go. When our heart is set on honoring the Lord, he will help us improvise ways to do that, even when circumstances make it difficult to keep our normal routines.

Q: *What if part of the family is gone?*

A: Again, there is no need to abandon the principle of family worship just because everyone can't be there. Of course, if you are reading through a book of the Bible and are discussing it as a family, you may want to set that aside until everyone is together again; but you can still read a psalm and pray together. If the absence of an older child is habitual due to too much activity, you will need to adjust their priorities to match those you set for the family as a whole. The normal pattern should be that all family members are present for family worship.

Q: *What do we do with disruptive younger children?*

A: Exercise patience and discipline. Expect young children to have less ability to concentrate and participate. Perhaps the two-year-old can play with a quiet toy by mother, but he should be required to stay by her. We have used a small rug when our children were toddlers; the child must stay on it and remain quiet during family worship, but I don't expect him to concentrate on all that goes on. We try to have some songs that the little ones like (with motions) as well as the great hymns (which they also learn to like). If most of your children are young, you can't expect to have a very long worship time. Bear with their weakness (Eph. 6:4a), but expect them to obey and never tolerate rebellion.

Q: *What if the children (or adults) are falling asleep during family worship?*

A: You must be having it first thing in the morning or last thing at night. The solution is more sleep. If you meet in early morning, you must establish an earlier bedtime. Late at night may be difficult even if everyone gets adequate rest. Try earlier evening, like right after supper. God has given us enough hours in the day to get enough rest *and* to worship Him. Just keep experimenting to find the most workable plan.

Q: *How do we keep our routine on trips, at other people's homes, or when we have guests at our house?*

A: The same way you keep other important routines, like eating and sleeping, under those circumstances: by making time for what is vital. Guests can be welcomed into your family circle for worship, or given the option of being absent while you conduct this important family time. (Who should get more honor: your guests or your God?) When you are guests elsewhere you could gather your clan in a bedroom before the start of the day, or perhaps your hosts would be happy to let you lead in a short devotion if you explain your routine—ask them. Remember, you don't have to do the whole deal every day if the schedule is off. Just a word of prayer can preserve the family focus on the Lord when everyone knows it is a substitute for a normally fuller practice of family worship.

Q: *What if my wife or children are clearly not happy with what I have decided to do—the time, the length, the contents, or whatever?*

A: Discern the cause of the unhappiness. If it is rebellion, pray for them privately and humbly remind them that you must obey the Lord in this. If they think it is too early or too long, communicate a genuine openness to do what is best for everyone. Be willing to try other ideas. Your goal is not to insist on having it one way; it is to lead the family to worship God. Listen to them; they may have good ideas to share. You want to make it work for the family, not against them.

Q: *What about single mothers?*

A: They are the head of their home and must take the place of the father who is not there. However, as they raise sons, they will want to be especially careful to train them toward leadership by teaching them to lead in parts of the worship. Teenage sons could begin to lead the whole thing, exercising a leadership function under mother's overall headship of the home.

Q: *I've blown it and failed to have family worship for two weeks after a really good start—now what?*

A: This is a critical moment. You will be tempted to give in to the lies of the evil one who wants you to believe "you are the lowest scumbag on earth, your family doesn't respect you (and why should they!), you will never be able to be successful in this," etc., etc. Focus on the Lord again. Dismiss those lies. Ask forgiveness of God and family and tell them you are ready to get back on track. Figure out if you need to adjust your schedule or modify the content of the worship to make it more realistic and doable. Better to succeed in a small effort than to fail in a grandiose plan. Just remember the Lord wants you to succeed in this even more than you do, and He is committed to helping you do it!

A Final Word about Priests: 'Sympathy'

As he represents his family to God through the practice of family worship and intercessory prayer, a father is functioning in his role as family priest. For him to properly approach God on behalf of his wife and children, he needs to exhibit a priestly quality that we see in Jesus. That quality is identified in this verse: "For we do not have a High Priest who cannot sympathize with our weaknesses, but was in all points tempted as we are, yet without sin" (Heb. 4:15). Jesus has sympathy for His people.

Jesus was able to become our representative, our priest, because He was one of us. "Therefore, in all things He had to be made like His brethren, that He might be a merciful and faithful

High Priest in things pertaining to God, to make propitiation for the sins of the people" (Heb. 2:17). Being one of us, He experienced life as we do (except for sin) and can truly relate to our condition. "He can have compassion on those who are ignorant and going astray, since he himself is also subject to weakness" (Heb. 5:2).

A father is able to represent his family before God since he is one of them. But this should mean more than that he is simply part of the group called a family. It should also result in his sharing Christ's ability to sympathize with his family.

Sympathy is the ability to enter into the experience and feelings of others and to share their interests and concerns. It results in having compassion, and compassion moves beyond feelings to actions. A sympathetic person doesn't just feel with another, he acts to relieve their distresses in any way he can.

The heart of God is a compassionate heart, and this quality is seen most clearly in the sacrifice and continual intercession of Jesus. His personal sacrifice on behalf of His people and His ongoing sympathetic interest in their welfare colors the exercise of His role as their king and prophet. He commands, but he does so as one who understands the weakness and temptations of those He commands. He instructs and disciplines, but He softens these acts with compassion because He knows the challenges of growing in grace. The sensitivity of the Messiah was foreseen by Isaiah: "A bruised reed He will not break, and smoking flax He will not quench" (Is. 42:3).

If he is Christ-like, a Christian father's leadership at home will be a compassionate leadership. He will not be overbearing and impatient, as if weakness revealed in his wife or children is something to be despised. A father is called to be a reflection of God Himself: "As a father pities his children, so the LORD pities those who fear Him. For He knows our frame; He remembers that we are dust" (Ps. 103:13,14). Since he himself is dust and subject to weakness, a father should patiently bear with the members of his household. He should lead not just from the front, calling the others to follow him; he should also lead from the side, putting his arms around those he leads and encouraging them on their way.

If Jesus, the sinless God-man, would condescend to show mercy to us, how much more should we sympathize with those whose weaknesses we share. The more a man reflects on his role as family priest, the more he will be a compassionate and sensitive leader.

This sympathy must begin with his wife, and we will deal with this in the next chapter as we take a look at the calling of the wife and how a husband ought to care for her as his helper.

CHAPTER 10

A Wife: To Love and to Honor

Husbands, likewise, dwell with them with understanding, giving honor to the wife, as to the weaker vessel, and as being heirs together of the grace of life, that your prayers may not be hindered.

1 Pet. 3:7

Abraham was a good man, a fine example of fatherhood, but he had some major lapses as a husband. Even though God had promised him a son, his faith wavered and he gave in to his wife Sarah's plan that he father a child by her maidservant, Hagar. After a son, Ishmael, was born to Hagar, Sarah became jealous and complained to Abraham, who allowed her to treat Hagar harshly so that she ran away (Gen. 16). Not exactly stellar leadership by Abraham! But that's not the worst of it.

On two separate occasions (Gen. 12,20) Abraham put Sarah in a very dangerous position to save his own hide. She was an exceptionally beautiful woman, and Abraham was afraid that first Pharaoh, then King Abimelech, would kill him in order to get his wife. So he passed Sarah off as his sister instead of his wife (a half-truth since she was his half-sister). In both cases, Sarah was taken into the homes of these men, where her purity was endangered, although on both occasions the Lord protected her. Abraham is a great example of faith, but on these occasions his faith lapsed—and his wife was the one who was imperiled by this failure.

Perhaps, then, we can understand why Peter mentions fear when writing to Christian women, whom he has just told to submit to their husbands, even if these men are unbelievers: "For in this manner, in former times, the holy women who trusted in God also adorned themselves, being submissive to their own husbands, as Sarah obeyed Abraham, calling him lord, whose daughters you are if you do good and are not afraid with any terror" (1 Pet. 3:5,6). Having to submit to husbands who are sinners puts wives in a vulnerable position, one in which they are likely to sometimes be afraid or downright terrified. Sarah must have known that feeling when she was in the houses of pagan men who didn't realize she was married. Yet she is commended for obeying her husband and entrusting herself to God who did, in fact, preserve her.

Now if were up to me, I would have told Sarah that she didn't need to go along with Abraham's scheme and allow herself to be placed in danger. It's frankly surprising that Sarah is commended for submission to her husband given how negligent he was of her welfare. The point of this passage, however, is not that Abraham's faults as a husband should be overlooked. The point is that when a husband acts poorly and fails to care for his wife, a wife acts commendably when she trusts God to take care of her. When she submits to her husband, calling him "lord," she is really simply acknowledging God's chain of authority and submitting to her husband's master, the Lord of all, who is able to compensate for her husband's failures.

But let this truth not be an excuse for careless husbandry! Instead it should be a wake-up call for men to realize what a difficult and defenseless position a woman is in when she entrusts herself to a man to become his wife. And it should help men realize how important it is that they take this trust very seriously and care for their wives with all diligence. Consider carefully the words that J.R. Miller wrote in the late nineteenth century:

> There is something very sacred and almost awe-inspiring in the act by which a wife, at her entrance into the marriage state, confides all the interests of her life to the hands of him whom she accepts as her husband. She leaves father and mother and the home of her childhood. She severs all the ties that bound her to her old life. She gives up the friends and the friendships of her youth. She cuts herself off from the sources of happiness to which she has been accustomed to turn. She looks up into the face of him who has asked her to be his wife, and with trembling heart yet with quiet confidence she entrusts to him and to his keeping all the sacred interests of her life. It is a holy trust which he receives when she thus commits herself to his hands. It is the lifelong happiness of a tender human heart capable of ineffable joy or unmeasured misery. It is the whole future well-being of a life which may be

fashioned into the image of Christ, or marred and its beauty shattered for ever....

Every husband should understand that when a woman, the woman of her own free and deliberate choice, places her hand in his and thus becomes his wife, she has taken her life, with all its hopes and fears, all its possibilities of joy or sorrow, all its capacity for development, all its tender and sacred interests, and placed it in his hand, and that he is under the most solemn obligations to do all in his power to make that life happy, beautiful, noble and blessed. To do this he must be ready to make any personal sacrifice. Nothing less than this can be implied in loving as Christ loved his Church when he gave himself for it. [22]

So important is a man's tender consideration of his wife that under biblical law he is given the whole first year of marriage to make a good start at the lifelong process of bringing her joy. "When a man has taken a new wife, he shall not go out to war or be charged with any business; he shall be free at home one year, and bring happiness to his wife whom he has taken" (Deut. 24:5). How many men place such a high priority on the happiness of their wives that it becomes a major project in their lives? Surely we men tend to undervalue the blessing of a wife. "He who finds a wife finds a good thing, and obtains favor from the LORD" (Prov. 18:22).

One of the reasons that patriarchy has earned a bad reputation (the caricatures of feminism aside) is because men so often fail to care for their wives. Women are truly vulnerable in this arrangement called marriage, and they are often hurt by thoughtless or downright reckless husbands. But as we have already seen, biblical patriarchy is not just about male leadership. It is also about men serving their wives and children. And the way to solve the problem of poor husbandry is not to abandon God's order for the family, it is to recommit ourselves to be husbands after the pattern of Jesus, the Servant-Leader.

I am always leery of men who begin their conversation about family order by talking about how wives must submit to their husbands. This is true, of course, but submission is the *wife's* duty. Our concern as husbands is with leadership and service. Let's start our conversations with *that* topic! And let's get beyond the heroic statements about being willing, if the need ever arose, to die for our wives. By all means, let's be prepared to do that, but it would be a lot more useful to them if we would consider dying to our own self-will for the sake of our wives—today.

After having addressed the women about the need to submit to their husbands and trust God for the outcome, Peter turns his attention to the men: "Husbands, likewise, dwell with them with understanding, giving honor to the wife, as to the weaker vessel, and as being heirs together of the grace of life, that your prayers may not be hindered" (1 Pet. 3:7). This charge is parallel to the more familiar words of Paul, "Husbands, love your wives, just as Christ also loved the church and gave Himself for her, that He might sanctify and cleanse her with the washing of water by the word..." (Eph. 5:25). These verses are consistent with the definition of leadership we discussed in chapter 5: a man leads by means of humble service; the best leader is the best servant. Taking these passages together, we conclude that there are three specific ways that a husband can love and honor his wife.

HEIRS TOGETHER

First, *a husband should honor his wife as his partner in life* ("…giving honor to the wife… as being heirs together of the grace of life…"). A woman has a dignity and value equal to the man. She, too, is created in the image of God (Gen. 1:27). She, too, is an heir of God and joint-heir of Christ (Gal. 3:28; 4:7). Her position in the home is just as important as the husband's. She, too, is a teacher (Prov. 1:8). Her labors are vital to building up the home (Prov. 14:1). Indeed, without her there could be no home (1 Cor. 11:11,12). A wife is due honor because she is fully a partner of the man by virtue of both creation and redemption.

The wife is the inferior of the husband only in the chain of authority. He is her head. A man is not given the superior position because he is better than his wife; he is given it because that is God's arrangement to maintain order and harmony in the home. The wife is in the glorious position of imitating Christ's humility as He voluntarily submitted His will to the Father, though He was Himself God! A woman submits to her husband because her calling is to show forth God's glory in her Christ-like submission. Just as the husband is called to exhibit Christ in his servant-leadership, the wife is called to exhibit Christ in her voluntary subjection to her husband.

Unfortunately, some men treat their wives as if they were children, commanding them with an imperious tone and displaying an attitude that borders on contempt. One of the worst offenses is for a man to correct his wife in front of other people. To humiliate his partner in this way is a sign that he needs some serious humbling himself! Such behavior is an affront not only to the wife but also to Christ.

One way husbands exasperate their wives is by making decisions without consulting them. Now the man bears the final responsibility for the decision, but to proceed without asking her counsel says that her perspective doesn't matter or that she has nothing to contribute to the decision-making process. One key way a man can honor his wife is to take her seriously as his most important counselor in life. Surely this is part of what it means for her to be his "helper" (Gen. 2:18).

A man needs constantly to remember that his position of leadership is a trust, not a right. The Scripture calls a man to love his wife and a wife to respect her husband, but the husband also owes his wife respect. He must choose out of obedience to God to honor his wife as someone who possesses with him the gifts of physical and spiritual life.

GUARDING THE WEAKER VESSEL

A second way that a man can love and honor his wife is *to have regard for her unique needs as a woman, a wife, and a mother* ("…dwell with them with understanding, giving honor to the wife, as to the weaker vessel…"). A wife is in a position of vulnerability as compared to her husband due to her role, her biology, and her unique duties.

The immediate context of Peter's words above is a fairly lengthy admonition to wives about their *role* in marriage: they are to be submissive to their husbands, even unbelieving husbands. As we saw, the passage included a reminder of the example of

Sarah who "obeyed Abraham, calling him lord, whose daughters you are if you do good and are not afraid with any terror" (1 Pet. 3:6). A woman's position of submission makes her vulnerable as she has to entrust herself to the care of a sinful and fallible man while learning to trust in God to protect her. A man ought always to keep before his mind what it takes for a woman to follow the leadership of a mere man. He needs to understand that she is truly exposed and can be hurt by his bad choices. This ought to make him all the more humble and careful about how he exercises that leadership and how he treats his wife.

A woman's *biology* puts her at relative risk and in need of understanding and sheltering by her husband. Although women tend to live longer than men on average and to be constitutionally more healthy, they are weaker in terms of muscular strength. Also, a woman's cyclical physiology can produce physical and emotional disturbances that are hard for an even-tempered man to comprehend, but he must make allowances for this aspect of God's design for producing godly offspring. Obviously a pregnant woman and a nursing mother need special care and protection (Matt. 24:19). The demands upon her body are enormous and the emotional strain can be considerable. Plus her physical activity is limited both by her physical changes but also by the sheer demands of carrying and nursing a child. Unsanctified men have a perverse tendency to despise weakness, and some men may get irritated by the reduced capacity of their wives physically, emotionally, and sexually during these times. Instead this "weakness" calls for thoughtfulness and protection.

In recent years there has been a renewed appreciation for the fruit of the womb, and couples have rightly begun to welcome as many children as God will give them. Wise husbands will be especially sensitive to the physical and emotional impact of this process on their wives. A woman who is continually either pregnant or nursing (or both!) needs extraordinary care from her husband. He needs to see that she has a good diet and he should try to protect her from any non-essential physical burdens. To live with a wife in an understanding way includes being thoughtful about the demands that childbearing places upon her.

Her *duties* as a wife and mother also put the woman in a position that calls for a husband's consideration. Although she is the primary caregiver for the young children, he ought to do all he can to make that job easier for her. When he is around the home or out with the family, he could take initiative to share the workload by holding or supervising some of the little ones. He could offer to care for the children periodically (or make other arrangements) so that Mom can get some time off from the relentlessness of her home tasks—she may enjoy some time to herself. It is good for her to have the opportunity to pursue those things which express her personal interests and exercise her unique gifts: reading for pleasure, playing the violin, or perhaps shopping flea markets for decorations to enhance the home. She also needs time to interact with other adults regularly. Some mothers with young children hardly ever talk with another adult. Rather than treating her like his servant, a husband ought to look for ways to serve his wife as she cares for his children.

The wife should also be the object of her husband's care in connection with her other home-centered tasks. If she has four children six and under, perhaps he can do the grocery shopping. Another very practical way for a man to honor his mate is to provide her with excellent tools for her domestic labors. Why is it that he can come up with money for a new computer while she is still struggling with the twelve-year-old vacuum cleaner that doesn't do the job anymore? For a man to honor his wife means that he will put her needs ahead of his own desires.

NURTURE HER WITH GOD'S WORD

A third way a man can love and honor his wife is *to nurture her with the Word of God* ("...that He might sanctify and cleanse her with the washing of water by the word..."). God's Word has a unique power to bless, and a man ought to use this power for the blessing of his wife. In the Ephesians passage the immediate subject of the sentence is Christ, who cleanses the church with the Word. God's Word is the primary means God uses to bring people to salvation and to build them up in the faith. As Jesus said while praying to His Father for His disciples, "Sanctify them by Your truth. Your word is truth" (Jn. 17:17). But the whole point of Ephesians 5 is that a man should pattern his treatment of his spouse on the way Jesus treats His church. This means the husband has a special responsibility to speak the Word of God into the life of his wife.

There are a number of ways this can be done. The foundation for this process ought to be family worship where the father exposes the whole family to Scripture and helps apply it to their lives. Beyond that, perhaps a man can have a Bible study time with his wife, exploring passages that address subjects they are dealing with together in their marriage, with their children, or in their church. Perhaps at a quiet moment during the day a man can make it a point to share with his wife some truth God has given him during his personal devotions, and he can ask her what she has learned in hers. Besides whatever planned means a man may use to expose his wife to the sanctifying influence of Scripture, he should always be alert to apply the Word to whatever circumstances they face together so that she can learn to see the world, her family, and herself through God's eyes. She needs cleansing in her spirit, and it is his job to wash her with God's Word.

HOW A WIFE TAKES DOMINION

Since this book is addressed to men, I have been addressing the man's role in the home and have said very little about the role of the man's wife. So we should pause to ask: How does she fit into the system of biblical patriarchy? Unless a man understands her role, he cannot properly lead her and enable her to reach her full potential as a wife and mother.

When we looked at Genesis we saw that the woman was created from the man and for the man. God made her to be "a helper comparable to him" (2:18,20). As the head of the human race, Adam bore the responsibility to fulfill the dominion mandate, to rule over the earth. But he couldn't do that alone. So God showed him that he needed someone else in his life and then made the perfect companion: someone enough like him to be his partner and friend and yet different enough to supply what he lacked. Together they could be "fruitful and multiply" and fill the earth.

Men and women have different orientations and different responsibilities. Feminism wants to deny these differences, but they are rooted in how God made man and woman and the distinct shape of their respective dominion tasks. Douglas Wilson addresses this point:

> This creation order means that all husbands are called to a particular task (in fact, the word *vocation* comes from the Latin verb, *voco*, which means *I call*). Their wives are called to the role of aiding and supporting them in their calling. This means, further, that the man is established by God as the authority in the home. Under God, he is defined by the work to which he is called, while she is defined by the man to whom she is called. As they turn to the task, since the work is his responsibility, she is his responsibility as well.
>
> This obviously collides with the idea that men and women both have an equal right to pursue their separate careers as they climb up the professional ladder. Unfortunately, this assumption is common in the evangelical church today. It is thoroughly unbiblical, but this problem was created, not by feminism, but rather by abdicating husbands.[23]

"He is defined by the work to which he is called, while she is defined by the man to whom she is called." This is the heart of the distinction between men and women. As we saw earlier, his focus is outward, upon his dominion task, epitomized in Adam's tilling of the ground. Her focus is home-centered, toward her husband and children. She, too, takes dominion over the earth, but her manner of taking dominion is as a helper to her man, the manager of his house, the mother of his children.

The woman exhibits the qualities that are evident in the roles of king, prophet, and priest, but not in the same way a man does. She rules under his authority: she is his queen. She teaches and disciplines as his assistant. She represents the family as worship leader and intercessor in his absence or as his helper when he is present. She shares many of the abilities of her husband; she just exercises them in a different way. And she has abilities he does not have. Only she can give birth to the child.

THE VIRTUOUS WIFE

The fullest description of a woman's role in all of Scripture is found in Proverbs 31:10-31:

10 Who can find a virtuous wife? For her worth is far above rubies.

11 The heart of her husband safely trusts her; So he will have no lack of gain.

12 She does him good and not evil All the days of her life.

13 She seeks wool and flax, And willingly works with her hands.

14 She is like the merchant ships, She brings her food from afar.

15 She also rises while it is yet night, And provides food for her household, And a portion for her maidservants.

16 She considers a field and buys it; From her profits she plants a vineyard.

17 She girds herself with strength, And strengthens her arms.

18 She perceives that her merchandise is good, And her lamp does not go out by night.

19 She stretches out her hands to the distaff, And her hand holds the spindle.

20 She extends her hand to the poor, Yes, she reaches out her hands to the needy.

21 She is not afraid of snow for her household, For all her household is clothed with scarlet.

22 She makes tapestry for herself; Her clothing is fine linen and purple.

23 Her husband is known in the gates, When he sits among the elders of the land.

24 She makes linen garments and sells them, And supplies sashes for the merchants.

25 Strength and honor are her clothing; She shall rejoice in time to come.

26 She opens her mouth with wisdom, And on her tongue is the law of kindness.

27 She watches over the ways of her household, And does not eat the bread of idleness.

28 Her children rise up and call her blessed; Her husband also, and he praises her:

29 "Many daughters have done well, But you excel them all."

30 Charm is deceitful and beauty is passing, But a woman who fears the LORD, she shall be praised.

31 Give her of the fruit of her hands, And let her own
works praise her in the gates.

This is a picture of ideal womanhood. It is probably not a
description of any particular wife—though, as an ideal, it is the
standard to which all wives should aspire. What do we learn
from the example of the virtuous wife? I see seven ways in which
she is a pattern for women.

1) *She is God-centered.* She is "a woman who fears the LORD"
(v. 30). The fear of the Lord is the beginning of wisdom for any
man or woman (Prov. 9:10), and this woman understands what
her life is about because she takes God seriously and follows His
plan for her. That is why she is "virtuous" (v. 10), a word that
carries connotations of valor, strength, and worth. Her strength
is in God and she finds her worth in Him.

2) *She exhibits godly character.* Because she lives with a
consciousness of God and desire to please Him, she reflects
His image in her attitudes and conduct. This woman displays
diligence as she rises early and stays up late to care for her family
(vv. 15,18). She is not idle (v. 27), but reveals great strength and
energy (v. 17). But she is not just a hard worker—she shares the
fruit of her work with those less fortunate than herself (v. 20).
Her whole life is characterized by good, not evil (v. 12).

3) *She is husband- and home-centered.* The very first statement
made about her is this: "The heart of her husband safely trusts
her; so he will have no lack of gain. She does him good and not
evil all the days of her life" (vv. 11,12). Her work is viewed in
the context of her husband and its effect on his welfare. He can
apply his energy to his work in the city gates because he trusts

her to run his household (v. 23). It is his approval that she works for (vv. 28,29). She is home-centered because she is husband-centered.

4) *She is a home manager.* Her calling is to help him by managing the household. Her authority is a derivative of his. Under the headship of her husband she is the vice regent of the home. "She watches over the ways of her household" (v. 27). Her servants receive assignments from her early in the morning (v. 15). As the manager, she sees that everyone in the household is cared for, having necessary food and clothing (vv. 15,21). But she is more than a manager: she herself is busy making things with her hands (vv. 13,19). And she finds time to take care of herself, making sure she is well-dressed and thus a good reflection on her husband (vv. 22,23).

5) *She uses the home to financially benefit her husband.* Instead of draining the family resources, she contributes to the economic wealth of her household. She goes into the marketplace to purchase the food and materials that her home needs to function (v. 14). She makes things at home, selling the products she produces directly to others or through merchants (v. 24). She invests in real estate, and out of her profits she makes other investments (v. 16). Notice that even her business concerns are home-centered. She does not become a merchant herself, leaving the home to work all day in the marketplace. She sells the products she has made at home. She purchases land to produce more wealth for the family. All this she does from her home. She is not an independent businesswoman; she is under her husbands' authority, acting as his representative.

This is consistent with the teaching of the New Testament. In Titus 2:5 the older women are instructed to teach the younger wives to be "keepers at home" so that the Word of God is not "blasphemed."

6) *She is a teacher.* "She opens her mouth with wisdom, and on her tongue is the law of kindness" (v. 26). Someone who manages others so effectively would have to be an able instructor in order to teach them their role in the household enterprise. When this woman speaks, it is with the wisdom that comes from aptly applying God's Word, and she has a special aptitude for explaining human relationships and helping people to live and work together ("the law of kindness").

7) *She delights in her calling.* This woman is no drudge, reluctantly doing a job she doesn't like. The text is permeated with a sense of her joy and energy in her work. She "willingly works with her hands" (v. 13). She gives her best strength to her work (v. 17). Just any old effort will not do: she loves to do *excellent* work (v. 18). Her hard work produces in her a quiet confidence because she plans ahead and is ready for anything (vv. 21,25). She enjoys being a woman and making herself attractive, first of all for her husband (vv. 22,23,29). But she is not shallow: she remembers that outward beauty is not most important (v. 30). Her own delight in her calling is matched by the recognition she gains in the community for her work (v. 31).

A Competent Helper

This ideal wife is not what modern people might expect a woman in a patriarchal system to be. Contemporary wisdom assumes that subordination means weakness, and that submissive women will be mousy and marginally competent. Not the virtuous wife of Proverbs 31. This lady is a powerhouse! She directs a large number of people with extraordinary competence. She shows initiative and creativity. She doesn't need her husband to micro-manage her life or the household. He trusts her to rule the affairs of the house on his behalf, and this gives him liberty to fulfill his dominion calling in the world. Stephen Clark offers this insight:

> This portrait of the woman amazes many modern people. They have the mistaken idea the Scripture pictures woman as weak, passive, and over-emotional. The mistake comes from identifying the Victorian ideal woman with the Scriptural ideal. The Victorian woman was supposed to be somewhat delicate, much in need of her husband's help. The Israelite ideal wife was a sturdy helper, able to shoulder significant responsibilities.[24]

In the Bible's vision of womanhood the wife is under the authority of her husband and derives authority from him. She is a competent helper to her husband who can be trusted as a steward of his family and goods. She is home-centered in her life and work, and she has great influence in the community because of her home-based vocation. Men and women have different callings, and their combined contribution creates the success of home life and the soundness of civilization.

Feminism rejects this balanced, biblical view of a woman's calling in life, and this rejection is not just a serious error; it is also pathetic. Feminists have to live in God's world whether they like it or not. They have to choose from the options God has created since they can't create anything new, and He only created male and female. (I'm not just picking on female feminists. I understand that many men are feminists, too, and that the movement would get nowhere without their encouragement.)

Here's what is pathetic: When feminists reject what is feminine, all that's left is what is masculine. So we find women renouncing their God given distinctiveness and trying to act like men. They want to be free from the burden of babies so they can be promiscuous (supposedly) without consequences like men, so they invent abortion and kill their babies—and their consciences. They want to compete with men in the marketplace, so they warehouse their babies in daycare centers with strangers. They want, like men, to be free of the perceived drudgery of housekeeping, so they end up simply adding the drudgery of commuting and punching a clock to the still unavoidable toil of home life.

The irony of feminism is that, while it hates men and wants to liberate women from men, the *masculine* is its standard of what is good and fulfilling in life. (It ought to be called "masculinism!") No one can escape God's order! All they can do is twist it, and in their attempt to change the unchangeable, damage themselves and those around them. In rejecting the Bible's definition of what it means to be a woman, women are rejecting their own humanity and condemning themselves to an unfulfilled life, and countless homes are a shadow of what they could have been if they had a virtuous wife within their walls.

How much better if we can all be what we were created to be: let men be men and women be women. A return to biblical patriarchy will mean that women will return to a biblical definition of womanhood. This is the only path to the fulfillment that women are seeking today in their strange and futile ambition to become like men. Our job as husbands is to help our wives see the glory of their femininity and all that it entails and, by doing our part right, to make it easier for them to embrace their role in God's plan.

Enjoy the Differences

While the differences between men and women ought to be celebrated, they are often the cause of much grief. I am referring to the broad personal and social traits that distinguish the genders from one another. If we understand these differences we can use their benefits to our advantage and we can work to counteract their pitfalls.

It should be no great surprise to us that God made men and women different because He had different roles in mind for them. Egalitarians rail against this fact, but its truth is evident to every parent. My ten-year-old daughter Alice (my youngest) fills balloons with water, paints faces on them, wraps them in towels, and carries around these "water babies" as if they were the real thing. I guarantee you that this project never occurred to my boys when they were that age, or any other age for that matter. They know that water balloons are for warfare! An experienced parent just laughs at the notion that these behavioral differences are the result of socialization and training. They're inborn.

Let's consider a couple of the more evident gender differences very briefly and thus begin to consider how to avoid their pitfalls and take advantage of their blessings. We recognize that the following statements are generalizations, but they are generalizations soundly rooted in both scientific study and common sense observation—and they are consistent with the roles God has given men and women.

Reason and Emotion

One of the dangers in making generalizations about the emotional and physical make-up of men and women is that there is no one-size-fits-all approach to understanding the sexes. Generalizations are just that—generalizations. A second danger is that when describing men and women we must, at all costs, avoid using humanistic categories of analysis that are foreign to Scripture, like many of those employed by modern psychologists. Yet another danger is that we may minimize the emotional and intellectual obligations which both men and women share, by categorizing the sexes with certain inevitable behavioral patters from which neither can escape. Our best approach will be to draw some basic conclusions from the creation patterns of Scripture and to build upon these.

The first step in understanding men is to know that God created them to perform specific tasks. Adam was placed in the Garden of Eden and given a job that required him to analyze, compartmentalize, and draw conclusions. This was, and always will be, an essential part of the make-up of a man. Eve was created to help her husband. Her goal was not to oversee all the projects, but to serve Adam in his tasks as he deemed best. She was created out of man, for man, and placed under man, which is why we should not be surprised to discover that she thinks and acts more as a responder than an initiator. She was made to respond to man, to adapt and adjust easily to whatever changing circumstances he initiates.

Consequently we should not be surprised to discover that men tend to have more of a differentiated personality while women have more of an integrated personality. Men are generally able to act out of part of their personality while ignoring others: their personality is more compartmentalized. For example, in the midst of a crisis or disturbing situation, men are generally better than women at isolating and ignoring their emotional response in order to concentrate on thinking through to a solution. The strength of the man's approach is that he is better at problem-solving and acting with reason in the midst of turmoil. His weakness, however, is that he tends toward insensitivity, reducing everything to abstractions of his reason and losing sight of the personal dimensions of the problem.

Women, on the other hand, tend to respond out of the unified whole of their personality, feeling what they are thinking about. A woman is sensitive to a problem's relational and emotional dimensions. Her strength is her more intuitive, immediate perception that often enables her to discern at a glance what her husband may never see with his more methodical application of logic. Her challenge, however, is that she has trouble, for example, in the midst of a crisis, setting aside her emotions enough to be able to reason through to a solution, when that is what is needed.

These differences fit well with our callings. God made man to have a personality that enables him to be a good leader, to remain calm in crisis, to apply reason and find solutions to problems. A woman's strength is that she is in tune with the emotional side of things: she cares about the people and the relationships involved. This is consistent with her nurturing, people-centered role in life. So in any particular situation, both the man and the woman bring something of real value. Her intuitive, people-oriented intelligence is a wonderful balance to his logical, idea-oriented intelligence. (Again, I realize that these statements are generalizations, but they are accurate as generalizations. They will be more or less accurate when applied to any particular man or woman.)

These differences can lead to trouble if we let them. Earlier in our marriage Pam and I had a serious disagreement (a.k.a., a fight). At one point she informed me, "I'm getting angry." My response was bewilderment, so I did the wrong thing: I laughed and said, "You're *getting* angry? What is that supposed to mean?"

You see, Pam was being a woman and reporting what was going on with her emotions and with our relationship, since she does not divorce her feelings from what she is thinking and talking about. I, on the other hand, thought that emotions had no place in what was supposed to be our very rational discussion and our attempt to solve a problem. If I had been a more understanding husband, I would have appreciated that Pam was doing something valuable for our relationship by sharing her emotional response, even though I couldn't identify with her way of responding. I hope I am learning that when I deal with people I need to consider them as whole persons, with emotions as well as minds, not just as problems to be solved.

One other thing I've noticed in connection with this set of differences: There have been numerous times through the years when Pam has perceived something about a person's character which she can't explain and for which she can offer no evidence. My tendency is to dismiss this insight as unfounded since it can't be rationally verified, and after all, I want to be careful when it comes to jumping to conclusions about people. But then, sure enough, her insight proves correct in time. It baffles me how she can recognize what is real so immediately, but I hope I am learning to respect the value of this female intelligence.

Of course, she may not always be correct in her intuition, so I can't simply abdicate my responsibility to evaluate and examine the data. But God has given me a helper whose gifts supplement my own, and I do well to take her very seriously as my counselor in reaching my own decisions.

Task and Relationship

Men are generally aggressive and goal-oriented, while women are nurturers who are oriented to personal needs. Men tend to see life as unfolding in a series of tasks—obstacles to be overcome. Women see life as a complex blend of interrelated tasks and relationships.

I once heard someone put it like this: Men approach their day like a rope with knots, each knot representing a task to be accomplished. When they get to one, they untie it, then they move on to the next. Women, on the other hand, approach their day like a web: everything is interconnected. They can move from one job to another, and back again, meanwhile answering several phone calls, changing a diaper, fixing lunch, and having a friend over for a chat.

A man is good at concentrating on the job to be done and sticking with it until it is completed, and paying no attention to what is going on around him. He does not do well, however, if he has several things that need doing at once, and he is more likely to get irritated by interruptions when he is working.

His wife, on the other hand, seems to thrive on having six chores going simultaneously. And it's a good thing because motherhood doesn't happen in discreet task units. She usually adapts well to having a chore interrupted by a person who needs her care.

God made men to work the ground, to take dominion over the earth. This requires defining *tasks* and moving methodically through them toward a goal. Dig up the ground, plant the seeds, water the plants, keep the weeds out, harvest the crop. This approach works very well when it comes to ruling the earth. But it falls short when it comes to dealing with people. People are not projects to be completed. So men have to work at being sensitive to other people and caring for them as whole persons.

God made women to help men, so their focus in life is toward other *persons* rather than tasks. Plus their very biology makes them the bearers and nurturers of new human life. They are instinctively oriented toward other people and have a built-in concern for the welfare of those around them. They are less inclined than men to focus on a single task and pursue it doggedly for hours or days at a time.

Ouch! Between the last sentence and this one, literally, I just had a good illustration of the downside of the male approach to life. I am in my remote office (just a few hundred yards from my house) where nobody is supposed to disturb me, and today I have been working at my computer for eight hours straight, with ten minutes off for lunch, writing this book.

Well, my friend Brian just showed up to wish me a happy birthday (that's right: men think working all day at something they enjoy is a fine way to spend a birthday). And what was my response? Rather than ask him right in, I stood at the door and asked what I could do for him. When he repeated his happy birthday greeting, I softened and let him come in (no one outside my family has even seen my remote office setup). We chatted for just a couple minutes, and he was on his way.

The fact is that Brian did a very thoughtful thing that showed a concern for our relationship. But my instinctive (and self-centered) initial reaction was irritation at having my project interrupted. I even let him know I was trying to get this chapter completed before supper. I think (I hope) I recovered enough civility to have been pleasant to my friend. But this showed me how I tend to value people less than work.

Every strength has a flipside. On the other side of the strength is a weakness that we must identify and counteract with conscious choices. Men need to learn to take the emotional, relational side of life more seriously. This takes work. Women need to learn to make decisions (and accept those that are made) without allowing emotion to override reason based on truth. This takes work, too.

To the extent that we understand that men and women are different for a good reason, given their distinct callings, we can then avoid unnecessary conflicts over our differences. Instead we can employ those very differences to our mutual advantage. *Vive la différence!*

UNDERSTANDING WOMEN

In the verse which heads this chapter, Peter instructs us husbands to live with our wives "with understanding." The fact that he would write this implies that there is something to be understood, that it may take some work to figure out, and that we had better get busy about doing it. But not many of us do this. We may joke about the differences between us, but we don't take this matter seriously as something that requires careful thought and determined action.

One of the most essential ingredients of a renewal of biblical patriarchy in our generation will be that men make it a top priority to live with their wives "with understanding." We must work hard to grasp the nature of womanhood, the role of wives, the essence of femininity. Then we need to make it a life's project to love and honor the woman God has given to each of us and to promote the full blossoming of her womanhood.

Being project-oriented as we are, men tend to revel in the challenge of winning a wife. Before marriage a man is focused, determined, moving toward a goal. He works hard to please his woman, to meet her needs, to show his love for her. The goal is to get her to the altar and to the marriage bed.

Once that task is completed, that goal met, he communicates (however unintentionally), "Good, now I have a wife. Let's get on with the rest of life." And he starts looking for his next challenge: finishing school, advancing in his career, building a house, improving his racquetball game. The woman who was so much an object of his attention during their courtship tends to be taken for granted. He still loves her. After all, look how hard he is working to provide a home and other material things for her. But she is no longer his preoccupation.

Combine this with the fact that he is often clueless when it comes to the emotional and relational side of life—and that this is exactly what is most important to his wife—and you have a recipe for some significant problems. The trouble is, it is the wife who suffers most, often in silence, from this change in the marriage relationship. She longs to be close to the man who was so enthralled with her during their engagement but who now seems so distracted and uninterested in her. Her whole life is focused on him, but he is busy about his dominion task, or his play, and she feels like she is just along for the ride.

The solution is that we men need to have as a lifetime project understanding and honoring our wives. Not that they become a project, as if we spend two minutes in the evening asking them how their day went and then put a mark on our checklist with our "relational" mission accomplished. No, we need to study what they are like, what their job is, and how we can make it easier and more joyful for them. Here is the model we need to follow:

Husbands, love your wives, just as Christ also loved the church and gave Himself for her, that He might sanctify and cleanse her with the washing of water by the word, that He might present her to Himself a glorious church, not having spot or wrinkle or any such thing, but that she should be holy and without blemish. So husbands ought to love their own wives as their own bodies; he who loves his wife loves himself." (Eph. 5:25-28)

CHAPTER 11

Patriarchy Beyond the Home

> You are the light of the world. A city that is set on a hill
> cannot be hidden. Nor do they light a lamp and put it
> under a basket, but on a lampstand, and it gives light to all
> who are in the house. Let your light so shine before men,
> that they may see your good works and glorify your Father
> in heaven.
>
> Matt. 5:14-16

As you and I shape our families according to the patterns of biblical patriarchy, the world around us will be affected. This will happen in large part because of our efforts, if we are faithful, to have God's Word shape everything we do outside the home as well as inside. But even apart from such conscious intentions, godly homes influence the societies of which they are a part by a very natural and inevitable process whereby the parts shape the whole.

Listen to how J.R. Miller describes the influence of the family in the opening words of *Home-Making* (1882):

> The benediction that falls upon the homes of a country is like the gentle rain that descends among the hills. A thousand springs are fuller afterward, and along the banks of a thousand streamlets flowing through the valleys the grass is greener and the flowers pour out richer fragrance.
>
> Homes are the springs among the hills, whose many streamlets, uniting, form like great rivers society, the community, the nation, the Church. If the springs run low the rivers waste; if they pour our bounteous currents the rivers are full. If the springs are pure the rivers are clear like crystal; if they are foul the rivers are defiled. A curse upon homes sends a poisoning blight everywhere; a blessing sends healing and new life into every channel.
>
> Homes are the divinely ordained fountains of life....[25]

God has designed the world so that it is shaped more by the accumulation of many small influences than by the one big influence. We see this in His kingdom as well: it is a bottom-up operation rather than top-down. God is changing the world through the quiet process of converting sinners one at a time, getting hold of their families, and thus shaping family lines, communities, churches, and whole nations. The influence spreads from the bottom up, from the lesser to the greater, from the individual to the family to the society. People are not converted by government decree by the thousands, but one-by-one and family-by-family. And changed people end up creating a changed society.

This is why mass education and legislation cannot actually create a better world, despite the grandiose claims of those who run our schools and governments. They don't deal with the heart and can't transform the person. The major influences that shape a Christian civilization are, first, the regenerate heart of the individual, and then the intimate connections of the home life. As godly patterns are established in thousands or millions of homes, the shape of a godly society emerges.

If our society is to be saved, it will be because men and their families are born again by the Spirit and then progressively transformed by God through His Word.

The home is where people are fashioned and it is where they live most of their lives, for better or for worse. The rivers of the community, the church, and the nation are all fed by the springs of the families that are part of the society. These larger bodies of people simply do not exist apart from the families that make them up. With the church in view, Rev. B.M. Palmer put it this way in 1876:

> Each pious household is a separate fiber of those roots by which the Church of the living God takes hold upon the earth, and preserves its existence in a sinful world.[26]

There is no church, no neighborhood, no city, and no nation apart from the homes that are the smallest social unit within each.

A return to God's patterns for the home will spill over into the rest of society. Let's now think more about that prospect. How will a return to biblical patriarchy in the family bring changes beyond the home? What should we expect to see and what should we work to see in society in general, in our communities, on the job, in civil government, and in the church? To answer these questions would take a whole volume. We'll just make a start here.

Male Leadership Throughout Society

As men and women practice their God-given roles within the family, it is only natural that the larger society will reflect and support these roles as well. The principle of male leadership will be expressed whenever groups of people join for a common purpose, be it a church, a voluntary association, or a county council.

Men are to lead and women follow. This is part of God's creation order that He established in the Garden at the beginning of history. The hierarchy of Adam over Eve formed the basis of a sound and stable family, and the principle of male leadership that God instituted during creation week flows outward beyond the nuclear family to inform the way in which all societal institutions should be structured.

It would be unnatural for a community group to reverse this pattern. Why would a woman who is used to affirming her husband's leadership and deferring to him at home then turn around and become the leader of men in the local neighborhood improvement association?

That men are to lead in organizations outside the context of the family is affirmed over and over again throughout the scriptures. Every time the Bible addresses the issue of hierarchy within a social group, men are always designated as the leaders.

The ruling office in the church is that of elder (or bishop), and men hold that office.

> If a man desires the position of a bishop, he desires a good work. A bishop then must be... the husband of one wife... one who rules his own house well, having his children in submission with all reverence (for if a man does not know how to rule his own house, how will he take care of the church of God?). (1 Tim. 3:1-5)

Furthermore, women are explicitly excluded from the position of authority in the church.

> And I do not permit a woman to teach or to have authority over a man, but to be in silence. For Adam was formed first, then Eve. And Adam was not deceived, but the woman being deceived, fell into transgression. (1 Tim. 2: 12-14)

The basis of Paul's command that men lead and women follow in the church is the creation order and the sinful forsaking of that order when mankind fell into sin in the Garden. So church life is consistent with home life in this regard.

Notice again the verses above from 1 Timothy 3. They contain an important principle that explains why there must be a continuity of practice between home and larger society: the home is the training ground for leadership roles beyond the home. The specific point of the text is that a man is not qualified to rule the church until he has proven his leadership ability within his family. But in general this means that family life is a preparation for life beyond the family and that the patterns of home life will become the patterns of life in other spheres.

It is proper for men to assume the lead whenever people get together since men reflect the headship of God the Father. Because this role is commanded in the home and the church, it follows by strong implication that it applies in the other spheres of life, be it civil government or in neighborhood or ministry associations.

The wisdom of this application was never questioned until egalitarianism began to make inroads into our culture. Now it is seriously questioned. Christians will often bow to God's commands for home and church, since they are so explicit in Scripture, and yet balk at applying the principle of male leadership beyond that. But it honors God and the order He has established to seek to create a society that is not at war with itself, with one standard for home and church and another for everywhere else. If God's people will shrug off the social pressures of feminism, they will see the wisdom of being consistent with the principle of male leadership in every sphere.

FEMALE FOLLOWERSHIP

If men are supposed to lead, then women are supposed to affirm and follow that leadership. We have already seen that women are explicitly excluded from the leadership function within the church. Nor do we have any examples that suggest otherwise.

Sometimes Christians will refer to Deborah as an example of how a woman might become a leader in the church or state (Jud. 4:4ff). Deborah was a "judge," an informal position of leadership, within Israel during the dark and unruly days before they had a king (Jud. 21:25). People came to her to have their disputes resolved because of the wisdom she displayed. But she did not seek leadership nor set up court. When it was time for war, she gave the man Barak God's plan for battle. He would not go to war without her, and although she accompanied him she also chided him for not being willing to act the part of a man and do his duty without the support of a woman (4:9). Part of what the account of Deborah is teaching is the *impropriety* of women being in the lead and how this exceptional situation reflects badly on men. We can't use Deborah to overturn the consistent testimony of Scripture elsewhere.

In the New Testament we have a strong statement against women taking the lead in a public meeting, even to the point of prohibiting their speaking. Here is 1 Corinthians 14:34-37:

> 34 Let your women keep silent in the churches, for they are not permitted to speak; but they are to be submissive, as the law also says.
> 35 And if they want to learn something, let them ask their own husbands at home; for it is shameful for women to speak in church.
> 36 Or did the word of God come originally from you? Or was it you only that it reached?
> 37 If anyone thinks himself to be a prophet or spiritual, let him acknowledge that the things which I write to you are the commandments of the Lord.

The context of these verses is Paul's regulation of speaking in tongues and prophesying in the church meeting. After addressing what to do "if anyone speaks in a tongue" (v. 27) and allowing that "two or three prophets speak" (v. 29), Paul then says that the women "are not permitted to speak" (v. 34). It is quite clear that what was allowed the tongues-speakers and prophets, was being forbidden to women in the meeting: namely, speech.

Paul piles up the commands and supporting arguments. 1) Women must be silent. 2) They are not allowed to speak. 3) This is a sign of their submission, which God's law requires. 4) They can't even ask questions in the meeting, but must ask their husbands at home. 5) It is shameful for a woman to speak in church. 6) Those who question this instruction are proud. 7) This is a commandment of the Lord.

It appears that God must regard any speaking out in the meeting of the church as a form of leadership since whoever is speaking is directing the whole group. Even asking a question sets the pace for the direction of the meeting.

This example strongly reinforces the notion that God intends men to lead in group settings. Godly women will defer to men and allow them to formulate the direction in such places, just as they do at home. This does not mean that women can never speak in any mixed-gender public settings, but propriety demands that they do so with caution, considering whether their speech amounts to leadership of the group. My wife says she always evaluates carefully whether to speak out in such settings since she knows that when she speaks it means a man does not have the opportunity to speak at that point, and she doesn't want to grasp the reins of the group.

Peter commends in women "the incorruptible beauty of a gentle and quiet spirit, which is very precious in the sight of

God. For in this manner, in former times, the holy women who trusted in God also adorned themselves, being submissive to their own husbands" (1 Pet. 3:4,5). The qualities of quietness and submission occur together in at least three separate passages in the New Testament that address the behavior of women, whereas men are instructed to speak, teach, and pray when the church assembles.

A godly society will honor God's order for relationships between men and women whenever a mixed group gathers, thus creating a seamless fabric of values throughout that society.

Children are instructed by God to honor their father and mother. Nowhere does Scripture say that they should honor the parents of their friend who lives down the street. Yet who would question the importance of their doing just that? How long will the children honor their parents if they are allowed to dishonor other adults? Patterns for relationships in the home are the model for relationships everywhere else. Male leadership and female followership ought to be practiced wherever men and women gather for a common purpose.

GOOD MANNERS

Another effect of a return to biblical patriarchy in the home will be the revival of good manners in the society. The necessity of practicing common courtesies is rooted in a biblical view of life. Courtesy grows out of two principles: First is a respect for the dignity of each person as a creature made in God's image. Second is a recognition of the position each person holds in the God-ordained social structure.

Every creature of God deserves honor as a fellow creature, especially fellow image-bearers of God. "Honor all people" (1 Pet. 2:17). But the way we demonstrate that honor will differ depending on the positions we hold relative to one another. A man must "honor" his wife (1 Pet. 3:7), and a woman must "respect" her husband (Eph. 5:33), but the expressions of honor and respect will not be the same in each case.

We have already discussed some of the ways a man ought to honor his wife: protecting her in her vulnerabilities, helping her with the difficulties her role imposes on her, encouraging her with the Scripture. Now we are thinking of the simpler, daily courtesies he shows her: opening the door, offering to carry a heavy object, holding her chair when she sits down to eat, holding an umbrella over her in the rain, rising to greet her when she enters the room after an absence, etc. Customs like these express important principles. He is physically stronger and as her protector bears burdens for her. She is valuable to him, so he shows that by greeting her when she returns home. Little courtesies are a constant reminder to both of the nature of their relationship.

Likewise, she should rise to greet him upon his return home. In a group, she should fall silent if she sees that he wants to speak. She should ask his permission before accepting a social engagement for the family. Such little courtesies express that she values him as her leader.

Good manners are a way of honoring God in every social situation by honoring other people and recognizing God's order for our relationships. Each person should show courtesy to all other people in a way that recognizes the distinct roles we play in the social structure. Men should demonstrate care for all women similar to that which they show to their wives, and women should show deference to all men to match that which they show to their husbands.

This does not mean that my wife must submit to you because you are a man: you are not her head and have no authority over her. However, she should practice a womanly deference and respect for you because you are a man. In God's chain of authority, men outrank women, and so a woman owes any man a measure of deference to his rank even though he is not in authority over her.

It's similar to how I had to treat those of higher rank in the Army. When I was a Major, I saluted the Colonel who walked past me even if he wasn't in my unit and had no authority over me in the chain of command. I deferred to him since I held a lower rank in the system. It's a way of showing honor and preserving proper attitudes within the military community. The attitude of respect I had for my own commander led me quite naturally to show respect to others of his rank. If I were allowed to neglect demonstrations of honor for others of superior rank, whoever they might be, I would find it harder to maintain respect for my own superiors.

Likewise, a man should extend to any woman the same quality of honor that he shows to his wife: opening a door for her, offering her a seat, rising in her presence, addressing her with gentleness and respect. However, propriety demands that he be careful not to be too familiar with another woman. He should show the same quality of care and respect but not to the same extent as to his wife. He should demonstrate care for other women without suggesting intimacy.

The way we treat each other socially should reinforce the principles that underlie a godly society. As fathers restore their families to God's ways, they should be teaching manners to their sons and daughters and demonstrating manners themselves, especially in how they treat their wives. Manners will then help shape a courteous society in which everyone is looking for ways to honor everyone else in a manner appropriate to their respective positions in God's order.

GETTING WIVES OUT OF THE WORKPLACE

A vital social effect of a return to patriarchy will be that married women will leave the workforce and return home. In an earlier chapter we mentioned how men have allowed the civil government to take over so many of the functions that previously were performed by families: child care, education, welfare, care for the elderly, healthcare. In a patriarchal renewal these functions must be reclaimed by families—and as the domain of family government increases, civil government will shrink.

One of the first effects of industrialism was the exodus of fathers from the home. In the last century, women have followed suit. Now the ordinary family has both husband and wife working in the marketplace, helping to put bread on the table. As we move slowly back toward a more family-centered way of life, one of the first needs is to get the wife and mother back home. Then the family will be able to begin the process of reclaiming the functions it has lost.

I recognize the challenge involved here. Since the whole structure of our society has changed in the last two hundred years to accommodate the new economic order, which tends to fragment the family into the workplace, schools, and other institutions, any progress made at restoring family functions will involve sacrifice, but must be done nonetheless.

The warehousing of babies and young children in disease-infested institutions under the care of strangers is one of the saddest side effects of sending mothers into the workforce. With mother home there is no need for the daycare center, and the little ones are provided with the best possible care by the person God designed to be their primary caregiver.

When the wife is home during the day, it also becomes possible to think of caring for an elderly parent who may need companionship or supervision. This is one of the chief ways in which children can honor their parents. "But if any widow has children or grandchildren, let them first learn to show piety at home and to repay their parents; for this is good and acceptable before God" (1 Tim. 5:4).

A mother at home is able to teach her children, thus fulfilling the mandate of Deuteronomy 6:6-9. The educational process was one of the first family functions ceded to the state, and its recovery by the family is one of the most costly commitments a father and mother can make in terms of time and energy. But reclaiming the educational role is probably the most effective step parents can take to revitalize their family and help assure that the Christian faith is passed along to the next generation.

Beyond restoring to the family the functions God intended it to perform, there are two other biblical reasons why we must get our wives out of the workplace and back into the domestic sphere.

First, *a wife is her husband's helper; she is not the helper of another man.* The woman was made from the man for the man, to be his companion-helper as he takes dominion over the earth. She is not the helper of men in general, but of the one man with whom she is one flesh (Gen. 2:24). His work takes him outside the home into the world. Her job is a domestic one. When a wife goes to work in the marketplace, she is shifting her dominion focus from her home to the world outside the home, and she is thus, to that extent, taking on the role of a man.

Furthermore, the working wife often becomes the helper of another man, be it her immediate boss or the company owner. She is helping him meet his dominion goals and is enriching his household as he makes a profit off her labor. Jesus said, "No one can serve two masters; for either he will hate the one and love the other, or else he will be loyal to the one and despise the other" (Matt. 6:24). While the immediate context of Jesus' words was the issue of money, the principle illuminates the problem created when a woman works for another man: her loyalties are now divided between her husband and her boss. Her schedule and how she occupies herself during the day are dictated by the demands of her employer, and her husband and children usually get the leftovers of her energy and attention.

One common side effect of women working for and with men in the workplace is infidelity. This is not surprising given human nature: you become close to those you work with every day. And there is a special bond that develops when a woman works directly for a man on the job. She is fulfilling a very feminine function by helping this man, and he is drawn to appreciate her as she assists him in his labors. The emotional attachments God meant to flower between a husband and wife are thus promoted between a man and woman who are not married to each other.

The second and most critical reason for getting the wife and mother back home is that *the home is a wife's God-appointed workplace*. In an earlier chapter we looked at the virtuous wife of Proverbs 31 and saw that she was home-centered in her work. Look now at this passage from the New Testament:

> But as for you, speak the things which are proper for sound
> doctrine: that the older men be sober, reverent, temperate,
> sound in faith, in love, in patience; the older women
> likewise, that they be reverent in behavior, not slanderers,
> not given to much wine, teachers of good things—that
> they admonish the young women to love their husbands,
> to love their children, to be discreet, chaste, homemakers,
> good, obedient to their own husbands, that the word of
> God may not be blasphemed. (Titus 2:1-5)

Paul is giving instructions to Titus about how Christians should live their lives, instructions he calls "sound doctrine" (v. 1). He tells the older women to teach the younger women to do several things, all of which center on the home.

In the midst of this he says that the women are to be homemakers. The actual word is a combination of "house" and "guard" (or "keep") and means someone who keeps or stays at the house; it is often translated "keepers at home." A related term is used in other ancient literature to mean "working at home," and refers to the domestic duties of women. So part of "sound doctrine" is the teaching that married women are supposed to work in the home and concentrate their attention on their husbands and children.

Notice how important this sound doctrine is: Paul says that the neglect of this teaching will cause the Word of God to be "blasphemed." This is serious. The Bible says that if your wife is not a keeper at home she is blaspheming the Word of God. God's Word must be followed, and it is the husband's responsibility to see that it is.

I am fully aware of how utterly challenging and counterculture this teaching will sound to most Christians today, tied in as we are to the modern economy which depends on working women. There is no way fathers can effectively turn their hearts toward home if their wives are not even there. But if we are to return to biblical patriarchy, to take up the mantle of leadership in our homes, we must lead our wives in their God given role and protect them from becoming "blasphemous," whatever the cost, whatever the sacrifice.

Family renewal will depend upon reversing the trends of recent years. Yes, it will take time. But the important thing is for us to believe what the Bible says and to set the direction of our lives in keeping with God's revealed will. It will take a while to rebuild families, and we may only make a start in our lifetimes, but let's at least make sure the goal is clear.

CHRISTIAN CITIZENS AND STATESMEN

In a society characterized by godly homes, the civil government will inevitably take on a different flavor. This will be another effect of a patriarchal renewal in our families. As families take back many of the functions they have ceded to the state, the scope of government activities will shrink drastically. As a result, the tax burden on families will be decreased and personal and family liberties will be increased: for example, no more mandatory school attendance statutes or threats of removing home schooled children from the home. These changes will not happen apart from Christian men shouldering the duties of citizenship. Some of us will even need to become Christian statesmen who will help lead the charge to implement the needed changes.

Over the last century too many Christians have shied away from involvement in politics and government, somehow considering these unworthy endeavors for believers. As we consider our role as Christian citizens, we should bear in mind the following principles:

1) *God's kingdom in this world begins as the Holy Spirit regenerates the hearts of individuals.* Christ's kingdom is most emphatically *not* established through the arm of government—and those who naively think that by electing the right man as president we will see righteousness reign in America are forgetting that God's kingdom grows from the inside out (it begins in the heart of individuals) and from the bottom up (godly leaders are a reflection of a godly citizenry). The starting point for renewal in our land is the preaching of the gospel to sinners, not political action.

2) *Every disciple of Jesus is responsible to apply God's Word to every sphere of life, including politics.* Discipleship is not just accepting Christ for eternal salvation and then ignoring God's will for life in this world. Discipleship is a life of obedience to Christ in every area of life.

Jesus' own definition of making disciples is, "teaching them to observe all things that I have commanded you" (Matt. 28:20). Since the Bible speaks to issues related to civil government, it is our responsibility as citizens to apply God's will to our political situation as He gives us opportunity. This duty is especially evident in a constitutional republic such as ours where the citizens create the government through their vote.

The substantially Christian character of early America was, in part, the result of believers applying their faith to the civil sphere. We must do the same today. We cannot abandon whole realms of life to the devil by failing to live righteously in those realms. Jesus has all authority in heaven *and* on earth (Matt. 28:18).

Our nation has slipped into wickedness and decline because Christians have failed to live righteously. We have accepted a truncated version of the gospel which reduces our faith to a private matter that is practiced in the home and church but not applied anywhere else. The enemy has had a heyday as Christians have withdrawn into their spiritual ghettos believing that religion and politics don't mix.

3) *A civil ruler is a minister of God* (Rom. 13:4). He lives in a world where Jesus is king. He is not a neutral moral agent who can do as he pleases. He is no less under God's authority than you or I. A true statesman will honor the law of God as

the basis for civil law, and godly citizens will hold their leaders accountable to that standard.

4) *Christians must submit to and honor civil authorities as a part of their allegiance to Christ as Lord* (Rom. 13:1-7). We must respect the leader because of the position he holds, even if he is himself a wicked person (Matt. 23:2,3).

However, it is not a breach of respect to identify the wrongs of leaders. We are instructed to expose the deeds of darkness (Eph. 5:11). Jesus lambasted the hypocritical leaders of His day (Matt. 23), and the prophets of Israel and Judah were forever naming names and condemning sin among the leaders of the nation.

Any criticisms of our leaders must be accompanied by a deep spirit of submission to the authority they bear. We should weep as we expose evil. The only pleasure that should attend our statements is the pleasure of our God. Concerning those rulers who take a stand against Him, Psalm 2 says, "He who sits in the heavens shall laugh; The LORD shall hold them in derision" (v. 4). We should expose the reasons for His derision, but God alone should scoff.

5) *We must always remember that our ultimate enemies are spiritual* and that our weapons of warfare are spiritual weapons. God's kingdom is established in this world not by might nor by power, but by God's Spirit (Zech. 4:6). Our trust must not be in ourselves as we vote, write to a legislator, or speak against a public policy or a wicked leader. Our confidence must be in our God who raises up leaders and brings them down as He wills. Our faith must be in the one who calls us to faithfulness, not

success, and who alone is able to bless us with spiritual renewal in our land.

Politics cannot become an obsession, nor can it be ignored. We may err in either direction. In a godly society Christian men will do their duty as citizens as part of their obedience to Christ even as they remember that civil government is not the means for bringing in the kingdom of God.

CHURCHMEN AND FAMILY-INTEGRATED CHURCHES

Before leaving our look at the broader effects of the restoration of biblical patriarchy in our homes, we should consider the church.

God meant family and church to work closely together in this age, and family men must be firmly committed to the church if their efforts at home renewal are to bear fruit over the long term. To be a Christian means to be part of the body of Christ, and it requires being part of a local manifestation of that body. The entire New Testament presents the necessity of living in fellowship with other believers (e.g., Heb. 10:24,25) and in submission to the elders of a local assembly of believers (e.g., Heb. 13:17). Being a committed part of a church family is every bit as important as seeking to implement God's pattern for life in our homes.

Each of us must make the commitment that we will not only be godly family men; we will also be godly churchmen. We cannot, we must not neglect this calling. God never meant for Christian families to live in isolation. He created them to be part of the extended spiritual family of the church. We cannot grow to our full potential alone or just within the setting of the family; we need the local body of believers. This is everywhere assumed and taught in the Scripture. (Acts 2:42-47; 20:7; Rom. 12:10,13,16; 15:7,14; 1 Cor. 12:7; Gal. 6:2; Eph. 4:3,16; 5:19; Col. 3:16; 1 Thess. 5:11; Heb. 3:13; 10:24; Jas. 5:16; etc.)

Now I realize that it is not easy to find a good church, or even an acceptable one. Many have compromised in terms of beliefs or in terms of practical Christian living. If a church doesn't teach some version of cheap grace, for example, it may pressure families to participate in a youth program that exposes children to evil influences. A father should find the best congregation he can and humbly work for change where it is needed, or he should help to start a new church that is closer to the biblical model. But neglecting the fellowship of the saints is not an option.

Those who are church leaders have a great opportunity in this generation. In chapter 2 we noted that the church has not effectively stemmed the tide as our culture has moved from its former biblical social structure over the last two centuries. In fact, the church has been a large part of the problem. It is time for the church to repent of its passivity and compromise and become firmly committed to the restoration of biblical patriarchy.

Pastors and elders should aggressively teach the biblical view of manhood and family while explaining and refuting the lies of feminism. The church is God's agency for promoting the truth and equipping families to live out that truth. Strengthening families is the best long-term strategy the church can have for expanding God's kingdom in the world. The family should be viewed as the primary missionary agency of the church.

One of the highest priorities of church leaders should be to disciple the men of the congregation in the principles and practices of godly manhood and to train them to be the primary teachers of their own families. For most churches this will require a substantial adjustment of ministry focus.

The leaders should change the structure of church life from a program-based, family-fragmenting model to one that encourages family-like, intimate relationships and multi-generational gatherings. A "family-integrated church" is just another description of the family-like church we see in the New Testament. It is a congregation where relationships are more important than mere activity, where discipling men and families is high on the priority list, and where the family is not divided up as soon as it enters the church door but is rather encouraged to worship and minister together.

While patriarchal families can indeed have a positive influence for change in their local churches, a wholesale return to biblical patterns of family and social life will not be realized unless and until pastors and elders make this their mission. The family is indeed the foundational institution of society and thus has the potential to shape the whole nation. But the church is "the pillar and ground of the truth" (1 Tim. 3:15) and ought to be at the forefront, leading the charge against falsehood and encouraging men and their families to get back to God's model for human life, back to biblical patriarchy.

CHAPTER 12

Rebuilding—
One Family at a Time

Those from among you shall build the old waste places;
you shall raise up the foundations of many generations;
and you shall be called the Repairer of the Breach, the
Restorer of Streets to Dwell In.
    Is. 58:12

Early in our marriage, Pam and I lived in an older inner-city neighborhood that was quite run down. Although the homes had been beautiful and full of character in times past, they had been allowed to deteriorate, becoming ugly, often dirty, and sometimes even unsafe.

Around the same time that we bought our house, others with an eye toward restoration were buying other homes in the vicinity. Over the years each family poured their loving labors into their own dwelling. Some renovations were total and involved the replacement of everything, including the electrical and plumbing systems, the walls and floors, and the fixtures in kitchen and bathrooms. Other efforts were more modest: repairing broken windows, applying a fresh coat of paint, planting flowers in the yard. The combined effect of these family efforts over time was amazing: the neighborhood was transformed. It began to regain the charm and character that had belonged to it in a former day, and it was again a pleasant place to live.

This renewed neighborhood was not the result of a government decree, nor was it the work of a corporation buying up all the properties and pouring millions of dollars into urban renewal. It was instead the fruit of many individual families taking responsibility for their own homes and doing what they could with their own hands and within their own limited means. It is an illustration of how family-sized efforts at renewal can result in changing a whole community.

Those of us who live in modern America (and similar lands) live in a giant slum, speaking in terms of the condition of our family life. The physical houses are, for the most part, structurally sound and reasonably attractive on the outside, but the families that inhabit them have deteriorated over the years to the point where they are barely holding together, if they are at all. Even the best of them are only a shell of what families once were, since the members of the household have little meaningful life together, and they are not fulfilling the callings God has given fathers, mothers, and children. They are badly in need of restoration.

The need is utterly overwhelming when viewed overall. But the solution is well within reach when viewed from the standpoint of each household. A father doesn't have to fix the whole society; he just has to fix his own family. And here is the amazing and hopeful thing about God's national rebuilding plan: *the renewal strategy that is within the reach of each father—making changes in his own home—is the strategy that will have the greatest overall effect for the kingdom of God.* As each of us sees to our own little sphere of dominion, our own families, the combined effect will be renewed communities, churches, and nations. In other words, as fathers turn their hearts toward home, God will be bringing in Christ's kingdom once again, and our nation can recapture the blessings that have been lost.

A national spiritual revival is clearly possible, by God's grace, but we should not wait passively for some spectacular operation of God's Spirit to bring it to pass. Why should God bless us with revival if Christian men are failing to be obedient to the calling He has given them in the home? If God has told us what removes His curse from the land and what prepares us to be a people He can use (and He has), why should we expect Him to work in any other way? (cf. Mal. 4:4-6; Luke 1:17) We can be part of a new revival and hasten its spread if we will turn our hearts toward our families and shape them according to the Word of God.

With the family in such disarray generally in our culture, the tendency has been to emphasize the individual and overlook the family. We have simply forgotten the enormous potential that home life has for transforming a culture. One of my purposes in writing this book is to help lay the foundation for a larger social transformation by encouraging changes within the home.

It is my firm conviction that if our nation is to be saved from going the way of decadent Rome and every other empire in history, its deliverance will be found in the restoration of patriarchal families that are part of biblical churches and the propagation of these Christian households by the thousands and millions across the land.

FATHER ABRAHAM

Perhaps you've heard the children's song: "Father Abraham had many sons, and many sons had Father Abraham. I am one of them, and so are you…" The words refer to the fact that any New Testament believer is actually a spiritual child of Abraham (cf. Gal. 3:29).

Abraham was just a family man. Actually he didn't even have a child until he was eighty-six years old! Yet God had promised Abraham that nations and kings would come from him and that through him all the nations of the earth would be blessed:

> Your name shall be Abraham; for I have made you a father
> of many nations. I will make you exceedingly fruitful; and
> I will make nations of you, and kings shall come from you.
> (Gen. 17:5,6; cf. 22:18)

Not only did he go on to become the patriarch of a whole nation, Israel (and the ancestor of its kings), but since the covenant God made with Abraham was fulfilled in his descendant Jesus Christ (the King of kings), he is also the father of all who believe in Christ as well. Since Jesus came, the whole earth has been blessed by the progress of the Christian faith, and will continue to be blessed—all because of Father Abraham.

Who in all of history, besides Jesus himself, was more influential than Abraham and his family? Not the Pharaohs, nor Alexander the Great, nor Plato, nor Caesar Augustus, nor Charlemagne, nor Isaac Newton, nor George Washington, nor Albert Einstein. No one has had more influence than this nomadic herdsman whose God-given name means "father of many."

There's no telling how influential one faithful father can be. But this is true not only of Abraham. It is true of every head of a family. The family is God's "secret weapon" for spreading His kingdom through the generations and over the globe.

Whether the Lord takes our efforts and multiplies them over the face of the land is His business. We can't control that. But even if He doesn't turn our nation as a whole back to Him, we can (God blessing us) create a little kingdom of God in our own homes and have at least some influence for good on those immediately around us. Our family, our descendants, and our neighbors will be blessed even if no one else ever is, and that ought to be enough to motivate us to action.

DEVELOPING A MULTI-GENERATIONAL VISION

After their return from exile in Babylon, Zerubbabel had the difficult task of leading the Israelites in the rebuilding of God's fallen temple. The temple that the remnant was building was a faint shadow of the glorious temple of Solomon that had been destroyed a couple of generations before, and some of the people were discouraged that their best efforts could accomplish relatively little.

In this context the prophet Zechariah spoke: "Who despises the day of small things? Men will rejoice when they see the plumb line in the hand of Zerubbabel" (Zech. 4:10). Through his rhetorical question—"Who despises the day of small things?"—the Lord was assuring Zerubbabel and the people that with His added blessing, their efforts to rebuild could accomplish much. Indeed, the contemporary prophet Haggai reported the Lord's assessment of this very temple: "'The glory of this present house will be greater than the glory of the former house,' says the Lord Almighty" (Hag. 2:9). This prediction was only fulfilled hundreds of years later as the Messiah Himself appeared in a later version of this temple.

Modern day fathers will, no doubt, be tempted to discouragement as they apply themselves to their restoration project. Rebuilding families takes time; rebuilding churches, nations, and civilizations takes even longer. Though some fruit will be evident in the short term, most of the fruit of our labors will not be seen for many years. It is essential that we, too, do not despise the day of small beginnings, and that we develop a long-range vision for our work.

Great projects always have small beginnings. Consider the tiny ship *Mayflower* with its 102 passengers, half of whom were dead after that first winter at Plymouth in 1620-21. Concerning them William Bradford wrote in *Of Plymouth Plantation*:

> Last and not least, they cherished a great hope and inward
> zeal of laying good foundations, or at least making some
> ways toward it, for the propagation and advance of the
> gospel of the kingdom of Christ in the remote parts of the

world, even though they should be but stepping stones to others in the performance of so great a work....

Thus out of small beginnings greater things have been produced by His hand that made all things of nothing, and gives being to all things that are; and, as one small candle may light a thousand, so the light here kindled hath shone unto many, yea in some sort to our whole nation; let the glorious name of Jehovah have all the praise.

The fathers who founded this great nation had a long-range vision. They did what they could, satisfied that their great God could take their "small beginnings" and multiply their efforts in time. The fact that you and I are considering this very subject today, as you read this book, is living proof that the faith of the pilgrims was not misplaced. We are their heirs, and we must share their vision.

Our calling is not just to fix our families until our children are grown. We should not just be looking for bandaids and temporary cures. Our aim should be nothing less than the flowering of Christian civilization, the fruit (to borrow the words of Bradford) of the continued "propagation and advancement of the gospel and kingdom of Christ."

God wants men to be men, to turn their hearts to their children in peculiarly masculine ways: in expressions of leadership, provision, and protection. And then, as these children grow up and have families of their own, they can repeat the process for the next generation, and so on. Listen to the long-range vision of Psalm 78:4-7:

We will tell the next generation the praiseworthy deeds of the LORD, his power, and the wonders he has done. He decreed statutes for Jacob and established the law in Israel, which he commanded our forefathers to teach their children, so the next generation would know them, even the children yet to be born, and they in turn would tell their children. Then they would put their trust in God and would not forget his deeds but would keep his commands.

The reason God turns the hearts of fathers to their children is so that His gospel and kingdom can be perpetuated and multiplied on the earth. God's plan is for each man to become the patriarch of a Christian clan, to have generation after generation of descendants who will follow him as he follows the Lord.

The Lord has graciously given me six children. If each of them has six, I will have thirty-six grandchildren. If each of them has six, I will have 216 great-grandchildren. If each of them has six, I will have 1,296 great-great grandchildren. Imagine, in four short generations I could be the patriarch of as many as thirteen hundred Christian families… if I faithfully turn my heart to my children and experience the blessing of God.

We must see the work of rebuilding our families as laying the foundation for a long-term process of growth. We cannot hurry the good fruit the Spirit will bring. *The best will come after we are gone.* We must be willing to be stepping-stones to others who will accomplish more, to light the first candle of thousands. As the psalmist states it: "Blessed is the man who fears the

LORD, who finds great delight in his commands. His *children* will be mighty in the land; the generation of the upright will be blessed" (Ps. 112:1,2).

You can see by now how Christian civilization, the cultural fruit of the kingdom of God in history, can be rebuilt. It will not happen tomorrow, nor in the next decade. But if we are faithful and train our children to be faithful, and if we pass on the vision to our sons and daughters, then by God's grace our great-grandchildren may yet live in a blessed land, a land that even exceeds the godly achievements of the generations of our pilgrim fathers.

If the rebuilding of families—and the civilization that rests on these families—is to succeed, it must be done God's way. We must use His tools and follow His blueprints. As the people rejoiced to see the plumb line in the hand of Zerubbabel, so our generation of Christians will rejoice when they see the plumb line of Scripture in the hands of Christian family men. Our families do not need therapy, they need righteousness; they do not need new ideas, they need wisdom (Luke 1:17). We must return to God's Word for direction on how to be a man and lead a family. Turning to our children and developing a multi-generational vision will do no good unless we also turn to the wisdom of the righteous revealed in the Bible.

One of the marks of a deep work of God is when men and women are willing to make great sacrifices to conform their lives to God's ways. That is what is exciting about the home education and Christian men's movements: there appears to be the beginnings of men turning toward home and toward God's

Word. But as we said in our opening chapter, the jury is still out on whether this initial effort will endure and bear long-term fruit.

CHRIST IS THE FOCUS, NOT PATRIARCHY

Perhaps this is a good place for a word of caution: People like me are people with a cause, and my particular cause is the restoration of biblical patriarchy in our homes, churches, and society (and maybe nearby galaxies!). People like me can lose perspective. We can come to believe that the principles and practices that we espouse are the most important thing in life, and to us they often seem to be just that.

But here's the point of my caution: these things are *not* what is most important. Let me explain.

One of the root human sins is pride. Our first parents were afflicted with it ("Let *us* be the judge of whether God or Satan is telling the truth"), and it is the sin behind any attempt of mankind to figure out his own way to solve the problem of sin and misery in the world (whether by jihad, education, religious pilgrimage, or legalistic righteousness).

People like me are seriously tempted to let our pride attach itself to the teaching and lifestyle that we call biblical patriarchy and make an idol of it. We may try to solve the problem of sin and misery in our families through perfecting our technique in the use of the rod, or through the choice of the perfect home school curriculum, or through avoiding church youth groups, or through leading our children to marriage through courtship, or through getting involved in a family-integrated church. We can easily come to rely on these very good lifestyle choices, and the biblical principles we believe lie behind them, as if these things themselves have the power to transform our families and assure that they will be followers of Christ. But they can't do that.

The inherent danger of being people with a cause is that we lose sight of our Cause. *Biblical patriarchy is not the meaning of life for the Christian. Christ is.* "For to me, to live is Christ…" (Phil. 1:21). Biblical patriarchy itself is not the secret for rebuilding our families, churches, and nation. Christ is. It is horrible to think that while focusing on the ingredients of a wholesome and biblical way of life, we may lose sight of the one who is the only source, guide, and goal of the Christian life, Christ himself.

When Paul wrote to the Corinthians about his former visit to them he said, "For I determined not to know anything among you except Jesus Christ and Him crucified" (1 Cor. 2:2). Now come on, Paul! Read the rest of your own letter. You address a lot of things besides Jesus Christ and His cross: unity in the church, church discipline, handling controversies, marriage and singleness, meat and idols, head coverings, the Lord's Supper, spiritual gifts, the resurrection, etc.

Obviously Paul doesn't mean that he never addresses other topics of importance to Christians. What he means is that no matter what topic, he wants to deal with it in terms of its relationship to Jesus Christ and His atonement. Nothing else matters. Nothing makes sense if considered apart from Jesus. And separated from Jesus Christ, all of these important issues can actually become stumbling blocks that prevent progress in the Christian life.

The very real danger is that we may attempt to substitute *a religious system* for the person and work of Christ. *If we make an idol of what we are calling biblical patriarchy, if in our pride we rely on our religious system to bless our families, we will lose our families in the long run.* Isaiah and the other prophets often warned about the danger of honoring the Lord with words and external actions but failing to have a heart for Him. The Lord says: "These people come near to me with their mouth and honor me with their lips, but their hearts are far from me. Their worship of me is made up only of rules taught by men" (Isaiah 29:13).

I hope that you and I don't see a return to biblical patriarchy as yet another technique to bring us the good life. I hope we see it rather as a matter of obedience to the one who is our Lord. Patriarchy is not the main thing; Jesus is. We should get back to patriarchy simply because it is part of the path Jesus calls His disciples to take through this world.

Having given this caution, let me return to our exhortation.

Needed: Obedience Not Sentimentality

Pollster George Barna created a stir two years ago when he said at the end of the high-flying decade of Promise Keepers, "Some good things happened among men during the 1990s, but it does not appear that there has been a massive reawakening of the male soul in the last 10 years.[27]

For a man to get charged up, shout, cry, and even do the wave at a huge rally is no guarantee that any substantial and lasting change is actually taking place in him. Since the time of the great "revivals" of the early 1800s, American Christians have believed that a shortcut to spiritual transformation can be found in the emotions: Get a man excited, and you have a new man. The problem is that this is simply not true, and that's the reason for Mr. Barna's comment. PK produced a lot of sound and fury during its decade of prominence, but it is fair to ask: Where is the fruit today?

We live in an age of sentimentality: the important thing is how you feel about something, not necessarily what you do about it. Sentimentality is *feeling* divorced from *action*.

I grieve as I look at myself and see how infected I am with this spiritual disease of modern man. How often I have heard myself professing some godly desire to a fellow believer, relishing the rightness of my feelings, but with no clear intention of doing anything about it and no actual change of behavior. Probably you have done the same thing. "I don't pray enough, and prayer is so important." "I haven't been spending enough time with my kids." "I ought to be memorizing Scripture." "I really should stop speeding." "I need to work at being on time." "I need to be more consistent in the discipline of my children."

It is easy to utter claims to right feelings, and even to feel a sort of piety as a result: "At least I *want* to do what is right!" We may even think that this is an expression of faith. But it is not! It may just be a cover for the intention to continue disobedience, or the lack of real intention to change, which is the same thing.

True Christian faith is not a pious feeling. Faith involves obedience; *faith shows itself as faithfulness.* You cannot separate the two. "Faith without works is dead" (Jas. 2:26). Abraham is the great biblical example of faith. Concerning him Hebrews 11:8 says, "By faith Abraham obeyed when he was called to go out to the place which he would receive as an inheritance. And he went out, not knowing where he was going." He didn't just agonize about the fact that he ought to go, he went! That is how you recognize true faith. "By faith Abraham obeyed…"

In the book that most clearly and emphatically teaches the doctrine of justification by faith alone, the apostle Paul describes at the beginning and again at the end of the letter God's great aim in salvation: "for *obedience to the faith* among all nations" (1:5); and "for *obedience to the faith*" (16:26). So we are not surprised to hear this report about the early spread of the gospel: "Then the word of God spread, and the number of the disciples multiplied greatly in Jerusalem, and a great many of the priests were *obedient to the faith*" (Acts 6:7). Not "excited about the faith," not "full of good intentions about the faith"—but "obedient to the faith!"

Sentimentality is not Christianity. Let's not deceive ourselves with righteous feelings divorced from action. The important thing is not how we feel about something but what we do about it. "Godly sorrow produces repentance" (2 Cor. 7:10), a change of mind, and a change of direction. God calls us to obedience, not good feelings.

While there is nothing wrong with big events, they are often a distraction. What Christian men need today is not an event but a commitment to walk in truth. Men leave events, but they can't leave their day-to-day lives, and it's what they do there that makes the difference. PK certainly attempted to follow up on its events and understood the need to build lasting change into its followers, but it fell short.

My contention is that the reason it didn't make a lasting impression on the male soul or the national soul was that it failed to ground its challenge to men uncompromisingly in the truths of God's Word. It failed to confront the lie of feminism head on, and it didn't call men to repentance for having flirted with this demonic ideology. It didn't challenge men to return to a fully biblical definition of manhood and family leadership. In short, though it certainly didn't need to use the term, it failed to call men back to biblical patriarchy.

Patriarchy is not something that a man feels at a rally. It is a way of life. To borrow from the title of a recent Christian book, it is "a long obedience in the same direction."[28] The masses of men today don't have patience for something that is not a quick and easy fix. We want to hear about "How to Renew Your Family and Restore Christian Culture in Three Easy Steps by This Time Tomorrow," and we would rather see it on a video than have to read the book. But getting back to biblical patriarchy will take commitment, sacrifice, and long-term vision; in other words, it will require faith and obedience.

RISE UP, O MEN OF GOD!

By God's grace, we are living at a turning point in history. There is electricity in the cultural air today as everyone senses the momentous changes in which we all seem to be caught up. Nations are transformed, and national borders become less important. Technology opens vast new windows of opportunity even as it complicates man's stewardship of the planet. Economies overheat and approach the exploding point as individuals find wealth both easier to gain and easier to lose. Old standards of morality collapse into the ruin of immorality. Men and women wander about searching for their identities, wondering why their families are crumbling around them.

When the need is greatest, the opportunity for God to work is also greatest. In the fullness of time God sent His Son into a lost world and into a generation of His own people who had forgotten Him. But He prepared a remnant that He could use, a remnant marked by fathers taking God's Word in hand and leading their families. Today, too, God is raising up a remnant, a people he can use to spread His kingdom once again. The need is great, but the opportunities are greater.

On the human level, everything depends on fathers and church leaders. The future course of the world will be determined by what men do in their families and in the churches. Will you study God the Father to learn what it means to be a patriarch? Will you submit wholly to your Servant-Leader, the Lord Jesus, and learn His ways? Will you submit to authority in your life, especially that of the local church? Will you yield your will for the welfare of your wife and children? Will you commit yourself to lead your family, to provide for them and protect them, not only physically but spiritually as well? Will you accept the stark fact of your responsibility for all that happens in your home? If you are a church leader, will you help move the church from its family-fragmenting, program-focused structure to one that makes the discipleship of men and their families a priority?

We still need to hear and obey Paul's exhortation to the Corinthians: "Be on the alert, stand firm in the faith, act like men, be strong" (1 Cor. 16:13, NASB). Let's commit ourselves to act like men—not like the men of our day who are preoccupied with money, with pleasure, with human power, and with selfish and merely temporal concerns. Let us act like men of God. And let's not attempt to be strong in our own strength. Rather let us remember that, "I can do all things through Christ who strengthens me" (Phil. 4:13).

Let's respond to the challenge given in William Merrill's great hymn:

> Rise up, O men of God!
> Have done with lesser things;
> Give heart and soul and mind and strength
> To serve the King of kings.

Will you commit yourself to give everything you've got to serve the King, and to serve Him by acting like a man? Will you help rebuild "the old waste places" and thus "raise up the foundations of many generations?"

Let's commit ourselves together to return to our God, to His Word, to our wives and children, to the church—to return to biblical patriarchy. Then the curse that we see spreading over our land may yet be removed, and ours may become a generation the Lord can use to spread His kingdom in a mighty way, a generation blessed by the Lord.

"Patriarchy"—A Good Word for a Hopeful Trend

The news media recently reported that the 1997 National Spelling Bee was won by a home schooler, a then thirteen-year-old girl from New York. The word with which she clinched the victory was "euonym," which means literally "a good name," or an appropriate name for something.

Another story that flows from the counterculture is not being reported by the national media, namely, the way in which thousands of fathers are turning their hearts toward their homes and pursuing a patriarchal lifestyle. It is true that reporters have noticed the "Christian men's movement" that fills stadiums with emotionally charged speakers and a revivalistic atmosphere. (Whether or not the men involved are being brought to a real obedience—expressed, say, in getting their children out of the soul-destroying government schools—is another matter.) But it is the quieter men's movement, one that is aptly described as getting *back to patriarchy*, which holds a real hope for national transformation. In times of spiritual decline God's work prospers, not among the masses, but within a remnant.

A Good Name

Patriarchy. Patriarchal. These are jarring terms to ears attuned to contemporary social language, fashioned as it is by the ideology and agenda of feminism. To be described as "patriarchal" is among the worst indictments that can be brought upon a group of people or a period of history, conjuring as it does vague images of domineering men and downtrodden women.

However, far from being a term to avoid as we begin the new millennium, this word is one we should embrace. It is, in fact, a euonym, a good name, because it suitably identifies the movement to which it refers. Not that we favor the cultural stereotype that enters the collective mind today at the sound of the word, but because we embrace a true and wholesome patriarchy, one vindicated by the Word of God and by history.

"Patriarch" was the first name I considered for a new publication I was founding in 1993, though I confess I initially set it aside in favor of less strident names. Both of the alternatives, however, had to be discarded because I discovered they were in use by other ministries and publications. So I came back to "Patriarch," gulped hard, and placed it on the masthead of the first issue. I have never been sorry for the decision, convinced that it was the providential choice.

Over the years I have participated in conferences named "Back to Patriarchy." In these meetings we present an expansive vision of spiritual renewal rooted in the choice of men to reclaim their God-given leadership role in the family. A patriarch is a man who reflects God the Father by embracing the biblical role of fatherhood. This domestic spiritual leadership overflows into the reformation of church and larger society under the leadership of godly men. A patriarchal society is God's ideal society, one shaped according to the principles and patterns of His Word.

Some might think that we should use less emotive terms to call men back to their manly duties. I must disagree. Let me suggest seven reasons why the term "patriarchy" is a good name to identify the movement of men back to their manly calling and the resulting reformation of family, church, and society.

1) *The term "patriarchy" points men to God the Father as the archetype for their renewal.* All fatherhood in heaven and on earth derives from God the Father (Eph. 3:15). He is the original pattern, the perfect example of fatherhood. If men are to rediscover their identity they will need to become reacquainted with the one who made them to be uniquely like Himself.

My generation witnessed the Jesus Movement back in the late '60s and early '70s, followed by a kaleidoscope of movements that have focused on the Holy Spirit and His work. It seems that God is now moving men to take a longer look at the Father and thus get back to the source of their identity and calling as men. Men need to go beyond the feminized emotionalism and sloppy doctrine of recent movements. Patriarchy accentuates not subjective religious experience but a manly pursuit of truth and a gutsy appeal to duty.

We need to study the Father to learn how to be leaders. We need to explore how He cares for His own so that we learn what it means to be providers. We need to meditate on how He defends the weak so that we learn how to protect those under our care. Fathers need to spend time with the original Patriarch.

2) *The term "patriarchy" suggests a call to personal holiness.* The biblical patriarchs were men like Abraham, Isaac, Jacob, and David (Acts 2:29; 7:8,9; Heb. 7:4). Though each of these men was a sinner, they were all approved of God and blessed by Him because they each had a heart for God.

To get back to patriarchy suggests a return to the faith of father Abraham (Rom. 4; Heb. 11:8ff). It suggests that a man be like Jacob, desperate for God's blessing above all else (Gen. 32:26). It suggests that a man aim to be called what David was called by God Himself: "a man after My own heart" who "will do all my will" (Acts 13:22).

To get back to patriarchy is to get serious about God again. A patriarch doesn't fritter away his life in front of the TV or on the golf links; he has more important things to do. He wants to walk with God and thus to change the world for good, just like the patriarchs of old.

3) *The term "patriarchy" communicates the biblical pattern of male leadership.* Although both men and women are made in God's image, the male reflects God the Father in a special way (1 Cor. 11:7) since he holds (in a delegated sense) the position of headship (cf. v. 3). It is not accidental that God is revealed to us in male terms, nor that men are called by the same name that God uses for Himself: Father. Patriarchy is God's idea.

The order of human social arrangements is not up for grabs. God made mankind to mirror His character and attributes, and

He made human relationships to reflect the order that exists eternally in the Godhead. Patriarchy is good because it reflects the very relationships that exist among the Father, Son, and Spirit, and it thus brings glory to God.

Our culture may think it has outgrown the practice of male leadership, but this only proves the foolishness of the current wisdom. We should not be apologetic about patriarchy. To abandon God's plan is rebellion against God. Patriarchy is submission to God.

4) *The term "patriarchy" implies the foundational significance of family government.* The biblical patriarchs were family leaders. To call men back to patriarchy is, first of all, to call them to be family leaders once again. The nation is a reflection of its communities and churches; a community or a church is a reflection of its families; a family is a reflection of its father. What men do in their homes will shape, for better or worse, every other institution in society.

This principle is stated explicitly in 1 Timothy 3:5 where, in the context of spelling out standards for church elders, it says that men must manage their own families well because "if anyone does not know how to manage his own family, how can he take care of God's church?" Family leadership is the training ground for leadership in the church, in business, in civil government, and in every other sphere of life.

If men are serious about making an impact in the world they will start by being good fathers. Too many men neglect the home because they believe that their work (or even their ministry) is so important that they don't have time for family.

However, if a man fails at home he is a failure. Period. No matter how successful he may be elsewhere. The health of the nation percolates up from the home. Patriarchy recognizes this truth.

5) *The term "patriarchy" recalls historical periods characterized by divine blessing.* Ancient Israel was, of course, the quintessential patriarchal society. The law of God provided for the rule of men in their homes, in the religious life of the community, and in civil matters carried on at the city gates. Under this system God's people prospered and were blessed by Him tremendously. Far from being oppressive of women, patriarchy offered them protection, provided for their needs, and gave them freedom to blossom in their unique calling as women.

In our own, more immediate past we find God's blessing upon the patriarchal society of colonial America. Never has God's smile been more evident on our nation than in those days when men ruled both at home and in business, cultural, and religious affairs. Like Israel of old, the colonies prospered greatly by both material and spiritual measures. And women were better off than in our day where, in their striving to be like men, they have lost security, contentment, and the pleasure of being who God made them to be.

Pointing men back to patriarchy is one way to stand at the crossroads and urge men to those ancient paths that God has blessed (Jer. 6:16). We don't aim to turn the clock back out of some sentimental longing for the past, but we do want to learn from those who have gone before. Patriarchy aims to build the future on the solid foundation of what has worked in the past. God blesses biblically structured patriarchal societies.

6) The term "patriarchy" constitutes a direct challenge to feminism. We have failed to stand for truth if we stand up for truth at every point except that which is under attack in our day (to paraphrase Martin Luther). Christians are too busy trying to accommodate feminism. They do this by allowing women leaders in the church, by encouraging the practice of women working outside the home, by married women sporting hyphenated last names, by importing "gender-inclusive language" into hymns and even Bible translations, and in many other ways. Feminism is winning the ideological battle for our civilization, and Christians are among its casualties.

The way to win the battle against an advancing enemy is to expose his position, attack him with force, and reverse the advances he has made. We need to expose feminism for the devil's lie that it is, attack it with the force of biblical truth, and seek to reverse the progress it has made in our culture.

The term "patriarchy" is an effective weapon in our arsenal. Its use instantly crystallizes the issues in the conflict. By defining the battle it forces men (and women) to take sides. It allows no neutral ground of accommodation and thus reveals those who are willing to compromise truth for social acceptability. The word "patriarchy" will make many uncomfortable, others furious, but for that very reason it serves well the cause of God and truth. "Patriarchy" is a call to action for men who want to deliver Western civilization from the cancer of feminism.

7) The term "patriarchy" stimulates a multi-generational vision in men. Those who in Scripture were called "patriarchs" were so named by those who stood many generations downstream from them. You don't normally call your dad "patriarch." A man earns that title through the honor accorded him by accumulating generations. The very term means "the first in a family" and thus "the family ruler." A patriarch is the head of a family dynasty.

Thus the use of the term encourages a long-range vision of a man's calling. I am not just Dad to a few children; I am patriarch to hundreds, thousands who will come after me. The preparation of my immediate children (the foundation) will affect the quality of many generations to follow (the building).

Contemporary men don't look very far down the road ahead. They might think about next month, next vacation, maybe even retirement, but it is a very rare man who is thinking about his children's grandchildren. We need to help men extend their time horizons generations into the future. Calling them back to patriarchy does just that.

The key to extending the kingdom of God is to disciple our children, who will disciple theirs, who will disciple theirs, and so on. In this way the gospel will keep pace with the geometrical increase of people on the globe. The current win-a-few, lose-a-few approach of the church is a model of defeat. Patriarchy is a model of victory. It is the way to actually fulfill the Great Commission that Jesus gave His church (Matt. 28:18-20). Multiplying Christian families through the generations is the means to the evangelization of the world. Patriarchy is thus central to the cause of Christ in this age.

A PATRIARCHY CULT?

Some might object that we are getting carried away here, that we are out of balance by placing so much emphasis on patriarchy. After all, the word is not used extensively throughout the Scripture. Isn't there something suspect about finding in patriarchy the key to fixing the world?

To be clear, we do not believe patriarchy is the central theme of the Bible. We are not trying to start some new movement based on a new understanding of Scripture. The opposite is true—our goal is to return to those ancient paths and rebuild the foundations which God has declared as the building blocks for victory. The sovereign purpose of God in the cross of Jesus Christ is the truly central issue of life and the power of individual and social transformation. Our passion is simply to see the gospel and kingdom of Jesus prosper in this world. A man's response to the claims of Jesus is the paramount concern.

Yet when a man is saved he is saved from sin and to a new life of obedience to everything Jesus has commanded (Matt. 28: 20). He is obligated to believe the doctrines of the Bible and to practice the lifestyle commanded in the Bible. It is here that we confront patriarchy because the Bible is clear about the duty of men. But again, the role of men is just one of many teachings of Scripture, so why do we make it so central in our teaching?

We emphasize the biblical doctrine of patriarchy, not because it is a doctrine above other doctrines, but because it is a keystone issue of our day. A keystone, of course, is the wedge-shaped piece at the crown of an arch that locks the other pieces in place. The effectiveness of every other stone in the arch depends on the presence of the keystone. The reason our culture is in decline, our churches are impotent, and our families are failing is the absence of patriarchal leadership by godly men. All other efforts at reform and restoration are failing and will fail unless men take up the full scope of their God-given duties, beginning at home.

Patriarchy is not the most important issue in life, nor even in itself a very remarkable thing. In times past it was simply taken for granted as the underlying framework that holds a civilization together, the pattern of relationships that allowed the truly important concerns to be addressed: evangelism, truth, justice, mercy, statesmanship, discipleship, discovery, dominion, and so forth. What is remarkable is the wholesale abandonment of patriarchy in recent generations and the utter devastation this has brought to every aspect of our culture. We look forward to the day when we can stop dwelling on patriarchy and move on to other less elementary things.

Our problem today is that the very foundations are being destroyed. We don't have the strong, godly men, the healthy families, and the sound churches that have held Western civilization together and made God-honoring progress possible on many fronts. We need to get back to patriarchy so that we can rebuild all that is fallen in our times and then build anew. Without the groundwork of patriarchy, no other efforts at renewal and progress will succeed. They will fall flat. No efforts of governments, churches, agencies, or organizations can compensate for the failure of men to lead their families.

Imagine what our nation would be like if in every home the father loved his wife sacrificially, trained his children in God's truth and disciplined them in love, took responsibility for the education of his sons and daughters, protected his family from evil relationships and influences, and led his family in worship and prayer. The land would be a veritable Eden.

There is nothing very remarkable about a nail, but when you are trying to build a house and you don't have any, they suddenly become very important! Getting nails becomes your top priority. The lack of patriarchy is like the lack of nails: you can't build anything without it. If men are not men, if they are not family leaders, then nothing else works. Each godly man is like a well-driven spike that contributes to the stability of the whole cultural house. You don't think much about his contribution until he is no longer there.

So should we use the term "patriarchy" and seek its restoration in our day? Absolutely. The hatred of this term is an evidence of the degeneracy of our culture. But it is, indeed, a euonym, a good name, and an appropriate designation for a very hopeful movement of God's Spirit. Because the path to future blessing is the path back to patriarchy.

APPENDIX   B

Living in the Open:
The Importance of
Accountability

"Two are better than one"

Accountability is inescapable: in the long run, we will all
answer to God on that great Day, the day of judgment.
"For we must all appear before the judgment seat of Christ, that
each one may receive the things done in the body, according to
what he has done, whether good or bad" (2 Cor. 5:10).

Every man will be judged for everything he does, even for
every idle word (Matt. 12:36), but the special roles a man is
called to fulfill in this life increase his level of accountability
considerably. As a husband and father a man must answer for
his stewardship of his wife and children. As a worker or a boss
he will be held responsible for how he conducts himself on the
job. If he is a church leader he must watch over the members
of his flock as one "who must give account" (Heb. 13:17).
Every position of *responsibility* brings with it the need to make
a *response* for his actions to God ultimately and to whomever he
must answer in this life.

As a man matures, he will aim to judge his own life before God or another person judges him. "For if we would judge ourselves, we would not be judged" (1 Cor. 11:31). A godly man is aware of the applicable standards of conduct and measures his own life by them, bringing his conduct into conformity voluntarily. He does this because he loves God and because he wants to avoid the pain that inevitably accompanies failure to perform one's duties.

But whether through lack of practice, laziness, or sin, you and I don't always do what we know we are supposed to do, and we find that we are not always able to overcome whatever obstacle separates us from success. That's why we need someone to help us.

Solomon wrote in Ecclesiastes 4:9ff:

> Two are better than one, Because they have a good reward for their labor. For if they fall, one will lift up his companion. But woe to him who is alone when he falls, For he has no one to help him up. Again, if two lie down together, they will keep warm; But how can one be warm alone? Though one may be overpowered by another, two can withstand him. And a threefold cord is not quickly broken.

This is a picturesque way of stating a basic truth of life: we need other people. We are not created for isolation but for fellowship, first with our Creator, but also with others made in His image. This is especially so for those who have been restored to fellowship with God in Christ. That is why there are so many commands in the New Testament letters that include the words "one another." Love one another. Serve one another. Teach and admonish one another. Be hospitable to one another. Our growth in Christ demands fellowship with other Christians, and an important part of that fellowship is accountability: being answerable to others for the conduct of our Christian life.

One of the signs of true maturity is a willingness to be transparent before other believers, even to the point of acknowledging our sins and failures. James wrote, "Confess your trespasses to one another, and pray for one another..." (5:16). Certainly this is the essence of vulnerability: to let others see the dark side of our lives, even our secret sins. But it makes sense for those who know that "nothing is secret that will not be revealed" (Luke 8:17).

We all need someone to help lift us up when we fall and to encourage us when we do well. This is part of what Paul had in mind when he wrote, "Bear one another's burdens, and so fulfill the law of Christ" (Gal. 6:2; cf. v. 1).

Don't Try to Go it Alone

Probably very few of those reading these words would dispute what we have said so far. It makes good sense, and besides, we have used a lot of Scripture to make our point, so who could argue, right? But the fact is that very few of us actually have adequate accountability structures in our lives. We tend to be Lone Ranger Christians, but the Lord didn't design us to function in isolation. We need one another to live the Christian life.

How about you? Are you alone? Who picks you up when you fall? If you are alone, please make it one of your highest priorities to place yourself in the kind of relationships that will build you up in your walk.

First, get into a good church; or at least get into the best one available in your community. It is foolish to risk spiritual isolation, and God requires you to be under spiritual authority—not to mention that you need to be setting a good example for your children.

Second, try to form or become part of a group of men who meet regularly for personal discipleship training and mutual encouragement. This may be something your church leaders would be happy to sponsor, or it may just be that you find three or four other men with the same vision.

It is impossible to be stagnant in your Christian walk if you have some plan for personal accountability in place. Go for it! Life is too short to be squandered with good intentions that are never realized. Make yourself accountable to other men in Christ, and as you "one another" you will begin to see a level of growth and victory that may be now only an empty dream.

God's ways work. And being a man under authority is one of God's surefire ways to help you grow to become the man He made you to be.

Stop trying to go it alone.

Endnotes

Chapter 1
1. Unknown origin.

Chapter 2
2. Brian Abshire, "Reconstructing the Family: The Industrial Revolution and the Sociology of the Christian Family," *Chalcedon Report #371* (June 1996), pp. 12-13.
3. Michiaki & Hildegard Horie, *Whatever Became of Fathering?* (Downers Grove: InterVarsity Press, 1993; first published in German in 1988), pp. 36-37.
4. Weldon Hardenbrook, *Missing from Action* (Nashville: Thomas Nelson Publishers, 1987), p. 31.
5. Edmund S. Morgan, *Virginians at Home* (New York: Holt, Rinehart & Winston, 1952), p. 45.
6. Mary P. Ryan, *Womanhood in America* (New York: Franklin Watts, 1983), p. 21.
7. Abshire, "Reconstructing the Family...," *op. cit.*, p. 13.

8. Allan Carlson, "From Cottage to Work Station and Back Again," *Patriarch* 36 (February 2001), p. 10.

9. Abshire, "Reconstructing the Family…," *op. cit.*, p. 13.

10. Horie, *Whatever Became of Fathering, op. cit.*, p. 39.

11. Michael G. Maudlin, "Why We Need Feminism," *New Man* (Nov./Dec. 1997).

Chapter 5
12. Douglas Phillips, ed., *Poems for Patriarchs* (San Antonio: The Vision Forum, Inc., 2001), p. 76.

Chapter 6
13. Jerry Bridges, *The Pursuit of Holiness* (Colorado Springs: Navpress, 1996, originally published 1978), p. 61.

Chapter 7
14. Stu Weber, *Tender Warrior* (Sisters, Oregon: Multnomah Publishers, 1993), p. 40.

15. *Ibid.*, p. 96

16. Steve Farrar, *Standing Tall* (Sisters, Oregon: Multnomah Publishers, 2001, originally published 1994), p. 13.

17. David Gergen, *U.S. News & World Report* (Sep. 29, 1997). Emphasis in original.

18. Stu Weber, *Four Pillars of a Man's Heart* (Sisters, Oregon: Multnomah Publishers, 1997), p. 43.

19. Stephen Clark, *Man & Woman in Christ* (Ann Arbor, Michigan: Servant Books, 1980), p. 52.

Chapter 9

20. James W. Alexander, *Thoughts on Family Worship* (Harrisonburg, Virginia: Sprinkle Publications, 1981, originally published 1847), pp. 58-59.

21. *The Directory for Family-Worship*, approved by the General Assembly of the Church of Scotland, 1647.

Chapter 10

22. J.R. Miller, *Home-Making* (San Antonio: The Vision Forum, Inc., 2001, originally published 1882), pp. 34,38.

23. Douglas Wilson, *Reforming Marriage* (Moscow, Idaho: Canon Press, 1995), p. 28.

24. Stephen Clark, *Man & Woman in Christ*, op. cit., p. 60.

Chapter 11

25. J.R. Miller, *Home-Making*, op. cit., p. 11.

26. B.M. Palmer, *The Family in its Civil and Churchly Aspects* (Harrisonburg, Virginia: Sprinkle Publications, 1981, orginially published 1876), p. 291.

Chapter 12

27. *New Man* magazine (May/June 2002), p. 33.

28. Eugene Peterson, *A Long Obedience in the Same Direction* (Downers Grove: InverVarsity Press, 2000).